What Environmentalists Need to Know About Economics

D1235615

What Environmentalists Need to Know About Economics

Jason Scorse

First published in 2010 by
PALGRAVE MACMILLAN®
in the United States—a division of St. Martin's Press LLC,
175 Fifth Avenue, New York, NY 10010.

Where this book is distributed in the UK, Europe and the rest of the world,
this is by Palgrave Macmillan, a division of Macmillan Publishers Limited,
registered in England, company number 785998, of Houndmills,
Basingstoke, Hampshire RG21 6XS.

Palgrave Macmillan is the global academic imprint of the above companies
and has companies and representatives throughout the world.

Palgrave® and Macmillan® are registered trademarks in the United States,
the United Kingdom, Europe and other countries.

ISBN: 978–0–230–10731–1 paperback
ISBN: 978–0–230–10729–8 hardcover

Library of Congress Cataloging-in-Publication Data

Scorse, Jason.
    What environmentalists need to know about economics / by Jason
Scorse.
        p. cm.
    Includes bibliographical references.
    ISBN 978–0–230–10729–8
    1. Environmental economics. I. Title.

HC79.E5S347 2010
333.7—dc22   2010013322

A catalogue record of the book is available from the British Library.

Design by Newgen Imaging Systems (P) Ltd., Chennai, India.

First edition: October 2010

10 9 8 7 6 5 4 3 2 1

Printed in the United States of America.

CONTENTS

Introduction   1

PART I
HOW ECONOMISTS APPROACH ENVIRONMENTAL ISSUES

Chapter 1.   The Root Causes of Environmental Problems   7
Chapter 2.   Determining the "Optimum" Amount of
             Pollution   17
Chapter 3.   Valuing Ecosystems   27
Chapter 4.   Putting Monetary Values on the Environment
             and Living Things   33
Chapter 5.   Valuing Future Generations   41
Chapter 6.   Tools to Address Environmental Problems: Taxes,
             Property Rights, Information, Psychological
             Insights, and Command and Control Regulation   51
Chapter 7.   Environment vs. Economy: Growth Rates,
             Jobs, and International Trade   71

PART II
PUTTING ECONOMIC ANALYSIS TO WORK

Chapter 8.   Climate Change   83
Chapter 9.   Forest and Biodiversity Conservation   101
Chapter 10. Agriculture   121

Chapter 11. Chemical Pollution   137
Chapter 12. Fisheries and the Marine Environment   145
Chapter 13. Population Growth and Technological Change   153
Chapter 14. Demand-Side Interventions   161

Final Thoughts and Additional Resources   167

Notes   169

References   205

INTRODUCTION

This book was inspired by the warm reception I received from a short essay I wrote in 2005 entitled, "Why Environmentalists Should Embrace Economics." I would like to thank the dozens of people from around the world who sent me encouraging messages and convinced me that there was a need for a larger treatment of the issues raised in this piece.

The target audience for this book is anyone interested in environmental issues with an eye toward actually solving them: students, citizens, policy makers, and activists. No economics background is required for this text, although some basic microeconomics knowledge is helpful. Even those with more advanced training in economics may find some new perspectives in this volume that they had not considered before.

The overarching goal of this book is to demonstrate why a solid grasp of economics is a necessary (though not sufficient) condition for addressing the environmental challenges of the day. For too long, there has been a lingering mistrust and skepticism among many environmentalists of economics and economists. There are many reasons for this, but one thing is certain: it has been to the detriment of many environmental causes. I am confident that the more environmentalists understand what economic analysis and reasoning entails, the more they will realize that economics can be one of their greatest allies. The bottom line is that more often than not it is distortions, imperfections, and perversions of economic systems that are the main drivers of environmental degradation.

Of the many criticisms of economists, one of the more truthful is that often they are poor communicators (even when they are *not* presenting complex mathematical models and abstract theories). For this reason I have tried to write this book in a clear and accessible manner with no graphs or charts and no mathematical formulas. The primary objective of these chapters is to help develop the economic intuition necessary to address a wide range of environmental issues; i.e., how to think like an economist in the environmental realm.

Given the complexity of the issues dealt with in this volume (each of which individually could span multiple volumes), this treatment provides nothing more than a basic foundation for future study, discussion, and inquiry. I have provided a short list of websites and periodicals at the end of the book where interested readers can continue to increase their knowledge of economic approaches to environmental issues. Because I also want this book to be rigorous, I have provided lengthy footnotes for those who want additional information.

Part I presents the basic intellectual architecture that underlies how economists think about environmental issues, and the tools and insights that they use to address them. Part II surveys the major environmental issues of the day and presents a range of solutions derived from economic analysis. It is recommended that readers read all of part I before they delve into the specific issues in part II. Part II does not follow any predetermined sequence, and therefore does not require following the chapters in order.

Throughout the chapters I try to differentiate the ways in which theory and theoretical conditions may deviate from real-world situations. In such instances, I present the key insights from the theories that are still applicable even if they do not perfectly mirror reality. In addition, because politics is so integral to getting environmental policies enacted and enforced, I provide political commentary where appropriate. All of this is for the purpose of increasing the relevancy of this volume for actually solving the world's environmental problems, which is the ultimate goal.

I would like to thank my advisor at UC–Berkeley, Michael Hanemann, who showed me that economics should always be relevant to real-life issues. Thanks also to all of the students at the Monterey

Institute of International Studies whose insights have helped me to refine my own. And a special thanks to Kira Darlow for her work as my research assistant.

I warmly invite all constructive criticism of the contents of this book, for which I am solely responsible. I can be reached at jason. scorse@miis.edu.

Jason Scorse, Central California, 2010

Part I

HOW ECONOMISTS APPROACH ENVIRONMENTAL ISSUES

CHAPTER 1

THE ROOT CAUSES OF ENVIRONMENTAL PROBLEMS

E nvironmental problems are extremely complex and varied, yet they almost always share similar features, be it air pollution in Mexico City or a village in Indonesia, habitat loss in Kenya or Brazil, or fisheries collapse in the Indian, Pacific, or Atlantic oceans.

Environmentalists trying to make sense of these issues are faced with difficult questions:

- Why do relatively rational actors buying and selling goods and services rarely take into account the toxic pollution that results from their choices?
- Why do fishermen routinely overexploit the fisheries that they depend on?
- Why are the ecological services provided by forests and wetlands, which produce tangible and wide-ranging value for society, usually not taken into account when decisions are made?
- How can food be so cheap when there is such massive pollution and resource use involved in industrial agriculture?

Economists have been studying questions like these for many decades and have devised a fairly comprehensive framework for understanding the root causes of environmental problems, which is where we begin.

Those who believe that the field of economics rests on an unalterable faith in the power of markets may be surprised to learn that one of the most robust areas of study within economics concerns the conditions under which markets *do not* lead to socially optimum outcomes, especially in regard to environmental issues.[1] In fact, in the environmental arena market imperfections are ubiquitous and often require some form of government intervention.

Readers may also be pleasantly surprised to discover that the economic theories that explain why markets fail also hold the keys to solving the myriad environmental problems we currently face. Virtually all of the environmental policies currently being discussed in the political realm, in the board meetings of environmental organizations, and on environmental websites can be traced to economic theories that date back to the 1940s and continue to be vigorously debated in academic settings.

The three most important sources of environmental problems are 1) market failure, 2) the tragedy of the commons, and 3) the underprovisioning of public goods.

MARKET FAILURE

One of the first principles of free markets is that for them to work effectively, the full costs of an activity must be borne by the involved parties.

For example, many types of air and water pollutants exact a significant price on human health and degrade ecosystems, yet they are not included in the costs of production or at the consumer level. These costs, which are borne by society but not the individual producers and consumers of the goods, are called *externalities*.

Externalities lead to *market failure* because in order for the market to supply the proper amount of goods and services, the prices must correctly reflect the true costs.

Nowhere is this type of market failure more common than in the environmental realm.

The following are some specific examples of widespread environmental externalities:

- Heavy metals emitted from power plants that cause cancer, birth defects, and harm animals and plants, but that most power companies and consumers of electricity are not required to pay for.

- Greenhouse gas emissions, which have no cost almost anywhere in the world (except in the EU and in some sectors of the U.S. power industry), so no matter how much a person or company emits, they pay no penalty for their contribution to global warming.

- Factory farms that emit more sewage than the entire human population, despoiling nearby waterways, but which are largely unregulated.

- Biodiversity loss from clear-cut logging, which timber companies can essentially ignore because there is no cost to factor into their decisions, and which consumers can ignore because they do not pay for the negative consequences of the forest products they buy.

The result of unaccounted for externalities is that prices for many of the most common goods and services are significantly lower than if they included their environmental costs. This leads to a gross misallocation of society's resources. Economists characterize a situation where the costs of environmental externalities are not included in the price of a good as a form of *passive subsidy*. Think of it this way: whenever we use power from a coal-fired power plant we receive energy at a price that is much lower than its true cost (once all of the harmful effects are calculated and included).

These harmful effects are not simply theoretical; **they represent real damages that have real monetary value**. In effect, our energy use from coal is being subsidized by all of the people who get sick from the resulting sulfur pollution, by the money lost when our natural heritage and infrastructure are degraded by acid rain, and by the communities whose landscapes are despoiled by mining operations (the worst being mountaintop-removal[2]). There is little incentive for people to switch to wind or solar energy when coal is cheaper, even though the low price of coal is largely illusory; society pays a heavy cost for our reliance on this extremely dirty form of energy.

If we lived in a world where prices fully captured environmental costs, our entire economies would look vastly different: we would have different modes of transportation, different layouts for our cities and towns, different dietary habits, and consumer goods would likely contain much less toxic material. Prices of environmentally harmful goods would rise and much more R&D would go into alternatives, thereby decreasing their price. In such a world society's resources would be invested in those things which bring the greatest social value.

This book discusses the various policies that can lead individuals and companies to take these environmental costs into account. Economists refer to this as the process of *internalizing the externalities*.

But externalities are not the only thing that can lead to market failure. In economic models of well-functioning markets, one of the strongest assumptions is that the parties involved have *perfect information* about products and services, including the consequences of the consumption and production of these goods. It doesn't take a critic of economics to realize that this assumption is very strong and is unlikely to be the case in the real world. Nowhere are the deviations from perfect information more prominent than in the environmental realm.

Even with major scientific advances, our knowledge of the interaction of many industrial chemicals is still incomplete as is our understanding of how ecosystems function. Even what we do know is extremely complex and beyond the comprehension of anyone but the most senior scientists. Producers and consumers of goods, therefore, must often rely on outside sources to make informed decisions about what they produce and what they buy. The market itself is not likely to provide the necessary information for people to make well-informed decisions. As forests are cut down how does this impact the watersheds and how is this information conveyed to the people that rely on them? How are municipalities supposed to decide whether they want to approve the development of a new factory that emits some quantity of air and water pollution? Precisely what information is needed and what is the best way to provide it? These are difficult questions even with very good information, but almost impossibly difficult questions when the relevant information is poor.

A third cause of market failure arises from the incomplete and/or nontransparent distribution of property rights. In situations where it is unclear who has the right to use an environmental resource, there may be little incentive for long-term management. For example, consider a country where land rights are uncertain and frequently contested. A farmer who currently resides on the land may want to invest significant resources into developing a more environmentally sustainable management regime. This may include drip irrigation, vegetative buffer zones, and integrated pest management (IPM). However, if she fears that someone may claim her land title, she has little incentive to make these investments. Instead, she may choose to get as much out of the land as quickly as possible and take her chances.

Clear property rights are also crucial for assessing liability in the case of environmental damages. If there is not a clearly identifiable party who owns the environmental resource in question or is responsible for its protection, it is difficult to collect damages or enforce regulations to hold them accountable in the event that they are breaking the law.

The issue of liability sometimes takes subtle turns that have large environmental consequences. In the famous 1989 *Exxon Valdez* case, an Exxon tanker spilled more than 11 million gallons of oil into the pristine ecosystem of Prince William Sound in Alaska. One of the key questions that arose was whether Exxon was responsible for the damage to this public resource above and beyond the cleanup costs. Put another way, did the public hold the right to Prince William Sound in its pristine state, or was a private company allowed the right to severely damage the resource without compensation, as long as they "cleaned it up"?

The courts held that Exxon was liable, and even though the initial case was ultimately settled outside of court,[3] the damage estimates that were calculated included a measure of compensation to the general public. It is now on record that oil companies operating tankers in U.S. waters are held liable for damages to the public interest, which in the Exxon case were estimated in the billions of dollars (Carson et al., 2003). The legislation that the U.S. Congress passed in the years immediately following the Exxon Valdez spill was supposed to enshrine into law oil companies' responsibilities in the case of future spills; ironically, the $75 million cap that was placed on liabilities (above and beyond clean-up costs) may have led companies such as BP to cut corners on safety.

From a purely economic standpoint, there should be no limit to a company's liability for environmental damage. Any limit will decrease their incentive to fully take into account the potential risks in their actions. Whether a higher, or even unlimited, liability cap would have led BP to invest in better safety equipment is hard to know (the company has had a terrible safety record for decades), but the 2010 Deepwater Horizon oil spill disaster is a reminder that there are significant hidden costs that come with oil production, one of which is the risk of the environmental catastrophe that is now unfolding.

It is important to point out that when economists talk of property rights, they do not necessarily mean private property rights. In the case of market failure, due to a lack of transparent and enforceable property rights, this can sometimes be addressed by assigning property rights to government agencies or a community organization. These options entail their own set of issues that need to be addressed, but it is not the case that defining property rights always necessitates private ownership.

A lack of clear and enforceable property rights leads to the most pronounced forms of environmental degradation in cases of open access resources, which were made famous by ecologist Garrett Hardin (1968), who coined the phrase "the tragedy of the commons."[4]

THE TRAGEDY OF THE COMMONS

Two of the world's most important environmental resources are the oceans and the atmosphere. The oceans provide not only huge quantities of fish and sea life that humans consume, but also immense quantities of marine biodiversity and critical ecosystem services, upon which much of the world's terrestrial biodiversity depends. Biochemical interactions in the atmosphere help to regulate climate and temperature, the ozone layer blocks harmful solar radiation from reaching the earth's surface, while clean air promotes human and ecosystem health.

But most of the world's oceans and atmosphere are devoid of property rights[5]; that is, there is no body, whether groups of individuals, private companies, or governments, that can claim ownership over them.[6] They are called *open access resources*, which anyone can use and to whatever extent they wish. From here on I will use this term instead of the term "commons" that Garret Hardin coined, because it is now understood that there are important distinctions between open access resources and those held as commons.[7]

Hardin's insights are truer today than when he first discussed them four decades ago. His essential insight is that open access resources will more often than not be exploited at unsustainable levels because there is a wide divergence between the private benefits that accrue to the individual users of the resource and the costs, which are diffused over the entire population.

When a fishing company decides how much fish to take out of the ocean, it is only thinking of the bottom line: how much profit it can make. It will increase fishing as long as it is profitable to do so. Fish are a renewable resource, but are potentially exhaustible if overexploited. Every time a fishing boat removes fish, it affects the ability of the species to repopulate and survive. From a sustainable use perspective, the problem is that this cost of reducing the viability of the fish population is spread over all of the fishing companies in the industry, and therefore will likely seem insignificant to the *individual fisherman* in an industry of thousands of boats and private firms.

In addition, given the open access nature of the world's fisheries, if one company decides to stop fishing in order to allow the species to recover, there is nothing stopping another company from taking the fish for themselves. This produces a very shortsighted "race to the bottom" mentality that we observe in virtually all of the ocean's international waters, and even domestic waters where property rights are not clearly defined. It is no surprise that fish stocks are at or near levels of collapse globally as a result.[8]

The atmosphere is a much different type of resource, one that is not actively harvested, but the essential logic holds. Because virtually anyone can dump as much greenhouse gases into the atmosphere as they want, there is little incentive for any individual company or nation to restrict their emissions. If they do so they will have to incur all of the costs of restricting their activity, while the benefits of reducing global warming (however marginal) will be spread out over the entire world.

Poorer nations, particularly island nations or those at or below sea level, who stand to suffer the most from global warming, have no recourse with which to demand that emissions be restricted, because there is no international body that has jurisdiction over the atmosphere.[9] While there are ways to address the issue of global warming short of creating property rights to the atmosphere, the key point is that the open access nature of the atmosphere has created the problem in the first place.

This brings up another essential point. Some claim that the commoditization of the environment and living things are the root causes of environmental problems; it is a world that assigns property rights to the world's environmental heritage and assigns them price tags that is the greatest threat to a more livable future.[10]

A careful examination, however, of the areas where we see some of the greatest environmental threats *leads to the exact opposite conclusion.* It is the fact that much of the world's oceans and the atmosphere are freely open to exploitation that drives the unsustainable levels of both fish harvesting and greenhouse gas emissions. The same is true for many areas of the Amazon rain forest, where property rights are nonexistent, nontransparent, or not enforced; as a result we observe massive deforestation.[11]

None of this is to suggest that addressing the problem of open access resources alone will be sufficient to solve major environmental problems. Market failure can still occur in cases when property rights are well-defined, whether due to the transboundary nature of environmental pollution or imperfect information. In addition, there is another serious reason to believe that environmental quality will be underprovided in a free-market system and require some form of intervention.

PUBLIC GOODS

Public goods are a specific class of goods that are nonrival and nonexcludable. Put simply, they are goods where one person's use of the good does not inhibit another's use of the good (nonrival) and where once the good is provided to one it is by definition provided to all (nonexcludable).

There are very few "pure" public goods, mostly because there are ways to exclude people from the enjoyment of what otherwise would be considered entirely public resources.

The following are examples of environmental public goods, along with the appropriate caveats:

- **Biodiversity:** My enjoyment of biodiversity doesn't limit your ability to enjoy it, and once biodiversity has been preserved, no one can be excluded from enjoying it (in the abstract; for example, if the blue whale is preserved, we all can take pleasure in this achievement, but access to viewing these whales will be limited by individuals' income and leisure time).

- **An intact ozone layer:** The protection I get from the ozone layer doesn't impede anyone else's protection, and once the ozone layer is protected, it is protected for all (this is close to a pure public good, but in reality, we do have a situation where the remaining hole in the ozone is concentrated over Australia and New Zealand, which until it is fully restored means that there are populations that are excluded from the full benefits of protection).

- **Clean air:** My breathing clean air doesn't prevent anyone else from breathing clean air, and once clean air is provided to my community, no one in the community can be denied access to it (but yet again, air quality may differ substantially within a community and it may cost more money to live in areas where the air is the cleanest).

- **A climate in which the threat of global warming is greatly diminished:** This may be the closest we can get to a pure environmental public good; there is no way to exclude anyone from a nonwarming planet, and one person's benefit from a reduction in the risk of global warming doesn't conflict with anyone else's.

Because of the nonexcludable nature of environmental public goods (however imperfect), we encounter what economics refers to as the "free-rider" problem. It is often difficult to get people to contribute to the provision of public goods because they know that once they're provided they can get them for free.

If the local people of Hawaii decide to protect their coral reefs, all U.S. citizens (and all citizens of the world) get the benefit of this enhanced biodiversity protection, even if they didn't contribute to this effort. If Brazil decides to fully protect the Amazon rain forest, all the countries of the world get the myriad benefits of rain forest protection for free as well.

This is not to suggest that there are not significant reasons for the Hawaiians to protect their marine resources or the Brazilians to protect their forests without outside assistance. There are direct benefits that accrue to the immediate parties, and the Hawaiians currently do a lot to protect their reefs and the Brazilians do a lot to protect their forests. Economic analysis only points out that if others who also benefited from the provision of these resources contributed to their protection, the extent of the conservation efforts would likely be much greater. It is not that public goods result in zero provision in the free market, but that they are often underprovided, which is the key insight.

SUMMARY

The economics profession is in many ways the study of markets. Markets for many goods and services often work very well and minimal intervention is needed to protect the public interest. But in the environmental realm, market failure is quite common and markets left to their own devices will not produce anything close to optimum social outcomes. The transboundary nature of environmental resources and pollution, the great complexity of ecosystems, incomplete property rights, and the highly imperfect information about the effects of toxins on health require adjustments to markets to make them function properly. More precisely, the prices for goods and services should include their full costs, consumers and producers should have the best and most up-to-date information about the products and services they buy and sell, and ownership over resources should be as clear and accurate as possible.

CHAPTER 2

DETERMINING THE "OPTIMUM" AMOUNT OF POLLUTION

A t first glance, determining an optimum pollution level may strike many environmentalists as strange or even heretical; there is an obvious "optimum" for pollution (despite what economists may think): zero.

Economic theory doesn't arrive at this conclusion, not because economists are callous to environmental concerns, but because pollution is a by-product of many things that we all value; therefore, some amount of pollution is warranted.

Take electricity, for example. Electrical generation produces pollution; even renewable sources produce some quantity of pollution. All of us benefit greatly from electrical power and would not be willing to give it up to decrease this source of pollution to zero.

Take another example: agriculture. All forms of agriculture require vast alterations of the natural environment, including various forms of inputs, organic and/or synthetic. To eat a varied and healthy diet, significant quantities of pollution are often generated even in the most ecologically designed systems. This is especially true when agricultural systems are required to feed large numbers of people who reside far from agricultural centers and the costs of transportation are included.

These are two basic goods that virtually no one would be willing to forego: electricity and farm-produced food. The list of pollution-causing goods grows exponentially once we start including the luxuries that most of us in the developed world now take for granted—airplane travel, computers and other electronic goods, furniture, modern houses—and which most in the developing world are striving to acquire as well.

Following this logic, it is easy to see why zero pollution is not feasible, at least given current modes of living and technology.

What about reducing pollution *as much as possible*? This sounds like a reasonable second-best option. But what does "as much as possible" really mean? In many cases reducing pollution is expensive. How much money should society spend to reduce pollution? And what should it give up in order to achieve these lower levels of pollution? Many people might have opinions on the matter, but how can we judge which views are more reasonable than others?

Economic theory provides a way to conceptualize the issue, which, while far from perfect, at least allows us to begin with a methodology that can be applied in a variety of situations and has some objective merit. As we will see, it does not completely solve the problem, and it also raises a host of other issues, but it's a start.

The idea is relatively straightforward (although putting it into practice isn't): the optimum level of pollution is the amount where the benefits of abating (getting rid of) additional pollution are worth the added cost.[1]

We can conceive of this from two different angles. First, let's assume that we are starting in a world with no pollution. We value some things more than having an environment entirely free from pollution, and we produce those things up to the point where we decide that additional pollution is no longer worth it. Or, more realistically, if we start from a relatively polluted world, we can ask ourselves how much pollution we would like to get rid of before the costs exceed the benefits of a cleaner environment.

Since this second perspective more closely mimics the situation we find ourselves in today, we will stick with it. The task we are presented with is determining how much to reduce various forms of pollution from their current levels.

For example, let's assume that we're talking about electrical production and the toxic emissions from power plants. Abatement can be achieved in many ways: by adding pollution-control equipment (such as scrubbers for sulfur in coal-fired power plants), switching to cleaner energy sources or technologies, or improving efficiency. These different ways of reducing pollution from power plants have very different costs; some may be relatively cheap while others may be very expensive. This means that we may be able to get some quantity of abatement for a relatively low cost, but if we want more, it may cost *a lot* more.

If we have a very dirty power plant with almost no pollution-control equipment, there are likely relatively straightforward and accessible options to help reduce some portion of its pollution. But as the plant becomes cleaner, the technology to improve it even more is likely to become increasingly expensive.

The same is true if we think of pollution not at the facility level, but at a regional or national level. The amount that it costs to decrease air pollution in a region becomes increasingly expensive as the area becomes cleaner. Reducing the smog in Los Angeles, while expensive, would be less expensive than improving air purity an additional step once most of the smog is removed. Often, it is these last units of pollution abatement that are extremely costly.

This phenomena is often referred to as the "low-hanging fruit" theory: there are almost always some pollution-reduction options that are relatively easy (they're within arm's reach), but once these are used up, pollution-abatement options become increasingly difficult (they're way up high near the top branches).

The benefits of reducing pollution exhibit the opposite relationship: they usually start out high and ultimately decline. Again, let's examine air pollution. The health and other environmental benefits of cleaning up a highly polluted airshed are many; they include significantly reduced mortality, reduced respiratory illness, better visibility, and a healthier environment for animals and plants. But once much of the smog has been removed and the air is reasonably clean, removing the remaining particulate matter, while beneficial, does not translate into nearly as much benefit as when the air pollution was at much higher levels.

Let's take a step back and think about all of this together.

The starting point is a city with a serious smog problem. The government wants to reduce pollution due to the myriad health and environmental problems through some form of new regulation (later, we will examine the various means of achieving a pollution-reduction target, but for now we're just interested in the target itself).

The city makes some estimates of the damages from the smog and the costs of abating it, and concludes that reducing smog by 50 percent costs only $10 million but leads to benefits of $100 million (for a net benefit of $90 million: 100 minus 10 equals 90). Next, the city considers whether reducing pollution by 75 percent is worth the cost. It determines that the additional 25 percent reduction costs a little more than first 50 percent reduction (another $12 million); the additional benefits are not as great (only $65 million this time), but the net investment is still positive ($53 million: 65 minus 12 equals 53) for going this extra step.

The city then examines the scenario of reducing the smog by 90 percent, and here is where the calculation changes dramatically. The additional 15 percent reduction (from 75 percent to 90 percent) turns out to be very expensive ($50 million for this incremental improvement), but this additional 15 percent reduction doesn't yield nearly as many benefits as the last phase of pollution reduction (now only $35 million). The net benefits of this final phase of abatement would actually be negative—to the tune of –$15 million (35 minus 50 equals –15).

A case can now be made that 75 percent smog reduction (or perhaps a little more since we didn't examine the precise scenarios between 75 percent and 90 percent) represents the "optimum" level of smog reduction for this city. We have arrived at this conclusion by quantifying the relative benefits and costs of smog abatement until we reached a point where the costs of additional abatement became greater than the additional benefits.

Before addressing the many caveats that accompany this logic, it is important to recognize that this is the same logic that we employ when choosing virtually any other good.

Take strawberries. Let's say the price is three dollars per basket. You go into the store and grab the first basket at the cost of three dollars, and then wonder whether you want a second. You decide that you do. Then a third—they are so delicious. A fourth? You think hard about it, but decide that three is enough. What made you stop? Simple, the marginal benefit of the fourth basket was not equal to the marginal cost of three additional dollars. If the additional benefit of that fourth basket was worth more than three dollars to you, you would have bought it (assuming you had the money).

Takeaway point: The theory of optimum pollution is premised on the same logic that economists use to analyze the markets for ordinary goods and services.

However clever this logic may (or may not) appear to you, you might already have questions regarding the actual implementation of this concept. To start, how are the benefits and costs calculated for pollution abatement? And, perhaps more important, how can we translate health and environmental values into dollars, which is what this methodology entails?

But first I want to make a couple of additional points about the concept of optimal pollution and its implications for real-world policymaking.

REAL-WORLD IMPLICATIONS OF OPTIMUM POLLUTION THEORY

The "optimum" quantity of pollution refers to what is most *efficient* for society as a whole. This is defined as the point at which society gets every bit of pollution abatement where the benefits exceed the costs.

What is important to recognize is that while efficiency may be a valid criterion, it is simply one among many. Efficiency says absolutely nothing about the ***distributional impacts*** of a given level of pollution. For example, an efficient solution could be entirely consistent with a situation where the pollution that is *not* abated is heavily concentrated in a poor minority community or in an area with lots of school-age children with asthma.

What is efficient, therefore, may conflict with what people consider fair, just, or equitable. And in current policy debates, fairness and equity are often what people are most concerned about. This doesn't mean that efficiency shouldn't be considered. In cases where what is efficient also corresponds with what the majority thinks is fair, we have a win-win situation.

A second key point is that economic models implicitly include costs and benefits that weight the decision-making process in favor of those with greater incomes and wealth.

Often, when health effects are calculated, lost productivity is partially determined by the number of sick days; a sick day for an engineer counts more in monetary terms than a sick day for a school-teacher because an engineer's salary is usually much higher. When the benefits of nature viewing are assessed, the wealthy traveler who spends thousands of dollars to visit a national park counts for a lot more than a person without a car who doesn't have the money to make such a trip. (One way this issue can be mitigated is to find the average of all people's values and use this as a representative of the population, which most studies do.)

Bottom line: the classical economic view of pollution doesn't take into account any notion of environmental goods as *rights*. For example, many people argue that access to clean air and water are human rights that society has an obligation to provide to all of its citizens.[2] While efficient solutions, as defined by economics, need not conflict with such notions of rights, they may, and sometimes do. There are cases where economists may use the above framework to define pollution strategies that are optimum, but that do not automatically guarantee all members of society some minimum level of environmental quality.

As a student of environmental issues for more than two decades, I have noticed that when economists and environmentalists discuss controversial issues, the economists often talk about efficient solutions, whereas the environmentalists talk about equitable solutions. In many instances there is a great deal of confusion as the parties essentially talk past each other. Environmental discussions and debates would benefit greatly if all parties could be explicit about when they are making arguments based on efficiency concerns and when they are making a case based on the distributional consequences of a policy independent of efficiency.

In cases where environmentalists want to argue that an efficient strategy for pollution abatement does not meet certain ethical criteria, it would be helpful if they acknowledged the potential losses in efficiency that these may entail.[3] Economists are used to talking about trade-offs and are not all coldhearted statisticians unable to be swayed by these modes of argumentation.

With respect to the earlier hypothetical case where our city's "optimal" reduction in smog is approximately 75 percent, what if the remaining 25 percent is concentrated in a poor minority community where rates of respiratory illnesses are significantly higher than the regional average? It would be entirely appropriate to make a case that what is optimum in this scenario from an efficiency standpoint may not be just, and imposes too heavy a burden on economically disenfranchised communities. What is efficient is not the "end all, be all" when determining the ultimate policy outcome.

There are other serious limitations of the optimum pollution methodology.

When attempts are made to quantify the costs and benefits of pollution reduction, analysts often compare aggregate costs of a given action to improve the environment with aggregate benefits; they usually do not search for the precise pollution level that will be most efficient. And typically, these benefit-cost analyses do not seriously examine the distributional consequences.[4]

Here are some suggestions for environmentalists when confronted with these types of studies:

- Take a close look at the scope of the benefits and the costs that are being examined. This is often where many assumptions are made and usually where many short-cuts are taken. Almost always, the direct health benefits comprise the bulk of the benefits side of the calculation, because politicians are usually swayed by these benefits more than benefits to plant and animal life,[5] which are in some ways more abstract. If this is the case, and there is a compelling reason to suspect that the effects apart from human health are significant, environmentalists may be justified in insisting that the benefits of the proposed policy are underestimated and may lobby for the inclusion of a greater scope of benefits, or at least an acknowledgement that the benefit estimates are incomplete.[6]

> Society expends its resources—financial, social, and political—on all sorts of things that it deems important, and which, one hopes, confer significant benefits to various groups of people within society and/or society as a whole. If we had a completely rational manner of distributing these resources, would it make sense to spend money on a program that cost $1,000,000 for every life saved when another program could save a life for $1,000? Put another way, wouldn't it make more sense to shift resources from the $1,000,000-per-life-saved program to the one that cost 1/1000th to save a life?

- With respect to costs, these usually include the direct and indirect costs of actually implementing the regulation. Typically, the bulk of the costs are the costs to industry for altering its production processes. These costs are often estimated based on estimates of the prices given *current technology*. But there are many examples where the costs of reducing pollution decrease dramatically once incentives for pollution reduction are created by new regulation. This often leads to an overestimation of the costs of pollution reduction.[7] Environmentalists should pay close attention to these costs estimates, and in cases where no account is made for technological progress, make the case that they need to be included.

- Uncertainty is very difficult to include in a benefit-cost analysis or optimum pollution framework because it is next to impossible to put monetary estimates on the unknown. The current state of our scientific knowledge of the adverse effects of many classes of toxic chemicals is poor or in its infancy, which only compounds the problem.[8] It may be reasonable to argue that an additional benefit of reducing pollution is risk reduction. Pollution reduction can be viewed not only as a means to achieve verifiable health and environmental benefits, but also as an insurance policy against many unknowns.

- Finally, environmentalists would be best served by prioritizing their environmental goals according to some level of rational calculus. This doesn't have to come from any central authority that speaks for all environmental organizations, nor does it need to be set in stone. *But not all environmental goals are created equal.* Figuring out which ones can achieve a high level of benefits relative to the costs is one way to couch them in economic terms, which often holds a lot of sway in the political process.

If we organized society according to this logic we would do things very differently. We would likely spend less money on maintaining thousands of active nuclear warheads and more money on prenatal and infant nutrition and education (which has huge societal returns). We would also likely shift environmental regulation more toward reductions in heavy metals such as lead, mercury, and benzene, and perhaps focus a little less on reducing chemicals that at current levels don't offer much more in the way of benefits, such as dietary exposure to some low-risk pesticides.[9]

WANT TO BE TOUGH ON CRIME?
BE TOUGH ON LEAD

Recent research makes a persuasive case that lead exposure can lead to increases in violent crime (Reyes, 2007), and conversely, that decreasing lead exposure can reduce criminal behavior. With crime rates always capturing a lot of public (and political) attention, this finding is something environmentalists would be wise to follow. If it can be further demonstrated that reducing some of the worst toxic heavy-metal pollutants can also help combat crime, this would provide a very powerful new argument in the environmentalists' arsenal.

SUMMARY

Economists approach the issue of pollution in much the same way as they approach the issue of how markets allocate other goods and services. Pollution is a bad thing, but many times it is the result of producing a good thing, *or at least a thing that people want.* Balancing the good and bad from pollution is similar to balancing the satisfaction (the good) we get when we consider buying a product or service against the amount of money we have to give up to get it (the bad).

However, this framework is an aggregate framework that does not deal with issues of equity and fairness; just as the market, when left to its own devices, does not guarantee everyone three meals a day and shelter, the market will not guarantee everyone relatively clean air and water.

CHAPTER 3

VALUING ECOSYSTEMS

In addition to addressing issues related to toxic pollution, conserving ecosystems and the species that inhabit them is the most important issue that confronts environmentalists. Rarely does a month go by without a major news story concerning ecosystems under strain or species facing extinction. Most people, even many who wouldn't consider themselves environmentalists, believe that we have a moral obligation to protect our natural heritage. For those who directly rely on ecosystems for their livelihood, it is often an issue of survival.

The problem, once again, is that preserving environmental resources is not only very difficult in practice, but sometimes also very costly. How do we prioritize what to conserve? What criteria should we use?

Once we have answered these questions, we then must determine who should pay for the desired course of action and how these decisions will be enforced. But first we need to think about what it is we want to conserve before we can formulate a strategy to get it done.

Ecosystems provide a wide range of benefits to society: they provide productive services such as food, fiber, and water; regulating services such as flood and disease control; wildlife services such as recreational and cultural benefits; and supporting services such as nutrient cycling that maintain the conditions for life on Earth.

While this broad range of services has been acknowledged by scientists (and economists) for quite some time, until relatively recently there have been very limited attempts to actually quantify them comprehensively to assign them economic value.[1] Unfortunately, the result has been that these benefits are often vastly undervalued in the public policy process. It is one thing to make note of the flood-control potential of a marshlands ecosystem, and another to say that it provides flood-control protection on the order of hundreds of millions or billions of dollars each year.[2] The latter is much more likely to get a policymaker's attention.

The absence of specific information on ecosystem services can be thought of as a form of market failure, as discussed in Chapter 1. Markets are very likely to undervalue ecosystem services (and therefore not preserve them to the extent that they should) if these services are not in some ways quantified and recorded, and the information disseminated. Only then can actors, whether they are private companies, local or national governments, or international organizations, take these values into account when deciding on alternative uses of ecosystems or the activities that will affect them.

In order to fill this void, numerous consultants, nongovernmental organizations (NGOs), and academics are busy trying to put monetary values on hitherto undocumented ecosystem services.[3] This work is going a long way toward demonstrating the tremendous economic value that ecosystems provide across a wide range of users.

Much of this work is uncontroversial, at least conceptually: Ecosystems provide many *direct* and measurable services, which even if difficult to quantify, are reasonably easy to catalog. For example, if a watershed above a city helps to purify the city's drinking water, which in turn saves the city the money required to build a water filtration plant, it makes sense to assign the value of water purification services to the watershed ecosystem.

If a river provides low-cost transportation in an area, then the difference between the cost of shipping goods using the river and the cost of using the next best option is one of the ecosystem services that the river provides. In economies that are dependent on extracting natural resources from ecosystems, such as timber, food, and medicinal plants, the *consumptive* value of these goods can be calculated in a relatively straightforward manner and attributed to ecosystem services.

In addition, we can often estimate the value of our recreational use of ecosystems because we leave *behavioral traces* when making use of these services, which can be quantified. Whenever we view wildlife, or go hunting, camping, rafting, surfing, scuba diving, or bird watching, we spend money along the way, which can be recorded and incorporated into an economic valuation. Revenue from tourist operations, park fees, the supporting services in the area such as restaurants, stores, and hotels, as well as the distance people travel to seek out nature recreation can be used to more precisely estimate the total economic impact of the demand for nature-based activities.

Again, this is relatively uncontroversial, even if the specific techniques are complex, imperfect, and require certain behavioral and statistical assumptions. It is reasonable that places people spend lots of money to get to and enjoy, such as Yosemite National Park, the surf breaks of Indonesia, or the dunes of Cape Cod, have more aggregate recreational value than locations that are rarely visited. (Remember, recreational services are but one among many ecosystem services, and a far-removed ecosystem that tourists never visit may still be highly valued for other reasons.)

Most controversial are the benefits that we derive *passively* from ecosystems. There are many places in the world that most of us will never visit, yet we care about what happens to them because we value their existence independent of whether we actually make direct use of them. We are happy to hear that they are being preserved and protected, and saddened when we learn of their destruction. Many of us give charitable contributions to organizations that help protect these distant ecosystems, which we may only ever see in pictures. Part of the value may be based on our desire to pass the natural heritage on to future generations, and perhaps because we want to reserve the option to visit these unique places one day, even if we may not actually get the opportunity.

Regardless of the reasons we care about those ecosystems that do not directly affect our daily lives and with which we have no direct experience, these passive-use (or nonuse) values are real. If we could somehow quantify them they would likely be very large, both because of the depth of many people's commitment to ecosystem preservation and simply because there are so many people on the planet. Some may suggest that contributions to conservation organizations capture the full extent of people's existence value for ecosystems, but this is not the case.

Many people believe that it is the role of government, not private charities, to protect our natural heritage. In addition, since nature conservation is a public good, there are many people who are content to let other people pay for ecosystem preservation while they sit back and derive the benefits. If push came to shove, however, and the fate of these ecosystems was dependent on their actions, most of these people would be willing to pay *some* amount of money to preserve them.

So how do we go about estimating these passive-use values for which we do not observe behavioral traces in everyday activity?

This is a very difficult task. The best economists have come up with is to devise surveys that attempt to elicit these values. They interview people and present them with hypothetical situations having to do with ecosystem protection or preservation. Ultimately, the participants are asked how much they would be *willing to pay* (WTP) to support a given action that will lead to improvements in the ecosystem, whether the purchase of new land, restoration efforts, or efforts to limit ongoing damage. This survey technique is called *contingent valuation*;[4] it used throughout the world to estimate the passive-use value of ecosystems. By posing realistic scenarios that confront people with difficult choices, contingent valuation surveys are able to elicit information that can inform us of the magnitude of the nonuse values, even when the ecosystems in question are distant.

Imagine that a government is considering a program to restore a degraded river. A contingent valuation survey would guide participants through a description of the current state of the river and what the government proposes to do to improve the fish and animal population and water quality. Then the participants might be asked if they would be willing to pay a given amount in extra taxes to enact this program.

The most important element of the survey is to convince the participants that their answer is consequential; that is, if they answer "yes" that they are willing to pay the given amount for the restoration project, this will influence the government's decision whether to proceed with the program and actually enact the tax.[5] If they don't believe that their answer will have any influence on the final decision, then they may simply answer "yes" to the payment question because it feels like the right thing to do, not believing that they will have to bear any real costs for doing so.

The contingent valuation method was famously used to help estimate the damage claims against the Exxon Corporation after the *Exxon Valdez* oil spill in Prince William Sound, Alaska, in 1989.[6] In a precedent-setting move, a federal court ruled that lost passive-use values due to the spill needed to be included in the damage estimates. This was the first time that a U.S. court explicitly acknowledged that citizens derive economic value from the mere existence of the ecosystems in the government's care, even if they do not directly use them and may never do so.

The contingent valuation survey estimated lost passive-use values of approximately $2.8 billion. The hypothetical scenario posed in the survey—that the government was planning on instituting a system of escort ships to prevent tankers from running aground—was eventually adopted.[7]

Contingent valuation studies can be very helpful for organizations that want to estimate the willingness to pay for entrance fees to parks or other environmental monuments. In many developing countries entrance fees to incredible natural treasures are often very low, and these nations are foregoing potentially tens of millions in revenue because they do not know the true value of their natural resources. Well-crafted contingent valuation studies can help them more accurately determine pricing and fee structures.

SUMMARY

Increasingly, efforts are underway to assign monetary values to ecosystem services. Some methods are much more straightforward than others, both conceptually and in practice, but by using a combination of tools, it is possible to capture a wide range of ecosystem benefits. This work is important because identifying both the source of the values and their approximate magnitude is an important first step in determining how best to preserve and protect ecosystems.

But monetary estimates of ecosystem services are just that: estimates. In many cases they may be extremely imprecise. At best these tools provide a reasonable range of values. They allow environmentalists to compare different sources of value, which is often important for figuring out the most effective conservation strategies.

If it can be shown that a wetlands ecosystem provides more value for storm protection than duck hunting, a stronger case for conservation may be made working with adjacent landowners than with hunting groups.

If both of these services combined provide more value than a proposed industrial development project, then these numbers may be used to sway the agencies in charge of approving the project. Of course, there is always the risk that the ecosystem benefits will actually be less than the value that could be generated by a new development project.

This underlies one of the inherent risks in assigning monetary values to ecosystems: *there is no guarantee that the ecosystems will always win in an economic calculus.* This is why some environmentalists are deeply suspicious of the race to put monetary values on environmental resources, even if they recognize the powerful economic forces at work that they must contend with.

Both the ethical and tactical problems associated with assigning monetary values to the environment arise in almost all economic policy responses to environmental issues. Whether they are made explicit or not, they are always just beneath the surface.

CHAPTER 4

PUTTING MONETARY VALUES ON THE ENVIRONMENT AND LIVING THINGS

The first three chapters outlined the basic conceptual framework of how economists approach environmental problems. Economists do not begin with the assumption that all pollution and environmental degradation should be eliminated; they believe that society must strike a balance between industrial development and environmental quality. Much of the methodology that economists employ to help society weigh the trade-offs between environmental goals and the production of goods and services relies on putting monetary values on the environment and living things.

Economists do this for a simple reason: money provides a convenient metric. To the extent that we can translate societal costs and benefits into monetary values, we can then easily compare them. This can help us choose priorities and make the most cost-effective choices.

But money is not the only metric we could use. In fact, there is virtually no limit to the number of metrics we could come up with.

We could measure things in equivalent amounts of copper or gold, pencils, computers, or children that could be fed.

There are many benefits of using money as the metric, as well as some significant drawbacks. The first I have already touched upon; there may be some things that we consider human rights, which should *not* be decided based on notions of cost-effectiveness.

Since access to clean water is considered a human right, we wouldn't want a government deciding not to build a new water delivery system because the monetary benefits of providing the water (however defined) were found to be less than the costs. Yet even in such a case, it would be reasonable to assess different costs of providing the water and using these to determine the most efficient way to provide this right.

The notion that certain levels of environmental quality and access to natural resources should be guaranteed is sometimes used as a way of saying that they are priceless. Many reasonable people argue that environmental treasures, such as our national parks, unique species, and human life are all priceless.

But the reality is that they are not; I have proof.

Consider the decision a person makes when deciding whether to take a vacation that will cost $1,000. What else could they do with the money? They could give it to charities that help starving children or AIDS patients, or to those like the Nature Conservancy that protect endangered ecosystems. And what if they don't? What if they decide to go on that vacation? Such a decision makes clear that, according to this person's calculus, the environment and living things are not priceless, not even close. If they were, they would certainly have sacrificed the relatively small sum of money for a luxury good (a vacation), and used it instead to protect and preserve life. The actions of this hypothetical actor are repeated billions of times a day in one way or the other, most of the time with a similar outcome.

FOR ECONOMISTS IT IS ACTIONS, NOT WORDS, THAT MATTER MOST[1]

Some may think that my example is unfair. Let me be clear: the person who takes the vacation may care a lot about the disadvantaged and threats to the environment. They may give a lot of money to charity to support these causes. And they are not alone; there are many incredibly charitable people in the world. But there is a point at which virtually all people stop giving. It is at a point well before they reach a simple subsistence lifestyle.

We may put a high value on the needs of others and the environment, but not a value that comes close to showing the type of dedication that would constitute a true belief that the well-being of others and the environment are priceless. Even those who are most charitable still put a premium on a high standard of living for themselves and their families.

There are many other ways to demonstrate that virtually no one acts in a way consistent with the view that the environment and human life are priceless.

Let's take the speed limit. In most states in the United States it stands at 65 mph. It used to stand at 55 mph. This increase of 10 mph has probably led to thousands of additional fatal accidents per year, because the speed limit is highly correlated with fatalities;[2] the faster we go, the greater chance that we die when we crash—and that we crash in the first place. And many of those killed in these accidents are completely innocent; they are simply the victims of other people's mistakes.

So why did we increase the speed limit in the United States? Because we valued the convenience of getting places faster more than we cared about the loss of life, even innocent life. In fact, if we really wanted to treat life as priceless we would make the speed limit very low, probably in the range of 15 to 25 mph. But how many people would accept this? Close to zero.

We can also see trade-offs at work even in the most basic environmental activity: nature viewing. Many if not most environmentalists are driven to protect ecosystems by a deep desire to commune with nature. But this desire to visit natural habitats and interact with natural systems exacts a price. The roads that we cut through wilderness areas to reach them, the diseases and invasive species we introduce, and the pollution we generate put strains on fragile ecosystems. If we truly wanted to maximize the survivability of these systems, in many cases we would protect them and leave them alone. But we don't.

One of the most dramatic examples in recent memory with respect to damage awards occurred in the decision over how to distribute funds allotted to the families of the victims of 9/11. Kenneth R. Feinberg created a detailed method for calculating benefits based on victims' ages, the nature of their employment, and their projected wealth (Chen, 2004b). This created a major controversy since the spouses of investment bankers received a lot more than the spouses of janitors. If he had to do it all over again, Feinberg said that he would simply give everyone an equal share (Chen, 2004a).

In fact, those of us who live in rural settings, perhaps to feel more in tune with nature and away from the hustle and bustle of modern industrial life, often impose more of a negative impact on just those natural systems that we want to protect. It is extremely inefficient and damaging to ecosystems to bisect them with country roads that serve very few people, and which require driving much longer distances to get to work, town, and school. From a pure conservation standpoint, urban living is much more efficient.

None of these critiques suggest that there is anything wrong or immoral about treating the environmental and living things as less than priceless. As economists have noted for a long time, humans are self-interested beings. We are often generous, compassionate, and charitable, but not in the extreme. We balance our own needs and desires with what we feel are our obligations to others, the environment included.

So while there are still problems with putting monetary values on the environment and living things, the "they are priceless" critique is not very persuasive.

The biggest issue with monetizing the environment and living things is not philosophical or ethical, but practical: how do we do it in a defensible way?

As mentioned in the previous chapter, some methods for assigning monetary values to environmental benefits are relatively uncontroversial. For example, if a fishery creates $50 million per year in revenues for the fishing industry and the surrounding local economy, then this is a reasonable *minimum* starting point for the total value of the fishery. If smog over a city decreases property values by $100 million, then this tells us something significant about the value that people assign to better views and breathing cleaner air.

The most difficult issue we face is putting a dollar value on human life and suffering, which is often necessary when trying to quantify the benefits of a given pollution-reduction policy. For example, if reducing mercury emissions would save fifty lives a year but cost $1 billion to implement, is it worth it?

Policymakers face these types of questions all the time. Probably the institution with the most experience dealing with monetary values for life is the court system. Damage claims for loss of life and pain and suffering are ubiquitous, and juries are often faced with the task of granting monetary awards to those who have lost loved ones or suffered due to someone else's negligence.[3]

Ultimately, there is no completely satisfactory way to place a monetary value on human life. One million dollars, ten million, twenty? There is always some degree of arbitrariness to the exercise. What economists have often done, which has filtered into the legal system, is to take the sum of the total of earnings over a person's lifetime. One way to make this equitable from a societal standpoint is to take the average across all people to determine the average lifetime earnings of the population; this ensures that poor and rich alike are weighted equally in the calculation. This doesn't address issues of the sorrow and pain that a person's family feels, but there is essentially no satisfactory way to put a dollar value on this.

We could begin to approximate pain and suffering damages by measuring the amount of lost time at work, but this only scratches the surface with respect to the true extent of the damages. In the courts, the accepted range for pain and suffering compensation is up to several million dollars, depending on the extent of the injuries.[4]

The problems don't end here.

One of the most interesting aspects of putting monetary values on human life is how dependent it is on the statistical nature of the lives in question. For example, let's go back to the issue of whether reducing mercury pollution that kills fifty people a year would be worth a cost of $1 billion. It is only when we talk about people in the abstract that we can even begin to make this judgment. What if, on the other hand, we knew exactly which fifty people were going to die? Could we then sit down and reasonably argue over whether it was okay to let these fifty people die instead of making the $1 billion investment? I doubt it. The same goes for our desire for the 65 mph speed limit. It would never be acceptable if we actually knew for sure which thousands of citizens would be mangled in the increased number of accidents.

But the randomness that comes with the costs of our actions makes them statistical exercises. We know that some people somewhere at some future time will die because of certain policy choices, but the uncertainty that surrounds the circumstances allows us to distance ourselves from these otherwise unacceptable costs.

This paradox raises some profound questions. Is this apparent contradiction actually beneficial? Does it allow us to bypass our sentimentality, which might otherwise cripple our material progress? And doesn't this material progress not also create the conditions for greater life span and prosperity?

There are no easy answers to these questions. The bottom line is that putting monetary values on human life will always be problematic, somewhat arbitrary, and subject to valid criticism.

For this reason, it is often preferable to think about environmental problems from another angle. What are the most cost-effective pollution reduction policies that will reduce the loss of life and improve health outcomes? This is often the actual task policymakers face; they are given mandates to reduce mortality and illness from pollution and then must figure out the best ways to achieve these results.[5]

Where these targets come from is worthy of an entire book unto itself. One of the first things one notices when examining many environmental targets established by government agencies is that they often come in round, even numbers—for example, reductions in pollution of 20 percent or 50 percent; it is rare that a government agency puts forth a plan to cut emissions by 13.7 percent.[6] Numbers are often chosen that are easily digestible by the public and that can demonstrate a clear commitment to pollution reduction.

However, in most cases there is at least some scientific basis that accompanies the given number. For example, in the 1990 U.S. sulfur dioxide "cap and trade" program, the goal was to significantly reduce acid rain, and the target chosen was based on an analysis of the reductions required. But even behind this decision lurked an implicit benefit-cost analysis and monetary valuations of human lives and the environment.

We know that the particulate pollution from sulfur dioxide leads to severe health problems, and that the initial 50 percent reduction from 1980 levels would not completely eliminate the acid rain problem. Why didn't the program call for immediate 60 percent or 70 percent reductions, which would have resulted in less smog and less environmental degradation? The likely answer is that there wasn't sufficient political will to push for greater reductions because there were limits to the costs that regulators wanted to impose on the coal industry. In effect, there was a point at which the agencies involved didn't think it was worth it to push for greater environmental improvements.[7]

Many U.S. environmental statues are unique in that they specifically mandate that agencies are *not* allowed to use benefit-cost analysis in their decision making. The Clean Air Act, the Clean Water Act, and the Environmental Protection Agency's (EPA) pesticide permitting process are all required by law to be carried out entirely on the basis of serving the public interest irrespective of the costs imposed on industry (and indirectly on consumers, who may face higher costs as a result).[8]

But is it possible for regulating agencies to truly divorce themselves from weighing costs and benefits when making important decisions about human health and the environment (putting aside for the moment whether it's desirable for them not to do so as the laws require)?

In a landmark 1992 study of the EPA's decisions regarding prohibiting the use of pesticides, a team of researchers discovered that while the EPA didn't carry out an explicit benefit-cost analysis when deciding which pesticides to ban under which uses, the agency did in fact weigh costs and benefits very much *as if they had* (Evans et al., 1992). Pesticides that posed a greater risk to consumers and pesticide applicators were banned more often than those that posed a lesser risk, while those pesticides that helped farmers the most were banned less frequently than those which were not as beneficial.

I suspect that if this study were updated today the results would hold. Regulators are faced with a wide variety of often competing interests, and they must find some logical way to prioritize their regulatory decisions. Some weighting of the costs of regulation against the benefits to human health and the environment are inevitable.

SUMMARY

Whether we explicitly assign dollar values to the environment and living things in the public policy arena, there is always an undercurrent of monetary valuation running just below the surface; it is inescapable. Economists contend that it is preferable to make these valuations and the assumptions that accompany them transparent and an integral part of the decision-making process. This does not mean that any action where *costs are greater* than benefits is unwarranted; only that good reasons should then be provided for pursuing such a course.

It is a misperception that assigning monetary values to the environment and living things automatically cheapens them and renders them mere commodities in the public policy process. In many cases, if attempts are not made to assign monetary values to the environment, the default value is zero or close to zero. As we continue to document the economic values of ecosystems and make them salient in the policy arena, it becomes much more difficult to ignore them.

There are cases where opponents of environmental regulations or environmental preservation may be able to use economic values to gain the upper hand; not every economic exercise will show environmental goals as the best choice for society as a whole. But environmentalists should not let this dissuade them from embracing environmental valuation.

Every day, scientists are discovering new ways that ecosystems provide societies with benefits and new ways that industrial pollutions threaten human health.[9] In addition, people all over the world are increasingly seeking nature-based recreation and enjoyment, putting a premium on environmental quality. Given these trends, the dollar value of the environment is poised to grow exponentially, which will help environmentalists make the case for increased preservation and pollution reduction.

CHAPTER 5

VALUING FUTURE GENERATIONS

f valuing *current* generations and their environmental needs wasn't difficult enough, policymakers also have to contend with how to value future generations. This is not an abstract issue; the biggest environmental issue of all, climate change, has huge implications for future generations (as well as current generations);[1] so do other issues, such as the depletion of nonrenewable resources, the degradation of unique and irreplaceable ecosystems, nuclear waste disposal, and the hole in the ozone layer.

A few questions naturally arise: How much voice should be given to the needs of the future when making decisions that affect us today? Put another way, if people from the future could influence our decisions, what would they ask us to do? And should we listen?

For many environmentalists the answers are obvious: future generations want us to dramatically decrease air and water pollution and increase the amount of biodiversity preservation so that they will inherit a cleaner environment rich with life, and one in which they won't have to face any catastrophic environmental risks.

Are these reasonable assumptions to make?

Since we have no way of interviewing future generations to elicit their opinions, it may seem impossible to answer this question. But we can look at the actions of generations before us and ask ourselves whether we would have asked the same of them.

There is little doubt that if U.S. citizens could go back in time they would tell the early settlers not to wipe out most of the buffalo population.[2] They would also inform those in the past of the risks of rampant and unchecked industrialization that made many cities nearly unlivable and exacted a terrible price on the environment that future generations inherited.

But if U.S. citizens compared their lifestyles today with those of one hundred or two hundred years ago, they would also likely acknowledge that some of the historical pollution and environmental degradation paved the way for the immense material progress they now enjoy. As with present-day environmental decisions, they would still be cognizant of the need to balance the benefits of smaller ecological impacts in the past against the benefits that were derived from them.

There is another angle to consider. Most of us alive today, especially in the developed world, are much wealthier than our distant ancestors. We enjoy better health, longer lives, more leisure time, and more choices. Would it be right of us to ask those in the past to cut down fewer trees and pollute the water less if these activities were integral to the modest improvements in *their* standards of living? Why should they have sacrificed so that we, who are immeasurably richer, could enjoy even greater prosperity today?

While these questions are somewhat abstract, it is not unreasonable to think along these lines. The future is uncertain and we may very well be passing down a planet in worse shape to future generations. But we might not—even the best ecological models are imperfect and highly uncertain. What we do know for sure is that in the areas of medicine, transportation, computer technology, and virtually every other field, the people of the twenty-second century are likely to inherit vastly superior technologies that will have the potential to markedly improve their well-being. Imagine if, by the end of the century, we eliminate cancer and heart disease or have computers that dramatically improve safety in all aspects of our lives. No doubt new technological improvements will also be made in pollution-control technology and renewable energy.

To the extent that there is a trade-off between spending more money on environmental improvements versus other types of investments, we have to be careful before assuming that future generations would automatically choose less pollution and more nature reserves. How can we be certain what balance of resources future generations would like us to invest in?

Nobel Laureate Robert Solow, in his classic 1991 essay "Sustainability: An Economist's Perspective," adds another wrinkle to his issue: we should be willing to sacrifice at least as much for *present* generations as we would be willing to sacrifice for future generations. In other words, it would be odd (some would say immoral) to incur costs today that would benefit people a hundred years from now and not make the same sacrifices for those who are living in squalor and misery today, which according to the United Nation stands at roughly one billion people.[3]

All of this raises a central question for economists, environmentalists, and policymakers: to what extent do environmental improvements actually require us to sacrifice resources that could be used to promote other goals? In other words, could we be at a point where current technology and know-how is sophisticated enough that improving the environment can be a win-win situation with positive economic returns?

Would a massive effort to combat global warming actually lead to the development of new technologies that would help grow our economies and increase employment? If this were the case, then we could be better off today *and* help secure a better environment for future generations; there would be no inherent conflict between the two, and in many ways the whole previous discussion would be moot.

The consensus view, however, is that we are not yet at this point; promoting many of our environmental goals *does* require incurring societal costs. For example, the Stern Review, which represents probably the most comprehensive analysis to date on the economics of climate change, estimates the costs of sufficiently reducing the risks of climate change at $1.35 trillion per year by 2050.[4]

If it is indeed the case that environmental goals require us to sacrifice resources, and hence some percentage of economic growth, we are back to where we started, confronted with the issue of how to weigh costs today against benefits in the future.

This is also the issue that the authors of the Stern Review had to deal with when it came to policy recommendations. Once they calculated the costs of greenhouse gas reductions, they needed to see how these compared to the benefits of the reduced risk of climate change many decades, even centuries, into the future.

How do we best do this? Should a dollar spent today to prevent climate change weigh equally against a dollar in benefits one hundred years from now?

To address these questions, we need to understand the role of *economic discounting*, which is highly controversial.

Discount rates appear in many discussions of environmental policy, particularly in the context of benefit-cost analyses and long-range environmental planning. They are expressed in percentage terms: the higher the discount rate, the more we value a dollar in hand today over one in the future (e.g., a discount rate of 10 percent makes the benefits of climate change prevention one hundred years from now worth much less than if the discount rate were 5 percent).

To compare costs today with benefits in the future, the authors of the Stern Review had to choose a discount rate that reflected the degree to which we as a society (or world community) value a dollar in hand today over a dollar in the hands of future generations.

Many environmentalists argue that the discount rate should be zero because it is immoral to value our well-being over that of future generations. But a zero discount rate implies behavior that we don't exhibit anywhere in the world: saving virtually all of our money to pass it down to our children and grandchildren.[5] If we really believed that a dollar in the hands of those in the distant future was just as important as a dollar in our hands today, we could put most of our money in the bank, let it earn interest, and make those in the future much better off. Why would we spend so much money on frivolous things when that money could grow and provide much greater happiness to others one hundred years from now?

We do, however, save some amount of our income for future generations and make investments that require us to sacrifice in order to make them better off. But not at levels that would justify a zero discount rate. We still spend a lot today on things that are purely for our own benefit and that are clearly luxuries.

If a zero discount rate is not consistent with how we actually behave (at least the overwhelming majority of the time), then what discount rate should be chosen? The answer has serious implications. Discount rates are applied exponentially per year; if we value something at 5 percent less next year than we value it today, we value it at 10.25 percent less two years from now (0.05^2), 21.55 percent less four years from now (0.05^4), and so on.

Put more concretely, if we estimated the benefits of climate change mitigation at approximately $1 trillion one hundred years from now and we used a discount rate of 5 percent, that $1 trillion would be worth only $7.6 billion today. If instead we choose a near-zero rate of 0.1 percent, then that same $1 trillion one hundred years from now would be worth over $900 billion today, more than one hundred times the amount!

Before proceeding with a discussion of what might be an appropriate discount rate and examine the choice made in the Stern Review, let me state bluntly that there is *no absolutely correct answer*. For decades, there has been intense debate about what the right discount rate should be for environmental projects, and there is still no consensus. However, there is a relatively high degree of agreement on what constitutes a *reasonable range* for the discount rate, and there are defensible arguments for choosing a rate within this range.

The *upper range* for the discount rate should be the average real long-term return on private investment, which has historically been in the range of approximately 9 to 12 percent per year for developed countries (and significantly higher for developing countries because of the higher risk).[6] This discount rate forces environmental investments to earn a rate of return greater than or equal to the return of private investment in order to pass a benefit-cost test. Those who propose this discount rate argue that environmental investments must compete on an equal playing field with all other types of investments that society makes; if an environmental project can't match normal private rates of return, then society's resources would be better invested somewhere else.

Others point out that the average return on private investment includes a premium for risk. Some businesses in developed countries return zero or negative profits (because they fail), while some yield much greater than 11 percent, resulting in the average of 8 to 11 percent. If an environmental investment is very likely to yield positive societal benefits, then the rate of return required to pass a benefit-cost analysis should be lower than the average private return, which factors in this risk premium (reward for taking the extra risk). Advocates of this view argue that the rate of return on government bonds, which are essentially guaranteed, makes more sense. Over the past decade the average long-term bond rate has been in the range of approximately 4 to 6 percent.[7] This discount rate forces environmental investments to earn a rate of return equal to or greater than the essentially riskless option of government treasuries.

Some argue that even this rate is too high. They advocate a discount rate of 2 to 3 percent because many environmental resources are irreplaceable; once they are severely degraded or damaged, this damage cannot be reversed. They believe that the special nature of environmental resources should tilt society more toward saving them for future generations. Unlike a new road, school, or factory, there is no substitute for a unique ecosystem, a stable climate, or an intact ozone layer; the more unique the resource, the lower the discount rate should be.

Environmentalists who find themselves in the position of having to argue in support of a particular discount rate almost always fall into this last category. Even those who in principle support a zero discount rate often concede that it not practical, nor does it best reflect actual human behavior.

But this group recently found a surprising ally for a close-to-zero discount rate in the authors of the Stern Review, which used 0.1 percent per year to calculate the present value of the benefits of climate change mitigation for future generations.

The report concludes by advocating an aggressive investment to prevent global warming *precisely because of this very low discount rate,* which makes future benefits appear relatively attractive when compared to the costs of reducing greenhouse gas emissions in the present. This is an absolutely crucial point: without the very low discount rate, the Stern Review would not have concluded that the benefits of mitigating climate change (which accrue largely in the future) are worth the costs incurred today.

The use of this near-zero discount rate has led to the accusation by many economists that the authors of the Stern Review "cooked the books"—a discount rate even in the low range of 2 to 3 percent would not have led to the report's favorable conclusions for immediate action. Many of those who otherwise view the report favorably have focused on the very low discount rate as the report's greatest weakness.

And yet, a few notable economists, including Martin Weitzman of Harvard (2007), have concluded that the Stern Review's conclusions might be "right for the wrong reasons."

This leads to a couple of final points on uncertainty and catastrophic risk that further complicate thinking about far-off environmental problems, and whether discounting them in the conventional manner makes sense.

Even though the science now confirms that human activity is contributing to global warming and that this warming is likely to continue if we do not dramatically reduce our greenhouse gas emissions, we are still highly uncertain as to what the end results of this warming will be (Parry et al., 2007). We can be sure about a few things—less Arctic ice, more storms, sea level rise—but the range of possibilities still includes some not-so-catastrophic outcomes along with some potentially cataclysmic scenarios, such as major new storm activity, sever drought, major species extinction, and major inundation of coastal areas.

Weitzman argues that a small probability of catastrophic damage may be enough to force us to err on the side of action over inaction, even if the most likely *average* future benefits of action do not merit such a response. Putting a high premium on worst-case scenarios tilts us in the direction of a zero discount rate *not* because we actually value benefits to people one hundred years from now as much as we value benefits today (as many environmentalists and the authors of the Stern Review would like us to believe), but because when our actions pose a reasonably significant risk of making the world *much less livable* in the future, then we have an obligation to go out of our way to reduce that risk.

This rationale is not operative when assessing the benefits of most types of environmental investments, because they do not pose such dire scenarios. For example, cleaning up a waterway or expanding open space, while perhaps in society's interests, will not greatly affect humanity's chance for survival or greatly affect overall living standards to anywhere near the degree that climate change might. When posed with these more common scenarios, we should revert back to the basic arguments for choosing the proper discount rate. These arguments are contentious and there is no consensus, but at least there is a range of reasonable values for which to make a case.

SUMMARY

Environmental planning almost always entails taking into account the well-being of future generations. All situations that require examining a stream of costs and benefits over time must confront the issue of choosing a proper discount rate, because a dollar in the future is not worth a dollar today (even after counting for inflation). Many environmental investments can be very sensitive to the choice of the discount rate; higher discount rates make current investments with benefits that accrue in the future appear less attractive, while lower discount rates make them appear more attractive.

To complicate matters, there is no correct discount rate.

The key for environmentalists is to understand the rationale for discount rates that are used in different environmental analyses and to craft an argument as to whether they are defensible. When dealing with especially unique and irreplaceable environmental resources, or in situations when future generations may be subjected to severe environmental risks, a very low discount rate, even approaching zero, may be warranted. The upper bound should always be the average private rate of return, which is the bar that private business investments must meet.

This upper bar will be higher in developing countries because their investments are typically more risky and require additional returns as compensation. In addition, in developing countries the average standard of living is lower and the balance between current consumption and the well-being of people in the distant future is arguably tilted more toward the needs of the present.

Another thing to pay attention to when assessing a study that makes use of a discount rate is whether alternative scenarios are presented using different discount rates to see whether they alter the basic conclusions. This is often referred to as "sensitivity analysis," presenting results under a variety of assumptions to show how sensitive the conclusions are to the different rates that are chosen. Studies with conclusions that are less sensitive to the choice of discount rate will be easier to defend. And as always, benefit-cost analyses are simply measures of aggregate efficiency, not equity or distributional concerns. These must be taken into consideration as well.

CHAPTER 6

TOOLS TO ADDRESS ENVIRONMENTAL PROBLEMS

TAXES, PROPERTY RIGHTS, INFORMATION, PSYCHOLOGICAL INSIGHTS, AND COMMAND AND CONTROL REGULATION

The field of economics would be of limited use to environmentalists if it was only good at examining the causes of environmental problems and offered little about how to actually solve them. Fortunately, this is not the case. This chapter provides an overview of the policy options for addressing environmental problems that economists have developed and the areas where they can be most effective. By and large, these policies fall under the heading of "market-based" mechanisms and are not at all controversial on the theoretical level; where disagreement exists is in the implementation and in the details.

At the end of this chapter I also briefly discuss "command and control regulation," which has traditionally been favored by many in the environmental community because of its clear and precise mandates and its long history of delivering tangible results. I argue that while market-based mechanisms are often more efficient than command and control regulations, optimum environmental policy often blends both approaches.

This discussion will form the basis for much of the discussion in the second part of the book, where we examine a range of current environmental issues and the best types of policies available to address them.

ENVIRONMENTAL TAXES

As discussed earlier, when the production of a good or service leads to damages that are borne by parties besides the producer and consumer, this is called an externality; environmental degradation is the classic example. In virtually all industries there is some amount of pollution or environmental harm that is imposed on those in the region or the greater society who neither produced nor consumed the good.

If we can calculate the damage from these external costs, we can partially correct for this market failure by levying an equivalent tax on the offending industries.[1] This is often referred to as the "polluter pays" principle, although this is a somewhat misleading phrase. In reality, it is highly unlikely that the price of the newly taxed good will rise by the precise amount of the tax. Depending on the relative slopes of the supply and demand curves for the good, the producers and consumers will share the tax burden in different proportions.

For example, if the good is something that consumers desperately need (or want) and has few substitutes, and hence their demand is not very sensitive to price, much of the environmental tax will be passed on to them in the form of higher retail prices.[2] For other goods that have more substitutes and that consumers can more easily do without, an environmental tax will be absorbed mostly by producers; here the polluter-pays principle is a more apt description.

Not only do environmental taxes generate the revenue needed to compensate those who are harmed by the pollution and/or to mitigate the negative impacts, but they also raise the price of the good or service in question, thereby decreasing the quantity demanded. This is exactly the result that environmentalists should favor: a shift away from environmentally harmful goods once their prices reflect the true costs imposed on society.

Putting aside for the time being the political issues associated with raising taxes, there are significant problems with this policy choice. While environmental taxes will reduce the production of environmentally harmful goods and encourage the production of alternatives, they may not reduce them significantly in the short term if the demand is not very sensitive to price.

Perhaps more important, environmental taxes do not address distributional issues. Over time they may lead to environmentally favorable shifts in patterns of production and consumption, but they are unlikely to effectively address situations where particular groups or resources are under immediate environmental strain and bear a disproportionate toxic burden.

Also, environmental taxes have to be thought out very carefully; if they are not applied to the root cause of environmental problem, they may actually make matters worse.

Let's examine the case for a gasoline tax for the purpose of reducing greenhouse gas emissions. At face value it appears like a sensible idea. Driving is the number one cause of greenhouse gas emissions in the transportation sector;[3] raising the price of gas (by the incremental damage of each gallon's CO_2 emissions) would decrease emissions both by reducing driving and creating incentives for more fuel-efficient cars and gasoline alternatives. The tax would also raise revenue that could be used to fund research and development in clean energy technologies and carbon sequestration, or that could be refunded to consumers.

The problem is that gasoline is not the only type of fuel that produces greenhouse gas emissions, and focusing only on gasoline (not the root source of the problem) could actually lead to a greater reliance on fuels that are even worse for climate change.

There already is a push toward plug-in hybrids as an alternative to gas-powered vehicles. But where will the electricity come from? If gasoline becomes more expensive through a gas tax, while the price of coal remains the same, increased coal generation could be used as the primary source of electricity for the plug-ins.

A carbon tax might be more appropriate than a gas tax because this would raise both the price of gasoline and coal accordingly; otherwise the tax could shift the economy to favor coal as an energy source, which could lead to a net increase in greenhouse gas emissions.

This still might not be sufficient. Carbon dioxide is not the only greenhouse gas emission, even if it is the most ubiquitous. Methane and other gases used for fuel are orders of magnitude more damaging for the climate than carbon dioxide.[4] If the ultimate goal of the environmental tax is to reduce the likelihood of catastrophic climate change, then it should focus on some weighted average of the total greenhouse gas impact for all types of fuels. This way, new methane farms, not just gas and coal, would face higher costs. Similarly, nitrous oxide is a potent greenhouse gas that is used in the production of nitrogen fertilizer; if this chemical were exempt from a greenhouse gas tax, the use of biofuels might increase without accounting for the additional nitrous oxide this would produce.

This example exemplifies why focusing on root causes of environmental problems is of the utmost importance in crafting environmental policy, especially when considering environmental taxes. *This is one of the greatest insights that economics can provide to environmentalists.* If this is not done, new distortions are created that may actually lead to a shift toward even more polluting industries and technologies.

There is a growing movement, especially within Europe, to move toward a tax base that derives a greater proportion of revenue from environmental taxes and less from labor income.[5] From an efficiency standpoint, there is a strong argument in favor of shifting society's tax burden toward environmental taxes instead of taxing labor income. Putting aside the issue of the proper size of government, no one denies that governments need to generate significant tax revenue to operate and provide the services that have been promised to the electorate.

Taxes by their very nature discourage the activity that they are levied upon because they raise its price. The higher the tax rates for labor income (all else equal), the less people will be willing to work. After all, if you are able to take home eighty cents of every dollar you earn, you will be willing to work more than if you can only take home sixty cents.

Taxing labor income is the predominant manner in which governments generate revenue throughout the world. The problem is that discouraging work is not good for society, since labor is the lifeblood of the economy. An optimal tax policy would have very low or zero taxes on labor income so as to encourage labor productivity and innovation. Environmental taxes, on the other hand, discourage exactly what society should be discouraging: environmentally degrading activity.

The challenge is figuring out what level of environmental taxes could provide the same revenue stream as taxing labor. Since no country has completely shifted to environmental taxes as its primary source of revenue, we don't yet have an answer, but we do know that they would be high. A society that went down this path would face much higher energy and food prices and costs for heavily manufactured goods, but would pay little to no income tax.

The question arises how the poor and middle class would fare under such a scheme. The middle class would likely do reasonably well; their overall level of taxation would likely stay about the same since they would be relieved of a major tax burden on labor but pay significantly higher prices for consumer goods.

Unfortunately, the poor would probably fare worse. Currently, they don't pay very much in income taxes, and hence they wouldn't benefit greatly from lower labor income tax rates, while they would face much higher prices across a wide range of goods.

The rich would likely be better off because they would be relieved of a huge tax burden. Although they consume a lot more than most people, as a percentage of their income they actually save and invest more.[6]

This leads to a major conundrum that plagues environmental policy. Many times what is most efficient is also *regressive*; is hurts the poor disproportionately more than the middle classes and the wealthy. Some might argue that the poor would be the greatest beneficiaries of a cleaner environment (which would result from much higher environmental taxes) since they bear a disproportionate toxic burden in society. This may be true and should be considered; however, this would likely not be sufficient to make up for having a much harder time buying enough food and heating their homes.

One potentially simple solution would be to use some of the tax revenue levied from environmental taxes to help subsidize the poor who would be hurt by this policy, perhaps in the form of tax credits or a minimum income. This would allow society to maintain equity and fairness while also benefiting from a shift in the tax structure that favors labor over consumption, and creates significant incentives to produce environmentally sensitive products and technologies.

PROPERTY RIGHTS: CAP AND TRADE SYSTEMS

The lack of transparent and enforceable property rights for fisheries, forests, and atmospheric resources has, in many cases, led to the classic "tragedy of the commons" scenario. On a theoretical level the solution to this problem is relatively simple: governments need to assign property rights to these resources, figure out a way to distribute them, and make sure that people don't use more of these resources than they are entitled based on their property rights.

These government-created environmental property right schemes are usually referred to as "cap and trade" systems. After the government determines the maximum allowable use of the resource (the cap), it allows actors to freely trade the rights to this utilization (usually in the form of permits), which in most cases greatly improves efficiency over a standard regulatory mandate (i.e., command and control regulation).

Efficiency gains are greatest in industries in which firms have very different cost structures, because the gains from trade arise from some companies' ability to reduce pollution at much lower costs than others. This typically occurs in industries where there is a mix of old and new, small and large companies, and that compete with foreign firms. A flexible system that allows pollution allowance trading, instead of a government mandate, allows the cleaner firms to gain an advantage over dirtier firms and earn money in the process.

The first issue that needs to be addressed when considering a cap and trade system is the appropriate level for the cap. For example:

- How much sulfur dioxide should be allowed in the atmosphere if greatly minimizing acid rain is the goal?
- How much greenhouse gas emissions should be allowed if we are to reduce the chance of catastrophic climate change?
- How much fishing should be allowed to maintain a fishery's sustainability?
- How much logging should be allowed to maintain optimal forest biodiversity and ecosystem services?

This is where the natural and physical sciences must play a huge role.

Fisheries biologists can help determine sustainable levels of fishing, ecologists can calculate with relative precision the optimal forest cover for habitat preservation and the provision of ecosystem services, while climate specialists have a pretty good sense of the maximum concentrations of greenhouse gases in the atmosphere that can insure us against climate catastrophe.

There are many uncertainties in all of these fields, which is why the caps should be subject to periodic review based on scientific updates and the best available information. Fortunately, our scientific understanding will only improve over time, and the scientific community can currently provide defensible baseline estimates to be used in cap and trade systems in a wide variety of contexts.

Economic considerations come into play as well, typically in some form of a benefit-cost analysis or other weighting of interests. Scientists can provide what they believe are the optimal levels of resource use from an ecological perspective, but to the extent that these recommendations require sacrifice in other realms of the economy, it is the job of policymakers to balance these with the economic interests at stake. The distributional impacts and the ethical implications of different courses of action must be addressed as well.

It is the job of citizens and environmental organizations to make their voices heard (and elect leaders who reflect those voices). One of the primary arguments of this book is that these voices will be most persuasive if environmentalists are able to speak the language of economics and understand its implications, as well as *substantively* critique economic analyses, especially if they believe that they are biased against environmental interests.

Cap and trade policies have become very popular because they allow for maximum flexibility in achieving their targets; once the cap is set, businesses and other actors can meet their obligations almost any way they choose. This creates room for innovation and adaptation that otherwise would be reduced if the government mandated certain technologies or practices. Similar to environmental taxes, cap and trade systems create incentives to move toward the development of environmentally friendly technologies because polluting or extracting a resource becomes more expensive; business are required to own a permit in order to exercise this right.

Some environmentalists criticize the basis of these programs because they create rights to pollute (or in the case of fisheries and forests, rights to exploit).[7] While this instinct is understandable, the appropriate question to ask is whether in the absence of explicitly recognizing these rights firms were limited in their ability to pollute or extract resources in the first place? In almost all cases the answer is no; the atmosphere and the open oceans are treated like free goods that everyone can pollute and degrade if they so choose; it is the establishment of the cap that actually limits what was otherwise an unlimited right.

Once a cap is chosen, how the rights to the resource are allocated raises important political and ethical issues that can have significant efficiency and revenue impacts. Economists typically favor the auctioning of resource permits; in this manner no actors are privileged and all must bid based on their valuation of the permits. This is equitable in that no firms are immediately favored over others, and future entrants aren't put at a disadvantage over existing businesses.

In reality, however, most of the time permits are allocated to existing businesses based on past performance; this is called "grandfathering."[8] This usually happens because it is politically the easiest way to get cap and trade systems passed in the legislative process. By freely giving out the permits to existing actors, these players gain a valuable resource, even if the caps ultimately end up constraining their activity. This has been crucial in generating the necessary support from industry for both sulfur cap and trade systems in the United States and the CO_2 trading scheme in the EU.

Allocating permits freely to existing industry raises serious issues, because in some way those with the worst environmental records are rewarded for their past bad behavior. In the U.S. sulfur dioxide trading program, established in 1990 (the world's first cap and trade system), the dirtiest plants were given the most permits while the cleanest plants given significantly fewer. The owners of the dirty plants could reasonably respond that their environmental performance was tied to the age of their facilities, which they shouldn't be penalized for, but many of them had for many years resisted making environmental improvements, thereby weakening this argument.

Not only does freely allocating permits create equity issues, but the government also loses a major source of revenue. With sulfur dioxide permits initially trading at approximately $170 per ton, the initial 226,384 permits were worth $38,485,280, which the U.S. government was unable to collect.[9] This money could have been used for any number of research projects such as cleaner coal technology, coal alternatives, or ecological restoration projects.

One of the benefits of permits is that since they are freely traded, environmental groups can participate in the market. Environmental groups that want to reduce sulfur dioxide by even greater amounts than the cap can purchase permits and not exercise them, thereby decreasing total sulfur dioxide emitted. (There are examples of environmental groups purchasing hunting permits and retiring these in order to decrease hunting below the maximum amount allowed.[10]) There is also nothing stopping environmental groups from purchasing CO_2 permits on the European trading market and retiring those in order to reduce carbon emissions at a rate greater than the EU has initially called for.[11] This takes money, but the mechanism exists.

Cap and trade systems work only in situations where the resource in question can be relatively easily monitored. For example, in the case of sulfur dioxide, there are a set number of coal power plants, and these all are equipped with instruments that monitor emissions levels. With respect to CO_2 emissions, firms must report the fuel they use, which can be converted into carbon equivalents.

The key is making sure that there are sufficient penalties for non-compliance with the permit allowances. If it's cheaper to pay a fine than to limit pollution or resource extraction, then a cap and trade system will break down almost immediately. Typically, the penalties have to be at least an order of magnitude greater than the benefits of noncompliance to truly deter cheating, since there is always a chance of not being caught.[12] Adding criminal penalties to noncompliance costs, especially those that may result in jail time, can also be very effective; it is one thing to pay a fine and another to do hard time behind bars.[13]

INFORMATION PROVISION: RIGHT-TO-KNOW PROGRAMS, ECOLABELS, AND R&D

Imperfect information is one of the primary causes of market failure; it is impossible for firms, policymakers, NGOs, and individuals to make well-informed decisions when the information at their disposal is limited and incomplete. If there is a factory on the outskirts of a town and the mayor and the citizenry are contemplating whether existing regulatory requirements are sufficient, they need to know what toxins the factory is emitting into the environment before they can evaluate the factory's impact.

In many parts of the world, a company's emissions are considered proprietary information that is not available to the public. This was the case in the United States until 1987, when the U.S. Congress passed the Emergency Planning and Community Right-to-Know Act (EPCRA), which mandated that virtually all manufacturing facilities in the United States had to annually make public the data on their emissions of hundreds of toxic chemicals.[14] The law led to the establishment of the Toxic Release Inventory (TRI), which the Environmental Protection Agency manages and disseminates to the public every year with updated emissions figures for more than 20,000 manufacturing facilities.

This "right-to-know" program was a revolutionary development in the environmental movement;[15] it has been heralded as a great success by many for its low cost, the breadth of information it provides, and its overall influence on how both the public and firms view environmental information. Although drawing a causal link between the establishment of the TRI and the subsequent drop in virtually all of the chemicals reported in the database (many by as much as two-thirds) is extremely difficult, there is a general consensus that the program has had an impact (Hamilton, 2005). Possibly the most powerful effect has been the ability to "shame" firms by directing media scrutiny to their poor environmental performance, which is often followed by political pressure to improve their management and reduce emissions.

Since the creation of the TRI, numerous countries have followed suit and established their own right-to-know programs, including the European Union and Canada,[16] and to a limited extent Mexico, Chile, China, Australia, India, and Indonesia.[17]

What is particularly fascinating about the experience of the TRI in the United States is that the emissions of many of the listed chemicals have dropped to levels much lower than those mandated by existing regulations (Roe, 2002). Some of these reductions may have occurred even if the TRI had never been established, but it is unlikely that they would have been so dramatic. The maxim in politics that transparency is a critical first step in minimizing corruption may have an analogous interpretation with respect to toxic emissions: transparency is the necessary first step to make firms take responsibility for their toxic emissions; or, put another way, being able to hide behind a wall of incomplete information may forestall greater improvements in emissions reductions.

Right-to-know programs are not without their critics, and they do suffer from a number of significant flaws. They are only as good as the quality of information they provide, which in many cases, especially in developing countries, is poor. In addition, while the provision of the information is often mandatory, the reports are provided by the firms with very little oversight as to their accuracy. This can lead to cheating or mistakes, which then weaken the effectiveness of the information.

Perhaps most important, emissions vary tremendously in terms of their toxicity. This requires skilled people to translate the raw data into information that accurately measures the health and environmental impacts of the various chemicals that are reported. A more than decades-old effort to translate the TRI data into a user-friendly form can be found at the Scorecard website.[18] Users can examine all sorts of geospatial aspects of the TRI database, including emissions in low-income and minority communities, and across a wide range of important categories, from reproductive toxins to ozone-depleting chemicals to cancer risks.

While right-to-know programs will continue to provide an amazing array of useful information to environmental groups, there is also a growing movement to offer more information directly to consumers at the retail level. This has led to the proliferation of dozens of "ecolabels," such as sustainably certified wood, dolphin-safe tuna, energy-efficient appliances, environmentally friendly cleaning supplies, and many others.[19] These labels help to provide some of the missing environmental information in markets by highlighting a product's use of nontoxic chemicals, energy efficiency, recycled content, or other sustainable practices. This then affords consumers the opportunity to put their "money where there values are" by supporting products with a lower environmental footprint.

The rise of ecolabels speaks to one of the larger ongoing issues in environmental policy: to what extent should individuals be allowed, through the marketplace, to choose the level of environmental quality they want versus the degree to which certain practices or standards should be mandated across the board by the government? While most environmentalists favor the latter course of action (and in many cases rightly so), they still recognize the tremendous potential for ecolabels to reshape industries.

The key for an effective ecolabel is to provide truthful and mean-ingful information to the consumer. Since eco-friendly products usu-ally carry a price premium, there is a great incentive for producers to exaggerate their claims, or make outright false ones.[20] This then requires some type of oversight, which can be governmental or by a credible third party.[21]

Modern technology is improving the legitimacy of ecolabels and is providing more informational power at the individual level. The Forest Stewardship Council, which certifies sustainably harvested wood prod-ucts, makes use of satellite technology to monitor forests and uses bar codes to ensure that they can trace all of the logs they certify.[22]

Technology to empower consumers has also moved rapidly to handheld devices, such as cell phones, iPods, and BlackBerries. The company GoodGuide has released applications for the iPhone that allow consumers to scan barcodes in retail stores to ascertain detailed environmental data on products.[23] The company also main-tains a website with the most comprehensive consumer product information in the world, which goes beyond simply environmental data to include issues of labor rights, the treatment of animals, and political contributions. Although still in its infancy, and with many gaps in product information, this new technology is ushering in a revolution in "ethical consumerism" that is sure to have profound consequences.

The power of information to influence consumer demand, as incredible as it is, is tempered by the fact that there is only so much information that individuals can reasonably be expected to process; there is a point where individuals experience "informational over-load" and stop paying attention. Where this threshold lies should be of great interest to environmentalists; surprisingly, however, there has been little research to date on this topic.[24]

Not only do consumers shut down when faced with too great an array of competing information and labels, but an even more pressing question arises: given the limited window to provide environmental information to consumers, what is the most important information to present?

Put another way, if we could influence consumer choices in only a few key dimensions, what would these be? Carbon footprint, toxic materials, unsustainable logging, food choices? Since the rise of ecolabels has been largely a bottom-up movement with no overarching strategy or public interest objective (aside from general environmental improvement), this question has never been addressed. It should be.

It can take years, or even decades, to cultivate consumer consciousness around a particular label or issue. The environmental movement would likely benefit if the major environmental organizations and institutions could agree on a limited set of issues to prioritize for information campaigns, and then stick to them, continually coordinating in order to reinforce them in the public consciousness.

We have seen this happen with recycling and to a lesser extent organic agriculture, but the question still arises whether these are the most effective areas for channeling individual action toward environmental improvements.

On the informational front there is ultimately nothing more pressing than the need for dramatic increases in basic research and development in all aspects of environmental science. Of the more than 42 billion pounds of chemicals entering the U.S. market every day, we have little to no information about the effects of more than 95 percent of these substances.[25] In addition, even the chemicals that have been studied have been in isolation; we have almost no knowledge of the synergistic effects of the varied combinations of these chemicals in the environment and our bodies.

Valuing ecosystem services can only be as good as our knowledge of the basic functions of these systems, which is in its infancy. More research dollars for understanding the roles of wetlands, savannas, tidal zones, forests, and the interactions within the climate system will only help us make better policy decisions.

More investment is also needed to research alternatives to toxic substances (i.e., "green chemistry") and for energy efficiency improvements across all sectors of society, from power plants to building to manufacturing. Private enterprises already have incentives to decrease their environmental footprint to save money, but since they don't reap all of the benefits of a healthier global environment, they are almost assured to underinvest in these improvements.

In the twenty-first century, we are going to witness massive economic shifts that we have barely begun to recognize; the economies of 2100 will be radically different in ways that we can only begin to imagine. One thing is for sure: whoever can lead the way in the development of green technologies is likely to have an advantage since this will be one of the biggest growth markets of the century.[26]

PSYCHOLOGICAL INSIGHTS

Over the past decades, a group of prominent economists and psychologists have been studying the various ways people think and act that are not in accordance with rationality as classically defined by economics. This has led to development of the field of "behavioral economics," which is becoming an increasingly influential school of thought within the discipline.[27]

While this growing subfield is too extensive to cover broadly in this chapter, environmentalists can get a sense for its potential for shaping environmental policy by examining the conundrums currently faced when trying to get residential customers to switch from dirty power to green power.

In the green power industry, one anomaly continues to attract attention: when people are surveyed and asked whether they would be willing to pay a small amount more for green power (typically 5 to 10 percent), overwhelming majorities say that they would; however, when these programs are made available, only a very small percentage of people actually make the switch to green power.[28]

Why the discrepancy? Is it that people just tell interviewers what they want to hear? Are people really not willing to pay more for green power?

Perhaps, but there is a more plausible explanation that comes from behavioral economics: *status quo bias*. In a landmark paper by Madrian and Shea (2000), the authors show (using the example of 401(k) retirement savings plans in a large corporation where enrollment was extremely low) that people tend to stick with default options and not switch even when it's in their economic interest; that is, inertia dramatically dictates a person's course of action.

In their research project, when the default option was switched to automatically enroll workers in the 401(k) plan, there was much greater participation in the plan than when the default was "not enrolled" and people had to opt in by calling the human resources department. This result was striking because retirement decisions are one of the most important we ever face, and yet inertia and procrastination prevented people from taking the time to sift through the information and make a simple phone call. This was even the case in instances where the company would match dollars one for one—an immediate 100 percent return on the investment in the 401(k) plan.

This finding is completely inconsistent with any conception of rationality that classical economics relies on, where all individuals are assumed to be able to make well-reasoned decisions about their future.

It very likely that status quo bias is also at work in a big way in electricity markets.

What if the default option when people moved into new homes was green power, and they had to call up the electric company to switch to "brown" power if they didn't want to pay a premium? Not only would we almost certainly see much higher utilization rates approaching those found in the surveys, but the psychology would be vastly different as well. When one is faced with the option of choosing green power, it is not hard to see how one can procrastinate; one has the good intention of switching but never gets around to it.

Once the default position is switched to green power, people would have to actively choose to switch to dirty power. How many people would really call up the electric company to request dirty power in order to save a few bucks? Some for sure, but this switch would make the issue much more salient because it would force us to focus on the ill effects of conventional electricity generation.

It is likely that status quo bias is ubiquitous throughout many sectors of the economy. It will force us to fundamentally rethink many of our policies in a variety of areas, including the environmental realm.

Another area where psychological insights can help guide policy is with respect to energy efficiency. Numerous studies have demonstrated that both individuals and companies often overlook large energy-saving investments, even when they are in their financial interest.[29] In the case of companies, the reasons for this oversight are likely bureaucratic inertia and the fact that many companies simply aren't accustomed to thinking about detailed energy-efficiency decisions in their business plans.

On the individual level, the reasons have more to do with a bias against energy costs over long time horizons versus the initial purchase price of appliances and other consumer durables (the discounting problem at the individual consumer level). People tend to buy lower-priced goods that are less energy efficient even when the cost savings over the lifetime of the product would make a slightly more expensive energy-efficient model significantly cheaper when the energy savings are factored in.

For this reason, governments may need to provide additional incentives or mandates to both businesses and individuals that favor energy-efficient purchases. For example, creating minimum efficiency standards for classes of appliances or electronic goods may actually benefit the environment and help people save money.[30] While classical economics predicts that people will always choose to save money without government interference, the reality is that most people simply don't pay attention to small savings over long periods, even if they add up to relatively large sums.

Another fascinating psychological insight with major implications relates to how people view their own household energy use. Researchers have discovered that the simple act of highlighting a person's energy use in comparison to their neighbors on their energy bill, accompanied with energy-saving tips, can lead to significant energy reductions (not huge percentage changes, but significant absolute changes when taken over an entire population).[31]

There is no question that the behavioral economics revolution is just beginning to be felt in the environmental realm, and will become increasingly important, especially as we tackle ever more complex problems.

COMMAND AND CONTROL REGULATION

There is no strict definition of command and control regulation; it generally refers to specific legally binding mandates regarding a company's production processes and/or emissions levels. A law that specifies a precise type of technology that all chemical plants must use is a form of command and control regulation, as is a law that limits the maximum amount of effluent that cruise ships may dump in domestic waters. (The previous example of minimum energy standards for appliances or electronic devices—such as the EPA's Energy Star Program—is also a command and control policy.)

The two defining pieces of environmental legislation in the United States—the Clean Air Act and the Clean Water Act—are command and control laws that include hundreds of specific mandates that firms must comply with regarding production processes, emissions limits, and rules for upgrading facilities. Despite the success of these signature pieces of legislation in reducing air and water pollution, they have been subject to severe criticism because of the burdens they impose on businesses and their lack of flexibility in meeting their pollution-reduction targets. There is no doubt that while these acts have been beneficial to society overall, they could have been achieved at a lower cost if firms had greater options for meeting the goals.[32]

Market-based mechanisms have the benefit of allowing firms multiple pathways to compliance, thereby allowing them to choose the cheapest. Market-based mechanisms are also generally much better at promoting innovation because they create incentives for the development of new cleaner technologies. This incentive is often lost under command and control regimes because specific technologies are mandated, or all firms are required to reduce pollution by the same amount, thereby eliminating the incentives for cleaner plants to make additional pollution reductions.

The focus of part II of this book will mainly be on the market-based mechanisms (largely) developed by economists, but where appropriate, attention will be paid to command and control options that can complement market-based solutions. It is often the combination of these policies that produces the best outcomes.

SUMMARY

The types of policies described above are the principle mechanisms in the economist's (and environmentalist's) tool kit that can be used to craft workable solutions to a wide variety of environmental problems. These policies can be characterized broadly as attempts to correct for market failures that are not self-correcting; they require some form of intervention, most often by the government. Governments can and do exacerbate many environmental problems through poorly designed policies (usually enacted to favor special interest groups) that are not designed to promote the public interest.[33] But these cases do not undermine the reality that market failure is pervasive with respect to many environmental issues, and that governments do have a constructive role to play in fixing them.

One of the main takeaways from this discussion is that there are many avenues with which to pursue effective solutions to environmental issues, many of which have been developed and tested over decades.

This brings us to a critical point: it is not the dearth of ideas in environmental and natural resource economics that impede a more livable future, but the lack of political will in the face of deeply entrenched special interests, as well as timidity in the face of uncertainty. We have the intellectual apparatus to solve most, if not all, of our global environmental challenges; we just need to put it into practice. This cannot be overstated.

Yet, for every policy that would result in significant benefit for *society as a whole*, there is some interest group or demographic that might lose out as a result. These groups will go to great lengths to stop progress and the promotion of the public interest. From an economic standpoint, their behavior is rational, even if rightly frowned upon.

At the extreme, economists use the term "regulatory capture", when industry groups gain so much influence over the policy and regulatory process that they in effect control the government apparatus that is supposed to be overseeing them.[34] Oftentimes regulatory capture occurs when former members of industry are given top regulatory posts, thereby perpetuating a "revolving door" in which conflicts of interests are rife and the public interest is scuttled.

Powerful interests will always do their best to influence politicians and block legislative and regulatory changes that will negatively affect them. In societies where the powerful are allowed to contribute to politicians without limit, where the public is less informed and mobilized, these interests are likely to have greater success in stymieing good environmental policy than in societies where the public interest is given greater prominence.

There is nothing mysterious or surprising about this. This is why ultimately environmental policy is driven by politics; this is not meant in a disparaging manner, but simply to indicate that policy is the result of the interplay of interest groups vying for power and influence.[35] Ultimately, all environmental (and public) policy is only as good as the people carrying it out; electing honest and competent politicians with a strong commitment to the public interest, and the resolve to stand up to powerful corporate lobbies, is an absolute necessity.

CHAPTER 7

ENVIRONMENT VS. ECONOMY

GROWTH RATES, JOBS, AND INTERNATIONAL TRADE

Before moving on to issue-specific discussions about economics applied to environmental policy, I would be remiss not to spend a few pages on the controversial topic of the "environment versus economy" debate. Environmentalists are often confronted with the claim that stronger and more far-reaching environmental regulations will harm the economy by decreasing economic growth, raising unemployment, and making the home country less competitive globally, thus weakening export markets and leading to outsourcing.

At face value these claims seem to follow a logical progression: stronger regulation leads to greater costs for industry, which decreases profits, leads businesses to shed workers, and makes other countries without these regulations more attractive. But this "conventional wisdom" is largely wrong, both because of theoretical considerations that render the issues much more complex, and because the empirical data for the most part does not support this view.

ENVIRONMENTAL REGULATION AND JOBS

There is no doubt that many environmental regulations cost money, whether for the purpose of installing new technology or monitoring equipment, switching to cleaner fuel sources, or changing production processes. While this may raise the cost of doing business in the affected firm or industry, if the demand for the goods in question are insensitive to price, this cost may be passed on to consumers without any appreciable decrease in output, and therefore with little to no employment impact. If the regulation calls for additional fixed costs only—such as requiring the installation of scrubber in a smokestack—this may decrease a firm's profits, but would not cause the firm to decrease production. In this case their variable costs haven't changed, and therefore the regulation represents a one-time write-off.

Environmental regulations can actually lead to increases in jobs because the laws can mandate the purchase of new technologies, which bolsters demand for the businesses that produce these inputs. Oftentimes regulations necessitate increased management and bureaucracy, which also increase jobs; complying with the U.S. Clean Air and Water Acts requires many forms and detailed monitoring programs that employ full-time workers at many large firms. Employment also increases at government agencies that need to enforce any new regulations. In large developed countries, environmental regulatory agencies typically employ tens of thousands of people.

The notion that environmental regulations will by default lead to increased layoffs is theoretically unfounded. They can harm industries and lead to net job losses, but they also can lead to net job increases, depending on multiple factors.

In industries dependent on natural resources—agriculture, forestry, fisheries, mining—the employment impacts of environmental regulation are equally nuanced. In most cases, employment is driven much more by technology than any other factor. Most people would be surprised to learn that U.S. manufacturing is currently producing record output.[1] Talk of the demise of U.S manufacturing is common throughout the media and has seeped into the public consciousness. What is true is that employment in manufacturing has declined dramatically. These two facts coexist—greater output with fewer workers—because of the tremendous technological innovations that have swept the industry. Modern market economies are extremely dynamic, and while there is less employment in manufacturing, there are a lot more jobs building the technology that supplies it.

This same technological trend has taken place in agriculture. In developed economies very few people work as farmers, but yields are at or near record levels.[2] Even in developing countries, where much higher proportions of people work in agriculture, this trend is observed; every decade fewer people work in the fields as societies industrialize. Agriculture is highly regulated, mostly for environmental health concerns, but it is hard to make a case that this is what has driven the employment declines.

These declines started more than a century ago, long before the environmental movement. One could actually make the counterargument that the lack of regulation for greenhouse gases has led to an artificially low price for fossil fuels and fertilizers, which has led to more automation than would have occurred if fuel prices included their true cost to society. If and when society aggressively addresses climate change, it is entirely possible that higher fuel prices will lead to less automation and more workers in agricultural fields. Organic agriculture is typically much more labor-intensive because of the demands of growing crops without pesticides or synthetic fertilizers, and therefore greater limits on pesticides and synthetics might also lead to greater agricultural employment.

Employment in forestry and fisheries is interesting to analyze because these are both renewable resources if managed well and require lots of manual labor. But many forestry industries have experienced significant employment declines. This has been driven largely by the practices in the industry and not due to environmental regulations. In most parts of the world forestry companies have either clear-cut or greatly exploited the old-growth forests with the biggest and most valuable trees. Since these trees take hundreds or thousands of years to grow, once they are removed simple mathematics dictates that there will not be as much biomass to harvest (for a very long time). This translates to a need for fewer workers. If the forests aren't replanted right away, the soils will erode into rivers and streams, making regrowth much more difficult, and the employment impacts will be even more severe. Here again, environmental regulations that mandate sustainable forestry practices can actually help maintain employment, especially in the long term.

The same situation exists in fisheries. A well-managed fishery can sustain employment essentially indefinitely, and the business is labor-intensive. Even with the advent of modern fishing technology, there is a great need for workers since there is only so much within fishing operations that can be automated. Where fisheries have collapsed due to excessive exploitation, it is precisely *the lack of environmental regulations* and limits that helped drive the demise. Given the current state of the world's fisheries, it is unlikely that they can sustain the current levels of employment. The trade-off is slightly higher employment now with all but guaranteed collapse in the future, versus a slight diminishment now but with sustainable employment indefinitely.

In the mining industry, once deposits nearer to the surface are mined, it becomes increasingly expensive to extract ore and mines have to be dug much deeper. This is extremely expensive. Many types of mines produce very large environmental externalities—both to the immediate surrounding environment and to air and water quality—and therefore are highly regulated in most parts of the world. This no doubt significantly raises the costs of mining operations, but the alternative is to allow them to despoil the environment. In the absence of these regulations employment might be higher, but again, the main driver of employment is the cost of extracting the ore ever deeper in the ground. These resources are nonrenewable, and regulation or no, they will always become increasingly harder to access. The challenge of reaching these deposits can actually employ many workers, and new exploration is also a continuing source of jobs.

Bottom line: There is no evidence that, overall, environmental regulation leads to job losses. In fact, many industries are created or expanded through regulation, and it is the absence of environmental regulation that leads many industries to seek short-term profit over long-term planning, which leads to employment bubbles that are not sustainable.

ENVIRONMENTAL REGULATION AND ECONOMIC GROWTH

But what about the impact on the overall growth rate of the economy?

There is no doubt that excessive regulation (of any kind) can dampen productivity and innovation in even the most dynamic economies. It is possible that environmental regulations, even well-crafted ones, can diminish economic growth as measured by GDP—through a net reduction in the production of goods and services—compared to what the economy would've produced in the absence of such regulation. But regulations can also help to spur innovation by forcing firms to cut waste or develop new technologies to become even more efficient.[3]

The right question to ask is whether the regulation is worth it, once all of its pros and cons are considered. Not everything society values shows up in GDP, and some things that show up in GDP—burglar alarms, medical costs, fuel spent sitting in traffic jams—do not necessarily correlate with a higher quality of life.[4]

While clean air and water laws might lead to lower economic growth rates if they are very costly to implement, it is still possible that they can be justified on economic grounds. The key is documenting and measuring the value of the contributions of such regulations to a society's overall quality of life, including those that aren't picked up by traditional market prices, and therefore don't show up in GDP.[5]

Given the widespread economic transformations and dislocations that serious climate change regulations will entail, it is entirely plausible and reasonable to suggest that they will decrease economic growth rates. Even if only by a tiny fraction of a percent per year, these reductions—since they are exponential—could very well mean that society will be giving up some significant potential wealth to take this threat seriously. But what we get in return is a much greater probability of avoiding catastrophic damages that may represent an existential threat to modern civilization. We will also get cleaner air and better energy security.

A government that decides to set aside a large portion of its undeveloped land for conservation will almost certainly forego some GDP growth since this action will prevent a significant amount of construction and industrial development. But the value that society derives from having these natural resources to visit and enjoy—much of which does not show up in GDP figures—must be taken into account. In addition, if these preserved lands help to clean the water that is used by nearby cities or provide storm protection for coastal communities, conserving them could actually have the perverse impact of negatively impacting GDP, despite being clearly beneficial to society. GDP would capture the costs of a water filtration plant or rebuilding after a storm, but not the ecosystems that provide these services naturally (for "free").[6]

Bottom line: Environmental regulations should be judged on the totality of what they contribute to society. Supporting or opposing environmental regulations on economic grounds is entirely valid, but care must be exercised when using GDP as the ultimate metric. GDP is highly correlated with many things that most of us value, and given a choice to live in a society with high per capita GDP versus one with low per capita GDP, most of would chose the former. But there are serious problems with GDP as on overall measure of well-being and we shouldn't be wedded to it. Even the economist who developed the concept of GDP (Simon Kuzents, who was awarded the Nobel Prize in economics) knew this, and rebuked those who thought that national accounts were direct proxies for a nation's well-being.[7]

ENVIRONMENTAL REGULATION AND INTERNATIONAL TRADE

Similar to the links between environmental regulation and jobs, the link with international trade is more nuanced than it first appears. To the extent that environmental regulation in one country leads to increased costs relative to another country that is not subject to these regulations, the affected industries may become less competitive. The key issue is whether the environmental regulation is significant enough to lead to outsourcing or a shift toward imports from other countries.

The first thing to keep in mind is that transportation costs for international trade can be very high, and if a product is competitive domestically, the environmental regulation would have to impose large costs to make paying these extra transportation costs worth switching to a foreign supplier. The electrical power sector, which is one of the most heavily regulated sectors, doesn't face international competition because power has to be consumed near to where it's produced. There are some cross-border power supply agreements between nations, but for the most part electrical systems by definition will always be domestic industries (this doesn't mean that the parts for the power plants or wind farms will be produced domestically).

In most industries environmental compliance costs are not a huge share of the operating budget. Labor, land, administrative, and materials costs make up the bulk of the total costs. Access to skilled and dependable workers, access to capital, a stable and reliable source of power, and political stability are all also hugely important for business operations and profitability. Ultimately, for most businesses environmental costs may lead to higher prices or reduced profitability, but they are not the main drivers that determine where a business locates or how much demand there is for their products.

There are some industries, however, in which environmental regulatory costs can be very large—in the range of 20 to 30 percent; notably, the chemical and petroleum industries. The question is whether these costs are high enough to drive these industries to countries with more lax environmental regulations, thereby creating "polluting havens." The only way to answer this is empirically because economic theory alone cannot provide an answer.

A study in the *Review of Environmental Economics and Policy* (Levinson, 2010) shows that over the past thirty years, the United States has been producing cleaner goods domestically *and* importing cleaner goods as well. The belief that our environmental regulation might lead us to import dirtier goods from abroad does not appear to be supported by the evidence. One explanation is that even in industries with high regulatory costs, the other benefits of locating in the United States trump these concerns. In addition, major advances in technology have allowed industries to comply with environmental regulations at lower costs, decreasing the incentive to relocate.

There is also no guarantee that countries with fewer environmental regulations will stay that way; as countries develop and become wealthier, they tend to increase their environmental regulations.[8] A company that sets up shop in a country solely to take advantage of lax environmental rules is taking a significant risk. And if this firm cares about its international reputation, it can suffer a serious public relations problem if it comes to light that it is poisoning people in order to save a buck or two. This is not to suggest that companies never do this, only that the risks are great enough that the practice may not be as widespread as some environmentalists fear.

How the relative environmental standards of a large developed-country multinational corporation (MNC) in its home country compare with its operations in poorer countries is an important consideration for the environmental community. Equally important, however, is how that company's environmental performance compares to the domestic alternative in the host country. In many developing countries, the domestic industry, completely free from any significant environmental regulations, may be even dirtier than a foreign firm that replaces it. Even if foreign firms do not employ all of the environmental mitigation techniques that they would at home, firms based in wealthier countries tend to be more efficient and employ newer technology. There is little evidence to suggest that a domestic Nigerian, Vietnamese, or Bolivian firm will be less polluting than a European and Japanese firm that operates in these countries.

If firms don't routinely seek out pollution havens in a "race to the bottom" for environmental quality, could there be examples where the opposite is taking place? Could international trade actually lead to a "race to the top," with firms competing to be the most environmentally sustainable? The answer is largely dependent on the domestic policies of the world's biggest markets. Many developing countries are very reliant on exports to the developed world for a large share of their GDP. If the countries they sell to demand greener products and production processes, they will make accommodations to secure access to these markets. There is evidence that the EU's increasingly stricter environmental regulations, especially with respect to toxic chemicals, are leading to the production of more environmentally benign goods in industries in the developing world (Schapiro, 2007). The EU is now the world's largest market[9] and their environmental policies hold tremendous weight globally.

Bottom line: The trade impacts of environmental regulation are ambiguous. While regulation can increase costs and diminish competitiveness, there is no persuasive evidence that major polluting industries are moving from the wealthier nations with higher regulations to poorer nations with weaker regulations. In addition, countries or regions with very strong environmental regulations can actually drive exporting countries to adopt stronger standards.

HOW U.S. TRADE POLICY HELPED DESTROY THE EVERGLADES[*]

The history of U.S. sugar policy and the state of the Florida Everglades are inextricably linked. For decades, the United States has protected the Florida sugar industry by levying significant tariffs on imported sugar. The Florida sugar industry uses tremendous amounts of water from the Everglades and discharges huge quantities of toxic chemicals, which have helped to drive the ecosystem's decline. Removing these tariffs and making the sugar industry pay for the pollution it emits would address one of the root causes of the degradation of the Everglades (the other major problem is commercial development). But in the Everglades Restoration Act (which began under President Clinton in 2000, continued under President Bush, and continues under President Obama), the U.S. government instead chose to spend billions on huge engineering projects to try to "fix" the problem. As part of the restoration plan, sugar producers are receiving hundreds of millions of dollars (or more) to retire their land from production. In the end, not only has the sugar industry benefited to the tune of billions of dollars in higher-priced sugar over the decades (taken from the pockets of U.S. consumers at the expense of producers in low-cost Caribbean and Central American nations), but it is now reaping an additional reward for bad behavior. This case

should be exhibit A for environmentalists on how trade protectionism at the behest of corrupt special interest groups
can wreak havoc on the environment and waste billions in
taxpayer money.

*For more information on the link between U.S. trade policy and
the decline of the Everglades, see Schwabach (2002) and Natta
and Cave (2010).

SUMMARY

The "environment versus economy" debate often generates more heat
than light. Economic theory does not offer black-and-white answers
with respect to whether environmental regulation is ultimately good
or bad for jobs, the economy, or trade; we have to turn to empirical analysis for the final analysis. While environmental regulations
can lead to job losses in certain industries, as well as lower economic
growth and diminished competitiveness, they can also lead to job
growth, innovation, and a "race to the top" in international standards. Modern economies destroy and create jobs at a furious pace,
but most of this "creative destruction" is driven by changes in technology and innovation, independent of environmental regulation.

All regulations, including environmental, should be judged on
their overall benefit to society. Economic considerations are extremely
important for decision making, but issues of fairness, rights, and
overall quality of life improvements need to be considered as well,
even if they cannot be easily translated into dollar values. Even if a
higher per capita GDP is correlated with material improvements in
the standard of living, it is only one of many metrics that can used to
assess a society's well-being.[10]

Part II

PUTTING ECONOMIC ANALYSIS TO WORK

CHAPTER 8

CLIMATE CHANGE

C limate change is the most daunting issue the environmental community has ever faced; it is fraught with huge uncertainties, requires intense international cooperation, and portends a major transition in almost all aspects of the global economy. The closest the international community has come to taking on an environmental issue of this magnitude was the effort to stop ozone depletion, which resulted in the one of the most effective international treaties ever enacted: the Montreal Protocol.[1]

Unlike the problem of ozone depletion, however, which could be traced to a relatively narrow group of chemicals with relatively minor global importance, addressing climate change will require reorienting our entire energy supply and making major improvements in efficiency throughout vast sectors of the economy. It is a much more complex and demanding task.

The problem is also compounded because the potential effects of climate change are more uncertain than the increased risk of skin cancer linked to the destruction of the ozone layer. Given the greenhouse gases currently in the atmosphere, some amount of global warming is almost assured (and is happening already).[2] The issue before us is at what concentrations could we significantly reduce the probability of severe and catastrophic climate change to acceptable levels.

Once again, we are faced with a trade-off: every incremental reduction in greenhouse gas emissions reduces the probability of catastrophic change, but also requires a greater societal transformation and more intrusive policies, which are costly, both in dollars (at least in the short to medium run) and perhaps more significant, in political capital.

With the myriad problems facing the world—the recent financial collapse and global recession, the tremendous toll from dozens of infectious diseases, the proliferation of weapons of mass destruction, terrorism, and global poverty—it will take a very courageous and determined leader to put climate change at or near the top of the list and make the demands on society that are required to tackle it. While global leadership is not necessarily a zero-sum game, in which focusing on one problem automatically detracts from another, the environment still ranks relatively low in the public consciousness;[3] therefore, significant political leadership is required to mobilize the public for dramatic action.

And dramatic action is what is needed, according to the International Panel on Climate Change (IPCC), the largest scientific body ever assembled. The IPCC's most recent report states that to limit CO_2 concentrations to 350 parts per million (ppm), the number suggested by NASA scientist James Hansen to prevent catastrophic climate change,[4] an 85 percent reduction in global greenhouse gas emissions is required with respect to 2000 levels (Barker et al., 2007).

Keep in mind, the world economy is expected to grow at an average rate of approximately 2.5 to 3.5 percent over the coming decades,[5] which means that these reductions will be much more difficult to achieve. If left unchecked, greenhouse gas emissions would likely grow by several hundred percent by midcentury.[6]

The remaining goal of this chapter is to outline the two main types of policies that are currently being discussed in academic and government circles (and in some limited cases already in action) to address climate change—an international carbon (or greenhouse gas) tax and an international greenhouse gas cap and trade system.

The critical component of both of these policies is to put a significant price on greenhouse gas emissions that increases over time; the tax does so directly (which is one of its strengths), while the cap and trade does so indirectly by direct limits on greenhouse gases emissions (which is one of its strengths).

Questions remain as to what the price of carbon dioxide (or the other greenhouse gas equivalents) pollution would need to be to get businesses and individuals to make the changes necessary to reduce greenhouse gases by 85 percent by 2050, which is the International Panel on Climate Change's goal. Nothing short of $35 to $50 per ton of CO_2 is likely high enough to initiate the full-scale transition that is required, but the price may need to rise as high as $100 per ton to make greenhouse gas emissions, and the technologies that generate them, prohibitively expensive.

Whatever the precise number, the cost of generating electricity from high greenhouse-gas fuels, particularly coal, must rise significantly, as well as the cost of gas for cars and heating. This in turn will decrease the relative power and profit of these industries (unless they can diversify significantly into the new industries that will comprise the green energy economy). It should surprise no one that the coal and gas industries have been at the forefront of campaigns to discredit climate change science and block or weaken comprehensive climate change legislation.[7]

INTERNATIONAL CARBON TAX

This is one of the most widely discussed proposals for tackling climate change. The logic behind it is relatively simple: carbon is currently underpriced in the market because the price does not account for the costs associated with climate change. By adding at tax to all carbon-based fuels that reflects the potential damage inflicted by each ton of carbon on the international community, users of these fuels will finally face the true cost of their actions. This will force them to shift to climate-friendly types of fuel or reduce energy consumption altogether.

As mentioned in Chapter 6, to be most effective, a tax should focus on the full range of greenhouse gas emissions, not just CO_2. While carbon dioxide is the most ubiquitous greenhouse gas, the last thing we want to do is distort the economy in favor of even more damaging gases. This could be accomplished by using carbon as the baseline for the tax and ratcheting up the taxes proportionally based on greater warming potential; for example, gases that have twice the warming potential would be taxed at twice the rate as carbon. (Therefore, while the term "carbon tax" is the most widely discussed in political circles, it is more appropriate to conceive of this policy as a "greenhouse gas" tax.)

Since the demand for fuel is relatively insensitive to price (inelastic—at least in the short to medium term) the tax would need to be relatively high to get significant reductions in fuel use.[8] This means that the prices of all forms of fossil fuel energy would have to increase significantly. At a time when oil prices have already risen dramatically, the price would rise even further, making driving as well as home heating and the cost of food more expensive.

But while taxes have this negative and regressive component, they also contain the source of the resolution: the tax revenue collected. A carbon tax could be refunded to consumers in the form of tax rebates or lower income taxes. Under most scenarios the revenue collected by the government could more than offset the higher costs of fuel for the lower and middle classes, even with the bureaucratic costs that accompany such a plan.[9]

Other proposals call for using the revenue generated to invest in research and development into alternative energy sources and energy efficiency, or the retrofitting of existing infrastructure. A combination of tax rebates for lower-income groups and R&D would be an attractive mix.

A significant advantage of a tax system is that it makes the cost of greenhouse gas emissions immediately salient to consumers and businesses in the form of higher prices. The best tax policy would be one that begins with a high enough tax to get people's attention andthen steadily increases over time until reaching its peak. This sends the signal to individuals and businesses that they had better make a transition to cleaner fuels or less energy use, and it gives them the time to do so, while also sending a clear signal that the pressure to reduce greenhouse gas emissions will only intensify in the future.

One of the greatest advantages of a tax-based approach is that it is transparent; it would be relatively easy to verify that nations were imposing this tax. In addition, this approach doesn't rely on having to verify the quantities of greenhouse gases emitted, only the quantities of energy bought and sold, which in most nations is already readily available or could be relatively easy to obtain.

From an outcome-based standpoint, however, this benefit represents the biggest downside to a greenhouse gas tax, because we wouldn't be able to guarantee a precise drop in greenhouse gas emissions. For example, a tax might be aimed at reducing emissions by 10 percent within the first five years, but actually lead to reductions of only 5 percent or 8 percent. This weakness could be remedied by annual adjustments based on what we actually observe once the tax is instituted. Some flexibility of this nature would be critical. It could work the other way as well; if demand turned out to be more sensitive to price than predicted, future tax hikes could be slightly curbed.

From a political standpoint, the biggest weakness of a tax is that taxes are highly unpopular. Making a greenhouse gas tax revenue neutral, or at least refunding some of the money to consumers, could help to overcome this aversion to taxes, but it would still be a difficult sell in many countries.

There also exists the potential for some countries to gain an immediate economic advantage by opting out of such a tax system; to be effective the tax would need to be truly international in scope (even major reductions in the United States and Europe are not sufficient to curb greenhouse gas concentrations to the levels that are required). Any country that refuses to enact the tax would lower the cost of doing business in the home country relative to other nations, which could increase foreign direct investment or give domestic industry a competitive edge.

This same logic applies to a cap and trade system (discussed below), and explains in no small part why the United States refused to sign the Kyoto Protocol or enter into any binding agreements with respect to greenhouse gases. Out of fear that U.S. industry will suffer unfairly, leaders in the United States for the most part have refused to sign on to any international agreements that mandate reductions unless the major developing countries, such as India and China, do so as well.

There is already a widespread perception among the U.S. public that U.S. industry is at an unfair disadvantage with respect to India and China because of currency manipulation (China) and weak labor and environmental laws (China and India), which drive down the price of labor.[10] In addition, if only a subset of countries makes serious efforts to reduce emissions, this may simply shift the emissions to other parts of the world and not result in net reductions (this is commonly referred to as "carbon leakage").

This potential for competitive advantage by opting out of costly climate change measures, while possible, may not be as significant as some suspect. Nations that impose serious measures on greenhouse gas emissions are likely to gain an advantage in the green technologies that will ultimately define the twenty-first century. While taxes can be viewed as penalties levied on business activity, they also provide strong incentives for change and innovation, and nations that take the lead on climate change may in fact gain the upper hand in developing new industries.

In addition, there are many local benefits of decreasing greenhouse gas emissions since fossil fuels, which are the dominant source of emissions, have many negative effects on air quality and human health. Any reductions in these fuels for the purpose of decreasing the likelihood of catastrophic climate change will also have many environmental co-benefits.

From the United States' standpoint, our oil dependency also creates a major foreign policy challenge since we are dependent on many hostile regimes for our energy needs, and thus a strong case could be made that independent of climate change, the United States should be raising the cost of oil.[11]

INTERNATIONAL CAP AND TRADE SYSTEM

Due mainly to the political aversion to new taxes (especially in the United States), an international cap and trade system for greenhouse gases has emerged as the preferred policy option for a post-Kyoto agreement that would take effect in 2012 and beyond.[12] Such a system would require not only coming up with a maximum annual greenhouse gas emissions target for the world as a whole, but also an agreement on how these allotments would be distributed among nations, and the rate at which the cap would decrease to arrive at the 85 percent reductions by 2050.

If all nations were equally responsible for the loading of the atmosphere with greenhouse gases and were at relatively equal stages of development, each nation could simply set their cap at a level that corresponded with an equal percentage reduction in emissions. For example, if the global cap required a 2 percent annual reduction, each nation would set the cap at 2 percent less than the baseline level from each previous period.

But the reality is that the industrialized Western nations are responsible for the overwhelming majority of greenhouse gases that fill the atmosphere,[13] and the majority of the world's countries are still vastly underdeveloped, with large shares of their populace living in poverty. This is particularly true in the large developing countries such as India, China, Brazil, and Nigeria, which are home to almost half the world's people.

Any international cap and trade system will need to recognize these disparities in historic greenhouse gas loading, and acknowledge that developed countries must bear a greater share of carbon reductions.[14] Arriving at consensus on distribution will be very difficult.

If it is achieved, a cap and trade system's most obvious benefit (at least on the surface) is that it can deliver a set target in reductions, unlike the international tax, which is less precise. This precision is perhaps the main reason that environmental groups seem to prefer a cap and trade system to a greenhouse gas tax.[15]

When in operation, there are potentially large efficiency gains from a cap and trade system since the ability to trade permits provides those with the lowest costs of greenhouse gas reduction the incentive to do so; they can then profit by selling their permits to those with higher abatement costs. Once again, environmentalists could also choose to buy permits from the market and retire them, thereby reducing greenhouse emissions beyond the global cap.

A cap and trade system and a tax should have almost exactly the same effect on prices since both raise the cost of emissions to the same degree if their target is the same. Politicians have largely promoted a cap and trade system as if it is relatively costless, when in reality its price impacts would be almost identical to a tax on greenhouse gases (which is one of the reasons they prefer it).

While many of the features of a cap and trade system are rightly attractive, there are some significant potential problems with the cap and trade system that merit mention:

1. Monitoring an international cap and trade system is a lot harder than monitoring an international tax. Once a greenhouse gas tax is instituted, it would be relatively easy to see if countries were uniformly imposing it since it would immediately be reflected in prices. A cap and trade system requires a much more comprehensive set of political and bureaucratic institutions to operate, and while the price effects should ultimately be commensurable with a tax, it would be much more difficult to see whether firms were actually being held to the limits imposed by their permit allowances.

2. Most cap and trade systems (at the international level, as well as in the United States) include provisions for "carbon offsets."[16] Carbon offsets allow firms to earn credits toward their emissions reductions by paying for emissions reductions in other firms, sectors, and even other parts of the world.[17] Under the Kyoto Protocol, these offsets are managed under the Clean Development Mechanism (CDM), in which firms can purchase offsets from projects certified by the United Nations.[18] There is also a growing market for voluntary carbon offsets (those that do not help firms meet legally mandated reductions obligations) that are being used to help companies burnish their green credentials or by groups and individuals who want to offset their own greenhouse gas pollution (in some airports, consumers can, with the swipe of a credit card, purchase carbon offsets for air travel[19]). Voluntary offsets are significantly cheaper than offsets sold in compliance markets because they are not part of a mandated regulatory regime (and some would argue are not as rigorously verified).

Carbon offsets are extremely attractive on a theoretical level because they allow firms to meet their obligations more inexpensively than if they were to reduce emissions in their own operations (which is why industries, and the politicians who represent them, fight vigorously to allow offset provisions into cap and trade legislation) and because often it is firms in wealthy developed countries that buy credits from projects in poorer developing nations. But in practice, it is difficult to verify at the project level that emissions reductions eligible for offsets are actually "additional"—that they would not have happened under a business-as-usual scenario.[20] The CDM has come under harsh criticism from a number of sources, both because of significant problems with additionality and the large lag time between project proposals and approval.[21]

The CDM has been an incredible experiment in using the power of markets to jump-start green projects in the developing world, many of which have reduced CO_2 more than under business as usual (even the strongest critics admit that some projects have been additional). The CDM has also helped to accelerate entire new industries. China didn't have a wind power industry before the CDM, and now it leads the world; some of this amazing growth can be linked to the incentives the CDM provided.

A strong case can be made that fixing the CDM is preferable to scrapping it, especially since it is not clear what would replace it. If no offsets are allowed under an international climate change regime, the price of reducing carbon will be dramatically higher, which will make it much more difficult politically to enact. In addition, developing countries are going to need significant inflows of capital to make the rapid transition to low-carbon technologies. The money flows under the CDM are mostly from private sources. If this dries up, the only substitute would be government money, specifically foreign aid flowing from developed to developing countries. It is hard to imagine that new foreign aid budgets would be sufficient to the task, because of both economic and political concerns. It is going to take trillions of dollars to transform the Chinese, Indian, Brazilian, Nigerian, and other major developing-country economies, and private capital will likely form the bulk of this investment, but only if the incentives are right. The CDM provides one set of incentives by providing revenue streams from carbon offsets.

Greatly streamlining the CDM process to make it much easier to navigate is critical. Since some of the credits the CDM issues are clearly "phantom credits"—ones that don't pass the additionality test—the system should err on the side of making very conservative estimates of how many credits to grant. If a large project is estimated to offset 500,000 tons of CO_2, this should be discounted by some "overhead" or "hedging" factor of, say, 20 percent (the precise number would need to be calculated by scientific experts) such that only 400,000 (80 percent of 500,000) actual credits are issued. This would provide a form of insurance to guarantee the environmental integrity of the CDM system. Project developers and developing countries would get less revenue, but environmentalists would be much more supportive overall of the CDM process and offsets more generally. There is so much potential money to be made in any post-2012 phase of offset trading that even with this insurance buffer there would still be plenty of money to go around.

One potential solution to greatly simplify the CDM system is to do away with much of the project-specific framework, which is paperwork-intensive and includes complicated methodologies, and instead create sector- or technology-specific "benchmarks" for greenhouse gas reductions. Instead of trying to determine whether a new wind project in China will be economical only if it receives carbon offset money (i.e., outside money that makes the carbon reductions additional), energy experts would determine how much new wind projects reduce China's overall carbon footprint, accounting for the fact that a lot of wind farms might be built without carbon offsets at all. Coefficients could be assigned to different classes of projects that would then generate offsets. A coefficient of 0.2 would mean that for every five megawatts of wind power, carbon credits equivalent to the coal burned to produce one megawatt with coal ($.2 \times 5 = 1$) would be earned and could be sold under the CDM.

A benchmark could also be constructed for the cement industry, based on an assessment of currently available technologies, such that if the industry as a whole, or individual plants within that industry, exceeded certain levels of energy efficiency, they too would receive carbon credits. Again, these credits could be issued based on very conservative formulas to ensure that they truly represent net reductions in greenhouse gases in the atmosphere.

Another potential change in the CDM would be to allow the aggregation of lots of small projects, which individually don't have much greenhouse gas impact but collectively do. If a million people in Mexico switch from incandescent to fluorescent lightbulbs, or if millions in China switch from cutting down trees for fuel to using propane cookstoves, the CO_2 reductions could be large. The issue is how to aggregate the impacts and verify them. Creating a system to allow these types of program activities in the CDM would also help steer money to poorer parts of the world, where huge manufacturing and power plants may not exist, but where greenhouse gas reductions can still be found.

None of these developments in the CDM would be free from problems, but they are worth trying.[22] The CDM process is flawed but not irreparably so.

3. How the permits from a cap and trade system are allocated can have large distributional consequences and also serious ramifications for the other types of policy interventions that are needed for a comprehensive climate change strategy. There is a consensus among economists that greenhouse gas permits should be auctioned off to firms since this doesn't reward firms for past bad behavior or create barriers to entry for firms that enter after the permits have been allotted, and it allows governments to generate revenue from the sale. This revenue can be used in the same manner as under the tax scheme. The problem is that there is tremendous political pressure to allocate permits freely to existing firms, and this pressure is hard for governments to resist.

To date, more than 95 percent of permits allocated under the EU cap and trade system have been given away for free (though this is supposed to change in the future)[23] and most current U.S. proposals call for free allocation of the overwhelming majority of permits. One notable exception is the Carbon Limits and Energy for America's Renewal (CLEAR) Act proposed by Senator Maria Cantwell (Dem.) and Susan Collins (Rep.), which auctions 100 percent of the permits in the cap and trade system, doesn't allow for any carbon offsets, and refunds 75 percent of the money from the permit auction directly to consumers in a lump-sum annual check, which would cover the increased energy costs for 80 percent of U.S. households.[24] It is a serious and promising piece of legislation that could provide a foundation for future national and international agreements (it still has significant flaws, however, and could be improved).

In summary, despite the benefit of setting a precise target for greenhouse gas reductions, there are serious issues with a cap and trade system for greenhouse gases. For these reasons (and a couple of other technical issues) William Nordhaus (2007), one of the leading experts on the economics of climate change, recommends the tax system over the cap and trade.[25]

COMMAND AND CONTROL POLICIES TO ADDRESS CLIMATE CHANGE

The longer we wait to address climate change, the more expensive it will be to make the transition to a low-carbon future. As the saying goes: "an ounce of prevention is cheaper than an ounce of cure."

Every new building that is built without the latest energy efficient technology creates more long-term demand for energy, and it is very expensive to retrofit them later on; every inefficient car that gets produced will likely be on the road for many years; every new housing development that is built without comprehensive transportation planning will lock in place wasteful commuting patterns for decades; every new coal or gas power plant that is built guarantees significant increases in greenhouse gas emissions for the life of the plant.

As the world waits for a new multilateral climate change regime that caps global emissions or puts a significant price on greenhouse gas pollution, we need to enact other types of policies that can get us started on the path to a low-carbon future.

Many of the steps that can be taken now fall under the heading of command and control policies:

1. Green Building Standards

Requiring a minimum level of energy efficiency in building design and construction, as well as incentives for even greater levels of efficiency, is one of the best ways for a city, region, state, province, or even nation to get a head start in the race to reduce greenhouse gas emissions. This is especially true in rapidly growing developing countries where the pace of construction is extremely high.

With China poised to increase its urban population by hundreds of millions in the coming decades (essentially building infrastructure equivalent to an entire new United States), the standards that are in place for this construction will have a tremendous impact on the energy and resource impacts for the country and the world. The Chinese government's Ministry of Construction has set ambitious targets for green building in the country and has developed detailed ratings system for new development projects.

Even the United States is expected to urbanize another 100 million people by midcentury, and given our much higher per capita energy and resource use levels, how we do this will have huge ramifications. Simple measures like skylights, the choice of paint colors, the type of insulation, and the types of indoor heating, air-conditioning, and light fixtures can significantly reduce energy and resource demands.

The U.S. Green Building Council (USGBC) is a leader in the effort to transition to more efficient buildings, and many international efforts modeled after the USGBC's Leadership in Energy and Environmental Design (LEED) rating system are in place around the world. While many of these green building standards are voluntary, governments are increasingly writing them into law to make sure that the infrastructure of tomorrow is the most efficient it can be. This will make the transition to a low-carbon future less costly.

2. Fuel Economy Standards

People drive less when the price of gasoline goes up, but this behavioral change may not last if the price goes back down.[26] Only a sustained high price of gasoline will lead to long-term shifts to more fuel-efficient cars and less driving by the average consumer. Until we have a price on carbon, the price of gasoline is likely to fluctuate a lot and not provide the type of consistent price signal that will lead to significant reductions.

While gasoline prices are the most direct way to get people to change their driving habits, governments can set average fuel

economy standards for car and truck fleets that can drive innovation
and reduce total gasoline consumption. In the United States these
standards are called Corporate Average Fuel Economy (CAFE) standards, and they are still relatively low, and are not slated to reach
more than thirty miles per gallon for cars and light trucks until close
to 2020.[27] China is pushing for standards that are more stringent,
with average fuel economy of over forty miles per gallon.

Fuel economy standards can be incorporated into their own type
of cap and trade system in which the cap is the average fuel economy
for the entire national fleet, and credits are earned by companies
that exceed these targets, which can then be sold to companies whose
fleets don't achieve the standard (e.g., if the standard is forty-five
miles per gallon, a company that makes cars that get fifty-five miles
per gallon could sell its excess credits to companies whose cars or
trucks don't achieve the forty-five miles per gallon target).

3. Efficiency Standards for Appliances and Electronics

Efficiency standards for durable goods (those with a product life of
at least three years) such as washers, dryers, televisions, refrigerators,
computers, copiers, and other household and office devices are an
excellent way to lock in energy efficiency across a wide swath of industry and sectors of the economy.

As already mentioned, the U.S. EPA's Energy Star program is one
of the leading examples of an energy efficiency rating system applied
to a large range of products. Energy Star products are indicated with
an easily recognizable label.[28] Such labels make it easy for households and institutions to identify efficient devices instead of having
to research them on their own, thereby greatly reducing transaction
costs and making green purchasing much more convenient.

4. Renewable Portfolio Standards (RPS)

As soon as greenhouse gas emissions have a price (whether directly
through a tax or indirectly through a cap), the economic attractive-
ness of low-carbon fuels will improve overnight. Resources will shift
to alternative energy sources such as wind, solar, geothermal, and

hydropower. But governments can start moving energy production in the direction of alternative energy sources right now through a variety of policies, including direct subsidies for different types of renewable energy generation.

The problem with direct subsidies is that they distort the market in favor of one technology over the other. Even if the technology being favored is preferable to fossil fuels, this biases investments against emerging technologies and can lock in place the least efficient of the renewable alternatives.

A better way to promote alternatives to fossil fuels is to set a target for renewable energy generation (at the state, regional, or national level) and then allow the utilities to meet this target in any way they like. Setting up renewable portfolio standards (RPS) allows maximum flexibility and doesn't distort investment decisions. RPS systems can have a cap and trade component in which utilities that exceed the targets can sell credits to utilities that don't meet them. One of the keys to a successful RPS is to make sure the definition of "renewable" is absolutely clear, consistent with the environmental goals of the program, and general enough to include new technologies that are either nascent or yet to be developed.

In the EU the preferred policy option is a direct subsidy to renewable power generators in what is called a "feed-in tariff."[29] Different types of renewable power are guaranteed a long-term price that is above the market price for nonrenewable power, thereby creating long-term demand for types of energy that couldn't compete on their own. Feed-in tariffs are used throughout the EU (and in many other countries) as a way to provide stability to the renewable industries so that they can grow to sufficient scale and ultimately become more competitive. While these policies are credited with the larger share of renewable in the EU's power system, from a strict economic standpoint RPS are preferable because they don't favor any one technology over the other, but allow for competition among renewable, including nascent technologies.[30]

5. Urban Planning and Smart Growth

As with green building standards, urban planning and zoning rules have a tremendous impact on the types of infrastructure that will

be built in the coming decades. Laws mandating high-density housing built around community gardens and business centers and criss-
crossed with bike lanes will have much different resource impacts
than laws allowing for low-density housing that continues to rely on
the city core/suburb model in which residents commute long distances to work by car.

Decisions over zoning ordinances and community growth plans
occur every day in city councils, state legislatures, and national planning meetings, and are extremely consequential in regard to what
our world is going to look like in the future.

"Smart growth" refers to an increasingly popular school of urban
planning that has evolved over the past few decades. It centers on
ways to make communities more environmentally sustainable and
increase the overall quality of life.

GEOENGINEERING AND FINAL THOUGHTS

With an issue as massive and complex as climate change, there will
(likely) be no silver bullet or miracle solution. An effective strategy
will make use of multiple policies and technologies, many of which
have yet to be invented (which in and of itself has major policy
implications).

One particularly intriguing possibility for addressing climate
change involves massive geoengineering projects. For decades people have floated ideas about how to tackle climate change that range
from the absurd (filling the oceans with Styrofoam to reflect sun into
the atmosphere) to the less implausible (seeding the oceans with iron
to spur algae blooms that absorb carbon).

Recently, there has been a lot of discussion about the possibility of injecting carbon underground, perhaps in empty coal mines
or oil fields, as a way to render fossil fuels carbon neutral. None of
these technologies are currently economically feasible, but they offer
promise and will no doubt continue to be investigated.

On the energy front, there is still the hope that hydrogen fuel cell
technology, a new generation of nuclear plants, or cold fusion may
one day deliver on the promise of virtually unlimited sources of clean

energy. Ironically, one of the more promising energy futures may rest with solar thermal—an essentially eighteenth-century technology that uses mirrors to heat water and power turbines—magnified to a massive scale. One recent study estimates that for a little over $400 billion, all U.S. power (for both electricity and transportation) could be generated in the desert by solar thermal and distributed around the nation with large transmission lines (Zweibel and Fthenakis, 2008). This would require massive government coordination, especially with the siting of thousands of miles of massive new transmission systems, but it is not entirely far-fetched.

Whatever the solutions to climate change, one thing is for sure: they all require a significant degree of government intervention in the marketplace and a serious and sustained commitment by the entire world community. The key is to get a significant long-term price on greenhouse gases so that all sectors in the economy begin the shift away from fossil fuels.

CHAPTER 9

FOREST AND BIODIVERSITY CONSERVATION

Preserving biodiversity is often considered the signature goal of environmentalism; along with pollution control, it has defined the movement since its inception. But preserving biodiversity is one of the most difficult policy challenges. It also raises very complicated moral and philosophical questions.

Economics is a discipline whose moral foundation rests on the utilitarian goal of maximizing society's welfare.[1] In economic analysis, intrinsic value rests with humans and humans only; **nonhumans have no intrinsic value whatsoever.** Nonhumans only have value to the extent that humans value them directly or if they help provide services that humans value; apart from these sources their default value is zero.

According to economic theory, whales have value because people derive pleasure from watching them and knowing that they exist out in the oceans; wetlands have value because they provide storm protection and help to purify water, in addition to providing habitat for many birds that people value.

Understandably, this strong form of anthropocentrism rattles many environmentalists. For most environmentalists, the great problems in the world stem from putting human values above all else at the expense of the natural world. The notion that all of nature's creation has no intrinsic value is anathema to the core environmental ethic that all of life has essential value and is sacred.

On the first day of class in my Environmental and Natural Resource Economics course, I present this conundrum to my students and pose the following question:

Is it possible to avoid anthropocentrism while making decisions about the environment?

It turns out that it's not as easy as many environmentalists make it seem. After all, if we decide that all life has intrinsic value, it is *we* who have decided it; that is, humans are deciding to assign values to nonhumans. In essence the anthropomorphism question is sort of a catch-22.

Putting aside the philosophical angle, it is very difficult to operationalize an environmental ethic that automatically assumes that all life has intrinsic value.

Does this mean that we should protect all species from extinction, even the ones that would go extinct through entirely natural processes (after all, 99.9 percent of all species that have ever existed are now extinct)? Does the intrinsic value of life apply equally to viruses and pathogens and parasites? Is it right to favor native species over invasive species? How do we prioritize what to preserve and protect if all life has intrinsic value?

This last question is particularly important for the environmentalist. Saying that all life has intrinsic value or is sacred is in some sense a way of saying that all life is priceless. The problem with such a view is that it is impossible to compare the *relative* worth of one form of life with another if they are both priceless.

If a subspecies of snail is priceless, then there is no way to say that saving the humpback whale is more important. If a rare subspecies of weed is priceless, there is no way of saying that saving a tropical forest ecosystem is more important. The strongest form of environmental ethic, while perhaps intuitively appealing to our moral sensibility, can actually paralyze the policy process—at a time when more than ever we need to focus resources and make hard choices about where to expend our energies.

Fortunately, environmentalists and environmental organizations are pragmatic and want to get things done. There is a growing recognition that time is not on our side and that we need to make great efforts to preserve the biodiversity that we *value most*, which is essentially a concession to the economists' view of the world (even if not explicit). Along with top natural scientists, many groups have identified "biodiversity hot spots" that they are targeting for preservation based on their ecosystem uniqueness and standing biodiversity, both on land and sea.[2]

The majority of these areas are in the tropics, particularly tropical forests,[3] which are some of the poorest regions in the world and under the greatest threat. This poses a particularly difficult challenge for conservationists since not only do these areas lack sufficient funds for conservation, but there is also immense pressure to exploit these resources and little institutional capability to prevent illegal resource extraction even when efforts are made to protect them.

The pressures on forests are varied, ranging from logging (legal and illegal), urban development, agricultural conversion, acid rain, and fire. Behind all of these pressures lie two driving forces of forestry decline: the de facto "open access" status of much of the world's forests and the underpricing of forest ecosystem services.

Similar to much of the world's oceans (for which property rights do not exist), much of the world's forests are located in remote areas with low population densities and where the enforcement powers of a central authority are weak to nonexistent. The result is a situation where property rights over forestry resources, even if they exist on paper, are often not enforced and are tenuous at best. This leads to a race to exploit forest resources before others can claim them, which in turn leads to massive deforestation.

Not only does the open access nature of forests lead to their overexploitation, but often there are additional incentives to cut down trees. Unfortunately, in many developing countries rampant corruption is often the norm; government authorities, in league with illegal loggers, engage in massive deforestation, even in areas that are set aside as protected areas.[4] In developed countries there is less outright corruption, but government subsidies for road construction and timber leases priced at well below the true market value result in much the same—excessive deforestation and abuse of the resources held in the public trust.[5]

The best way to decrease deforestation would be to directly address these issues: improve the system of property rights and decrease corruption in developing countries, and get rid of government subsidies for timber companies in the developed world (there are instances where these recommendations would apply to both sets of countries). The impediments within the developing countries are obvious; establishing and strengthening the rule of law is much easier said than done. But the obstacles in the developed world, while easier to solve theoretically, are also difficult because of the power of the timber companies and a lack of public awareness about the ways in which government actively exacerbates deforestation (this is similar to the situation with regard to agricultural subsidies).

But even if we could miraculously improve the institutions of governance in developing countries and diminish the perverse policies in developed countries that promote deforestation, there would still remain serious threats to the world's forests and biodiversity through the other channels mentioned above. Development pressures would still exist and agricultural conversion would not go away.

This brings us back to one of the central intuitions from the economics of the environment: the goal is not to reduce deforestation to zero, but to balance the legitimate uses of forest resources with the needs of preservation. Currently, the ecosystem services that forests provide are vastly undervalued; in fact, they often are taken completely for granted.

It is critical for environmentalists to recognize that most biodiversity resides on land that is privately owned. These landowners must be given incentives to conserve their resources if it is not currently in their economic interests to do so.

Economics poses a relatively straightforward solution to this challenge (at least theoretically) with the concept of *payments for environmental services*. Those who derive the most benefit from environmental resources should pay for their preservation.

REDD

A significant amount of time at the recent United Nations Climate Change Conference in Copenhagen was devoted to the how developing countries can receive carbon credits for *not* cutting down their forests, and hence preventing the release of the CO_2 stored in them into the atmosphere. This was done under the proposed Reduced Emissions from Degradation and Deforestation (REDD) framework.[6]

Trees sequester carbon, and therefore release carbon when they are cut or burned. Currently, a company that cuts down a tract of forestland and releases tons of carbon into the atmosphere pays no price for this carbon pollution. Conversely, developing countries that decide to halt deforestation receive no compensation for the carbon that they sequester. Without any funding for the environmental service of carbon sequestration, simple economics often dictates that cutting down the forests is the best course of action for developing countries to take. The poorer nations view REDD as both a way to recognize the global value of their forests and to secure outside funding to ensure their preservation.[7]

It is very likely that some version of REDD will be ratified and become an integral part of any post-Kyoto climate change agreement in 2012 and beyond. REDD's theoretical premise, just like the central tenets of carbon offsets more generally, is sound: a ton of carbon not released into the atmosphere, which would have been released had a transfer payment not been made, should be considered a reduction in global CO_2 emissions. In the case of REDD, this emission reduction is achieved through a payment for forestry services and allowing trees to stand.

But as with other carbon offsets, the additionality problem is paramount. It is very difficult to determine that a tree that is not cut down would have been cut down had someone not paid the owner a carbon credit. REDD tries to ensure additionality by creating baselines of deforestation for countries and then establishing what deforestation rates would be under a business-as-usual scenario. Any amount of deforestation less than this projected amount is then eligible for carbon credits. One potential problem in this system is that if one country reduces deforestation, what is to stop the deforestation from moving to other countries, especially ones where historical deforestation rates have been low, and therefore the countries don't have the potential to earn many carbon credits under REDD. This problem is known as "leakage" and it is a serious enough concern that provisions to artificially inflate historical deforestation baselines for low-deforested countries are being considered.[8]

REDD has generated so much attention in the environmental community because not only can it help reduce global carbon emissions, but also the co-benefits of biodiversity conservation that would come with significantly reducing deforestation are potentially large. It is rare that a proposed solution could address so many critical environmental priorities at once.

I wish that I could enthusiastically and without hesitation endorse REDD, but the economist in me remains skeptical. The problem is not in paying people in developing countries to preserve their forests—that makes complete sense and should be increased—but in coupling these payments with carbon credits, since big problems arise if these credits aren't truly additional. While I am not prepared to recommend scrapping the REDD framework altogether, it may turn out that decoupling payments for forestry services from the carbon markets will be necessary to ensure the integrity of a climate change regime. If avoided deforestation is decoupled from carbon credits there will be less money for it, but this trade-off may be worth it in order to guarantee greenhouse gas reduction targets (the last thing we need are millions of "phantom" reductions bringing us closer to a climate tipping point). As with most policies, the "devil is in the details," and environmentalists will have to examine very closely any final REDD agreement before rendering a judgment.

OTHER ENVIRONMENTAL SERVICES FROM FORESTS

Carbon sequestration is only one of many ecosystem services that forests provide. Water filtration, storm protection, habitat for biodiversity, clean air, and protecting against soil erosion all have tremendous economic value but are rarely even measured or enter into the decision-making process when forests are cleared.

Multiple efforts, however, are underway to estimate the values of forest ecosystem services and create mechanisms by which communities can be rewarded for preservation efforts.[9] Probably the best example of such a policy in action is in Costa Rica, where since 1997 the country has embarked on an ambitious plan to pay landowners for forest preservation based on the valuable ecosystem services they provide (Chomitz et al., 1998). The program has largely been a success and is heralded as a model for other countries to follow. In the first phase, approximately four thousand projects received approximately $65.8 million to conserve approximately 300,000 hectares of forestland across the country (Sanchez-Azofeifa et al., 2007).[10] One problem with the program is that funding comes primarily from a fuel tax, which is regressive and disproportionately affects the poor (which could be mitigated in the future by outside funding from REDD).

Some other excellent examples of forest ecosystem services incorporated into economic decisions in novel ways include:

Panama: To decrease sediment runoff into the Panama Canal (caused by deforestation), which leads to expensive dredging efforts, the government is paying people to plant trees in areas adjacent to the canal ("Are You Being Served?" 2005).

Belize: The government accepted funding from Shaman Pharmaceuticals to preserve 2,400 hectares of forest as an ethnobiomedical reserve in exchange for the rights to the discovery of new drugs (Spiro, 1998).[11]

New York City: The city bought the forestland in its upstate watershed since the trees provide water purification more inexpensively than an industrial water purification plant (U.S. Environmental Protection Agency, 2008).

Niger and Kenya: Recognizing the value of trees for soil protection and as a renewable source of food and wood products, these governments have provided many incentives for tree planting to local communities (U.S. State Department, 2004; World Agroforestry Centre, 2004).

CREATING NATIONAL PARKS AND PROTECTED AREAS

Setting aside large swaths of land for protected areas or national parks, particularly where biodiversity is most concentrated, is also a worthy goal. Governments around the world are increasingly recognizing the importance of conserving entire ecosystems, both because of their cultural and historic value, and their economic importance. Yet, only slightly over 12 percent of the world's terrestrial resources are under some form of legal protection, and less than 6 percent of the world's marine resources (Ervin et al., 2010).

For decades, in an effort to increase global conservation efforts aimed at the world's most threatened biodiversity hot spots, organizations like the Nature Conservancy (TNC), Conservation International (CI), the International Union for the Conservation of Nature (IUCN), and the World Wildlife Fund (WWF) have been channeling donations from primarily wealthy donors in the developed world to conservation projects throughout both the developed and developing world.

The willingness and capability to devote significant monetary resources to biodiversity preservation is much greater among the wealthy for the simple reason that they have more disposable income, and because biodiversity preservation is in most cases a luxury good (the richer one becomes the greater percentage of one's income one is willing to devote to this cause).[12]

It is almost certain that the people of the United States and Europe have devoted more money to rain forest preservation in the Amazon than the people of South America. This is not because the people of South America don't care about the fate of the Amazon (or to imply that they aren't doing anything to preserve it), but at their current stage of development preservation is not as great a priority as economic growth and raising material standards of living (rapidly exploiting their natural resources is exactly what the now-developed nations did during their industrial rise).

But contributions by private organizations will never be enough, because too much habitat is under threat and people can "free-ride" on the preservation successes of others. All of the great work done by TNC, CI, IUCN, and WWF is enjoyed by everyone, regardless of whether they ever contribute a dime to any of these causes. This is why public goods like biodiversity conservation will always be underfunded (relative to the total benefits of global biodiversity conservation goals) if left to the whims of the market system.

Fortunately, many developed-country governments and international organizations like the United Nations Environment Programme (UNEP) have also contributed billions to global conservation initiatives in dozens of countries to protect some of the world's most fragile ecosystems and spectacular natural resources.

Not only is funding for conservation from rich countries to poorer countries efficient—matching demand with supply—but it is also equitable. After all, if the rain forests are truly the "world's lungs," and provide environmental services to billions of people outside of the countries where they are situated, then it is only right that the rest of the world contribute to their preservation. This can be viewed as a corollary to the "polluter-pays principle"—the **beneficiary-pays principle**.

In addition, many of the world's biodiversity hot spots are under strain from climate change and the huge global demand for natural resources, both of which have been fueled for centuries primarily by the industrialization of the developed world. Now that the wealthy countries have achieved very high standards of living, it is arguable that they have a responsibility to devote a growing share of their wealth to preserving the most threatened areas of the natural world.

In order to dramatically increase worldwide conservation to the levels that many scientists believe is necessary to stave off a major reduction in global biodiversity, rich countries would need to transfer a significant amount of wealth to poorer nations over the coming decades—on the order of at minimum tens of billions of dollars.

To put things in perspective, in the post-WWII era the richer countries have already transferred (in the form of foreign aid) in excess of two trillion dollars to poorer nations, often with little to show for it (Easterly, 2006). If even a fraction of the hundreds of billions of dollars a year that the rich countries spend subsidizing their farmers (often at the expense of the environment and many poor-nation farmers) was devoted to greater global biodiversity preservation efforts, momentous progress could be made. Investments in conservation corridors that run north–south across countries (and continents) and allow species to migrate as the climate changes offer excellent returns on conservation dollars.

The key is to ensure that any money transferred from developed to developing nations results in tangible conservation benefits, and does not simply line the pockets of corrupt or ineffective politicians. With modern technology it is now much easier to monitor environmental impacts through satellite photos or wildlife tracking sensors, which should make it easier to hold governments and organizations accountable to their conservation agreements.

One policy mechanism that is once again gaining traction is "debt-for-nature" swaps, in which outside funders purchase a portion of country's international debt (at pennies on the dollar) in exchange for conservation commitments equal to the face value of that debt. In this way, poorer countries get much-needed debt relief and conservation sponsors get habitat protection at a large discount.

Debt-for-nature swaps began in the 1980s during the time of the major debt crises in Latin America, and since then some important lessons have been learned.[13,14] It is not enough for developing country governments simply to promise to protect areas and nothing more; they must create detailed management plans and commit resources to their enforcement. This puts more onus on the recipient countries, but also creates a mechanism for accountability and ensures that real conservation is taking place instead of nothing more than the creation of "paper parks." Recent examples of such transactions occurred in Guatemala and Costa Rica.[15]

IT WILL TAKE MORE THAN MONEY

Money alone is not sufficient to ensure that biodiversity is preserved. Billions of people currently live in the areas that have been identified as biodiversity-rich areas.[16] The old-style belief that somehow we could cordon off the world's natural treasures is giving way to a more balanced and nuanced approach that takes into account continued human presence in these areas and the needs of local populations.[17] This requires much more than simply buying up areas and designating them as natural parks or protected areas. Conservation plans now must provide serious alternatives to natural resource extraction and incentives for local groups to take an active role in preserving the surrounding areas over the long term, both of which require significant investment of money and capacity-building for effective monitoring and enforcement.

A 2004 article entitled "A Challenge to Conservationists" sparked a furious debate in the environmental community because it accused three of the biggest environmental conservation groups of ignoring the plight of indigenous groups in and around the areas that they tried to protect (Chapin, 2004). The author paints a picture of these groups as arrogant and out of touch with the needs of local people and their historical rights to their natural resource base. Needless to say, the article produced major responses from the accused parties and a lot of discussion.[18]

The net effect has been a healthy discourse; environmentalists are beginning to grapple more effectively with how to incorporate models of "sustainable development" into forest conservation plans, and to treat ecosystems as arenas of human-nature interaction, instead of simply zones for wildlife and biodiversity protection. This is a crucial development because the majority of the world's forests will remain in private hands. We are past the time when the choice was between forest conservation or meeting human needs; they must both be accomplished to guarantee sustainability.

There are also many conservation challenges that are much more local in nature and do not require large-scale wealth transfers across countries. At the national, state, provincial, and city and town levels, pitched battles for conservation and biodiversity preservation occur every day. These conflicts sometimes pit farmers against developers; commercial fishermen against recreational fishermen; energy, mining, and timber companies versus local landowners—and environmentalists are almost always on the side of those favoring more conservation and less exploitation of the natural world. As with virtually all public policy decisions, these conflicts entail inherent trade-offs that result in winners and losers.

ASSIGNING "NONMARKET" VALUES TO ENVIRONMENTAL RESOURCES

Environmentalists are often at a disadvantage in the public policy process because the benefits to resource exploitation are easier to quantify than the benefits of preservation. The economic gains from fisheries can be captured by valuing the amount of fish harvested and applying a multiplier factor that captures the overall economic impact to the local community, but the benefits of less commercial fishing to the tourist sector or the sea otter population are more difficult to quantify.

The same goes for agriculture versus development. Developers have an array of market prices with which to assign values to agricultural land conversion, which will almost always exceed the value of the crops currently grown on the land, while the value to the community of having a viable agricultural sector is hard to put a monetary value on.

With extractive industries such as mining, energy, and logging, the current price of these commodities is transparent and provides a clear signal of the value of removing these natural resources, while there is a not readily apparent market price for the value of maintaining pristine ecosystems and open space. Sometimes these non-market uses of natural resources are referred to "nonconsumptive" uses since they do not rely on significantly altering the resources and the activities in question leave the resources reasonably intact.

Economists have developed many techniques for what is referred to as "nonmarket" valuation, which attempts to assign monetary values to the environmental goods and services that are not readily accessible in the marketplace. These techniques can help provide a more comprehensive and accurate account of the wide range of values that people derive from the natural environment.

Many of us derive considerable value from viewing wildlife and pay significant sums of money to partake in this recreational activity. In instances where we pay to go on tours (or full-scale safaris or scuba trips for those of us that are fortunate enough) there are readily available market prices with which to gauge the direct economic value from visitors. But what about those of us who simply visit public parks or drive down the coast, stopping along the way to take in the views and watch the animals? There is no simple way to gauge our economic value for these excursions, but economists have come up with ways to estimate them.

One of the most common and well-respected methods is called the "travel-cost method." It originated in 1947 when economist Harold Hotelling was tasked with trying to estimate the public value of the U.S. national park system.[19] Hotelling discovered that although entrance fees couldn't provide an accurate valuation of the parks (since they are set by the government and not subject to supply and demand forces, and capture only one dimension of the cost of visiting the parks), the amount of money people spend trying to get to them can provide a reasonable estimate of their direct value to citizens. By collecting information on how far people drive to get to the parks, economists can estimate a "virtual" demand curve for park recreation, and thereby estimate the public's total benefit. Thousands of travel cost studies have been done over the years, and since they rely on actual behavior that is quantifiable, the results are taken quite seriously. These results can not only help environmentalists determine values for environmental resources that are not available from market data, but they can also help to prioritize efforts by highlighting the types of things that people value the most. Travel-cost studies can be used to estimate environmental values for a variety of resources, both terrestrial and marine.

Another interesting and well-tested method for determining nonmarket values is called "hedonic estimation." It is based on the principle that when consumers buy goods, they are really buying bundles of attributes.[20] When someone buys a house, they are buying a collection of things, such as the number of rooms, the view, the safety of the neighborhood, the quality of the schools, and the proximity to other resources they value. What if one of those attributes is open space? How could we determine how much of the home price can be attributed to being near a park or forest?

In principle, if we could somehow find two identical houses in every way *except* that one was in the middle of a residential area and the other bordered the open space, the difference in price would tell us how much the open space contributed to the value of the house (if at all). Since in practice this is not possible to do, what economists have developed is a method by which large samples of data, which differ on many dimensions, can be used to "tease out" the distinct contributions each attribute makes to the final price of the good. This has proven particularly effective in determining the value of cleaner air, the absence of traffic noise, or proximity to a landfill.

What is important for environmentalists to take from these examples is that while economics may threaten to reduce environmental resources to monetary values, it can also help assign monetary values to resources that usually are considered secondary in public decision-making. Environmentalists should take heart that in many instances (though not always) the nonmarket and nonconsumptive values for natural resources are actually greater than the market values based on extraction.[21] It is often the case that a full accounting of the values that society derives from natural resources favors their preservation over exploitation. One of the primary challenges for environmentalists is to make sure this full spectrum of values is taken into account in the public policy process, and not just the interests of the extractive industries.

ECOTOURISM (NATURE-BASED TOURISM)[22]

One of the more promising avenues for promoting economic development and environmental conservation at the same time is ecotourism. Though not without its critics, ecotourism is an attempt to directly link conservation to economic benefits, which does not necessarily require elaborate funding mechanisms or transfers of wealth, but instead relies on tried and true business principles. Ecotourism matches the growing demand for nature-based tourism with the desire by local inhabitants to find alternative ways to promote economic development that also provide incentives for biodiversity conservation. I was somewhat skeptical of the potential and efficacy of ecotourism as a preservation model until I heard a lecture by a famous National Geographic photographer.

During his talk he retold the story of a trip to the Pantanal in Brazil (the world's largest freshwater ecosystem, which is an amazing example of South American biodiversity) in which he saw a rare and endangered bird and asked the local guide about it. The guide's response was that it tasted good. Aghast that people were eating this endangered animal, the photographer told the guide that he would pay $100 if he could help him get a good photo of the bird. This was an incredible amount of money for the guide and he proudly helped the photographer get some close-up shots. The photographer then told his friends about the guide and promised him future business, premised on the guide's ability to ensure future visitors such great access for viewing.

Immediately, the guide's view of this endangered bird changed. No longer did he view it as a source of food, but as something to cherish and protect, both because of the tremendous revenue he could generate by protecting it, as well as the pride he took in knowing that people from the outside valued his local wildlife.

This anecdote impressed upon me the power of economic incentives at the grassroots level. Most people want to preserve the natural world, but their economic circumstances often force them to exploit it for short-term gain if they are struggling to survive and improve the lives of their families. The poor often do not have long-term time horizons because they do not know if they will even be alive in the distant future. By creating direct economic values for local conservation, ecotourism is filling a crucial need in the environmentalists' toolbox.

This leads to a larger point that is often overlooked by economists: *people only can value things that they are aware of.* For example, people who don't know about the environmental benefits of forests or that a rare type of freshwater dolphin just went extinct in China cannot attribute values to these things (Lovgren, 2006). For this reason environmental education is extremely important in providing a foundation for promoting the values of biodiversity preservation. Every time a person experiences the majesty of nature or learns to appreciate human dependence on ecosystem services, it is very likely that their valuation of a whole host of environmental resources will increase.

From 1995 to 2000 Mitsubishi had plans to open a major saltworks operation in Baja, Mexico, near one of the most pristine and largest lagoons where gray whales congregate every year. The Natural Resources Defense Council (NRDC) worked tirelessly to fight this development, and just when it seemed like they were going to lose, an interesting thing happened. Mexican minister of natural resources Julia Carabias convinced then Mexican president Ernesto Zedillo to come out with them to the lagoon and see the whales firsthand before making the final decision on the project. President Zedillo took along his young children on the small dinghy boats into the lagoon. Once on the water, they were soon surrounded by the gray whales, with one of them coming close enough to touch.[23] Needless to say, the president and his son were deeply moved by this experience. The next day the president rejected Mitsubishi's plans for the saltworks. It's not possible to attribute this decision solely to the experience on the boat trip, but from all accounts this intimate encounter with the whales was a deciding factor (Smith, 2001). Personal experience and direct contact with nature's bounty is one of the best ways to instill a conservation ethic, or from the economist's point of view, generate additional value for environmental resources.

OTHER IMPORTANT LESSONS

1. The Failure of "Bioprospecting"

Whereas ecotourism holds great promise for future conservation efforts, it is instructive to examine the widely held belief during the 1980s and into the 1990s that the great potential for pharmaceutical discoveries in the natural world would provide significant incentives to halt deforestation and species extinction. The essential logic behind "bioprospecting" was that companies and local communities would do better economically scouring the forests for new medicines than cutting down the trees. While a few joint agreements in Costa Rica and Belize between western pharmaceutical companies and local governments produced economic development opportunities, conservation victories, and some minor discoveries with economic value, overall the bioprospecting movement has been a great disappointment.[24]

The reality is that many plants contain the same elements as others, thereby making conservation of large tracts redundant, and synthetic chemicals have been replacing naturally derived medicines, further limiting the economic potential of new discoveries of plant-based compounds (Simpson et al., 1996).

2. The Threat Posed by the "Bush Meat" and Exotic Wildlife Trade

The global demand for "bush meat" (animals caught in the wild and sold for food), animals and plants for jewelry and medicines, and exotic pets is exacting a terrible toll on the world's biodiversity. In particular, the demand for shark fins is devastating many marine ecosystems and entire shark populations, and the demand for wild meat throughout Africa is leading to massive depopulation of numerous threatened species of primates.[25] Not long ago, the demand for ivory decimated the world's elephant population, and the current demand for tiger bone has led to dangerously low levels of these majestic animals.

The trade in virtually all of these commodities is not driven by the desperate poor struggling to survive (although they are often the ones engaged at the supply side), but by the middle class and the wealthy in both the developed and developing world who are willing to pay high prices for these products. Much of the trade in these wildlife products is illegal, but as visitors to open-air markets throughout Asia and Africa can attest, in many places enforcement is lax or nonexistent.

As with the illegal drug trade, the only way to stop the supply is to decrease demand at the source. Organizations like WildAid have been very effective at airing commercials using famous celebrities that implore people to stop buying things such as shark fin soup (these have starred NBA player Yao Ming and movie mogul Jackie Chan).[26] Effective education campaigns that shame people may be one of the most effective ways to combat the demand for bush meat and exotic wildlife.

As a side note, the development of Viagra has supposedly decreased the demand for some rare animal parts known for their aphrodisiac properties ("Kindest cut of All," 2002).

3. Too Much Focus on "Charismatic Megafauna"?

Within the environmental movement there has always been a tension between the popular demand for the preservation of "charismatic megafauna," such as whales, dolphins, polar bears, bald eagles, and seals, and the conservation of other strata of species, such as reptiles, amphibians, and small plants and animals that may play just as important a role in ecosystem functioning but don't capture the public's imagination to the same extent.[27]

In some sense, this problem can be viewed as one of education: people simply need to be informed of the ecological importance of these less "sexy" animals and plants and be made to appreciate a wider spectrum of environmental resources. Some argue that since the megafauna are often dependent on a whole host of lower species that support the ecosystem, making this leap shouldn't be too difficult.

There is a counterargument that says there is nothing wrong with people valuing animals like whales more than salamanders, since it is *we* who have to decide what to prioritize and we should be able to focus on the things that give us the most pleasure. This may seem shortsighted to some conservation purists, but we are all likely susceptible to this logic to some extent; after all, if we had the choice, how many of us would choose saving a salamander over a whale?

But clearly, economic criteria are not the only criteria for determining value, and it may well be the case that the public's infatuation with charismatic megafauna has channeled money and resources into some areas that do not represent the best conservation options or "bang for the buck." Working on establishing a greater role for purely science-based measures of conversation priorities in the public-policy process may be a fruitful strategy for environmentalists to pursue, along with greater educational efforts.

SUMMARY

The basic economics of forests and biodiversity conservation posit that private investments will never be sufficient to meet all of the world's conservation goals, because people can "free-ride" on the investments made by others. There is a role for governments both to promote biodiversity conservation in their own countries and to assist with global conservation goals, especially in biodiversity hot spots.

Since most biodiversity exists on private lands, providing incentives for landowners to conserve their natural resources is critical. The most effective means of doing so is through a system of payments for environmental services, in which the primary beneficiaries of the services pay those who are providing the conservation benefits.

Even if putting a monetary price on natural resources is antithetical to most environmentalists, priorities for conservation must be made given limited resources. Shining a light on the values that we derive from forests and the world's plants and animals can actually elevate their importance in the policymaking process.

CHAPTER 10

AGRICULTURE

Agriculture is the greatest human alteration of the natural world. Currently, more than 38 percent of the world's land has been converted to agricultural production (Food and Agriculture Organization of the UN, 2004). In most cases the conversion to agriculture causes a dramatic decrease in biodiversity, since forests are often cleared to make way for crops. In addition to losses in biodiversity, agricultural production is rife with externalities caused by pesticide use, soil erosion, and water and energy use.

Given agriculture's scope and its dramatic effects on the environment, it is surprising that agricultural policy rarely garners the attention from the environmental community that it deserves. Agricultural issues are by no means ignored by the major environment organizations, but as their monthly periodicals and newsletters can attest, issues such as oil drilling, whaling, and climate change receive disproportionate attention.

I am not exactly sure why this is the case, but it likely has something to do with the romantic notion of farming that still persists, ironically, in the developed countries where so few people actually farm. There are no doubt tens of thousands of farmers who live up to the ideals of proper land stewardship, but agriculture is big business, where profits often trump environmental concerns; even many "family farmers" are not immune to practices that are severely damaging to the environment.[1]

The negative environmental impacts of agriculture must be weighed against the tremendous benefits that it has brought to humanity.[2] The agricultural productivity gains of the twentieth century were the foundation for much of the economic growth that propelled the United States and Europe and helped to free up resources for other aspects of industrial development. These gains were not just relegated to the developed world. The "green revolution" technologies that dramatically increased yields are estimated to have saved the lives of hundreds of millions of people around the globe. For this reason, Dr. Norman Borlaug received a Nobel Peace Prize for his work in the area of plant genetics.[3]

Agricultural innovations are constantly changing the dynamics of global food production; Brazil's soybean industry has been catapulted to number three in the world, behind the United States and China, after major breakthroughs in plant breeding and fertilization techniques. Many countries in Africa, which continue to lag behind the world in agricultural productivity, are poised to reap the benefits of modern technology and improved management if the right incentives are put in place.

When dealing with something as pervasive and fundamental for society as food production, it is difficult to accurately quantify all of the myriad benefits that come from a strong agricultural sector and low-cost nutrition.

From an environmentalist perspective, it is much easier to identify specific aspects of the agricultural system that are clearly counterproductive—those that promote negative environmental outcomes with few or no counterbalancing benefits.

AGRICULTURAL PRODUCTION SUBSIDIES

The massive agricultural production subsidies that persist in the United States, Europe, Japan, South Korea, and a few other developed countries[4] total over $200 billion a year and result in huge environmental damage (Organization for Economic Co-operation and Development, 2004b). Most of these subsidy programs were first instituted in the early twentieth century, around the time of the Great

Depression, when large segments of the population worked in agriculture and agricultural production in many regions had come to a standstill. Production subsidies were used as a way to sustain farming and rural livelihoods and have stayed with us ever since. Unfortunately, not only have they greatly outlived their usefulness, they contribute to massive overproduction, besides being a colossal waste of taxpayer money that could be used for much more worthwhile causes.

Production subsidies pay farmers a per unit amount to produce certain crops—mostly commodities such as wheat, rice, soy, corn, and cotton—usually based on the difference between the current market price and a predetermined price floor that is significantly higher.[5] With the promise of subsidy payments, farmers produce much more than they would in a free market system. Not only do they expand acreage, but much of this expansion occurs on marginal lands, since the best lands are used first. These marginal crops require even more fertilizers and pesticides, and are grown on soils that are prone to erosion. All of this leads to unnecessary environmental harm.

In addition, most of the subsidies go to larger farmers who own the most land. In a process called "land capitalization," the subsidies ultimately result in higher land prices, as the value of the guaranteed government payments gets absorbed into the land price. This creates a barrier to entry for aspiring farmers who want to enter the agricultural sector, and directly harms those who lease their land, which are often the small-scale producers.

The obvious solution is to eliminate agricultural production subsidies by slowly phasing them out over time to give farmers sufficient time to adjust. This would not only yield tremendous environmental benefits, but also save taxpayers billions of dollars a year that could be devoted to dozens of other causes that merit greater investment.

Unfortunately, due to both the disproportionate political power that agribusiness maintains throughout the world and a lack of knowledge on the part of the public,[6] there is little indication that there is the political will to diminish the role of production subsidies in the agricultural sector in most countries anytime soon. Undoing the U.S.

system of agricultural subsidies is particularly difficult since the main agricultural states have disproportionate representation in the U.S. Senate and are also some of the major "swing" states in national elections, which politicians must pander to for votes.[7]

One interesting campaign in the United States that is drawing public attention to the issue of agricultural subsidies is being led by the Environmental Working Group (EWG), which hosts a website that lists every farmer in the country who receives agricultural subsidies along with their exact annual payments.[8] This information has been reported in various media outlets and has led more people to question the efficacy and fairness of the system.

The inability to significantly reduce agricultural subsidies[9] is one of the main reasons that the most recent Doha Round of multilateral trade talks reached an impasse. Many developing countries rightly contend that the overproduction caused by production subsidies decreases the world price of agricultural commodities, which then harms their producers, who do not have the benefit of wealthy governments to subsidize them. It is estimated that food-exporting nations are harmed to the tune of tens of billions of dollars a year because of artificially depressed world prices for their crops.[10]

While the multilateral process has stalled, there have been some positive developments coming out of the World Trade Organization's (WTO) judicial body. Since agricultural production (and export) subsidies greatly distort world trade in agricultural goods, the WTO has repeatedly ruled against the United States in cases brought by developing countries harmed by U.S. agricultural policy.[11] While the United States has been slow to heed the WTO rulings—as evidenced by new farm legislation that maintains most of the current subsidies[12]—the EU has made some great strides in moving away from production subsidies over the past decade.

Even though the EU still greatly subsidizes its farmers, the farm payments are now largely "decoupled" from production; they are not linked to how much farmers produce, and therefore do not encourage as much overproduction. The EU has largely shifted to a system where farmers receive lump-sum payments as a form of minimum income insurance, as well as payments to engage in specific agricultural practices that are more environmentally benign.[13] This is certainly an improvement over the production subsidy system, and may present a model for other countries to follow. Large agribusiness interests who stand to lose tens of millions in direct payments will still resist it, but at least it presents a compromise that many parties have already accepted.

Ideally, farmers should receive no subsidies, since workers in many industries face uncertainties and risks just as great as in agriculture. Farmers can purchase crop insurance on the private market, just as other businesses buy insurance for all sorts of potential losses.

New Zealand was one of the first developed countries to scrap its entire agricultural subsidy system in 1984–1985.[14] Today New Zealand's agricultural sector is thriving, with farmers competing on global markets through innovation and efficiency, and free from government support (Birrell, 2007; Sayre, 2003). Not all New Zealand farmers are still in business, but turnover exists in every industry, and overall New Zealand's agricultural sector is strong.

There is one last point regarding agricultural subsidies that has important global ramifications, especially for the poor. It has been noted that by depressing the global prices of agricultural commodities, production subsidies harm agricultural exporting nations in the developing world. But those developing countries that are *net food importers* actually benefit from cheaper food on world markets—at least, the urban consumers benefit.

Any change in the global subsidy system that led to an increase in world food prices could hurt these poor food-importing countries. Two important things to keep in mind: the poorest of the poor in most of these countries are in the rural areas, and the extent to which their income could be boosted by higher prices for their crops would be a plus; also, the money saved by wealthy countries by eliminating the subsidies would be more than enough to make up for the increased food prices in the poorer countries. A multilateral agreement that combined a reduction or the elimination of agricultural production subsidies in the developed world with increased assistance to the developing world would likely be a win-win scenario for the environment and the world's poor.

AGRICULTURAL SUBSIDIES AND HEALTH IMPACTS

Agricultural subsidies in the United States have dramatically increased the production of corn and lowered its price; this is one reason corn syrup is so cheap and ubiquitous in food products. Corn and soybeans (another subsidized crop) are now the primary feed for livestock, so these subsidizes are also indirect subsidies for the meat and dairy industry, also lowering their prices. The net result is that calories are cheaper now than ever before, which is one reason obesity is on the rise. In addition, agricultural subsidies are partly responsible for the extremely low prices for a wide variety of fast foods that contribute to heart disease, cancer, and diabetes. These diseases take a tremendous toll on human health and cost huge sums of money to treat. Because the prices of unhealthy foods are artificially depressed, the relatively higher prices for fresh fruit and vegetables (which receive no direct subsidies) further discourage their consumption. From a public health perspective this is completely backward—if anything should be subsidized it is healthy foods, but the opposite is the case in the United States and throughout much of the world.

SUBSIDIZED WATER

Water scarcity is becoming an increasingly important global issue. Already there is talk of water becoming the new "black gold."[15] There are some regions of the world where water shortages are so persistent that there is literally not enough water to maintain a reasonable standard of living for the populace, let alone for other economic purposes or to support local biodiversity.

But in most parts of the world, even those regions where fresh water supplies are decreasing, the primary issue is not one of *absolute* water scarcity, but how the water is distributed. And in many regions and countries the bulk of fresh water resources go to agriculture, often at highly subsidized rates, which is both environmentally damaging and a waste of public resources.[16]

My home state of California is a perfect example.[17] Here, 80 percent of all of the states' water goes to agriculture (Office of Water Use Efficiency, 2008), and at prices that are a fraction of its true value, both with respect to what others are willing to pay for it and the costs of capturing and transporting it. The result is that in California a huge amount of water is wasted; hundreds of thousands of acre-feet of fresh water are used inefficiently for relatively low-value crops in areas that couldn't naturally support such production. Not only does this lead to much less water for residential use, but the environment has been one of the biggest losers in the state's water wars.

Many rivers in the state have been deprived of sufficient water to maintain healthy levels of fish and other biodiversity, leading to large areas that are essentially devoid of sustainable biological populations—this in a state where river recreation and wildlife tourism is extremely popular and lucrative. This practice is technically illegal in California, but that has not stopped many water districts from taking more than their share of the state's water for their agricultural interests for decades.

One of the state's longest-running lawsuits pitted the Friant County Water District against the Natural Resources Defense Council (NRDC, which represented the people of California). The NRDC claimed that the Friant County Water District was legally obligated to leave sufficient water in the San Joaquin River to maintain its historic salmon populations, when in fact the district for decades had removed so much water that large stretches of the river were rendered virtually lifeless. After numerous appeals and decades of legal action, the NRDC won its lawsuit in September 2006 ("Water to Flow," 2006; U.S. Bureau of Reclamation, 2006) and the San Joaquin River is being restored with hundreds of millions of dollars in state money.

California is not alone in having a highly inefficient system of water distribution in which the environment and consumers are the net losers. The question is how to move to a more equitable and efficient distribution system.[18]

It is often the case that changes in water policy are precipitated by legal challenges such as the one described above; water interests are so entrenched, the historical claims so complicated, and the stakes so large that protracted court battles are required to settle them. The legal process is costly, both in time and money, but routinely necessary.

Since water is considered a public resource virtually everywhere in the world, the government is the principle arbiter of establishing a baseline of rights and distribution. Ironically, the fact that in so many parts of the world so much water is being wasted is *good news*; it means that there is sufficient water available for both human and environmental needs if a sensible distribution system is put in place.

One of the policy recommendations most popular among economists is to create water markets, which allow users to buy water rights from farmers, and for farmers to trade among each other. This can go a long way to dealing with the efficiency issue; farmers that grow low-value crops will have an incentive to sell to higher-value users, including other farmers, residential users, industry, and environmental groups.

It is estimated that if we had a fully functioning water market in California the agricultural sector would shift considerably; we would still have large-scale production of high-value crops such as nuts, tree fruits, wine grapes, and avocados, but little to no alfalfa or rice production. This shift would free up water for many of the state's beleaguered rivers as well as for increased residential uses to meet the needs of the growing population.

Creating water markets requires first and foremost the clarification of property rights over water so that traders can be confident that they are obtaining contracts that are legally binding. In addition, a trading system has to be established along with methods of transporting water from one user to another, which requires significant infrastructure. Water markets do not address the equity issue as to whether the existing rights to water are fair or not, but they do at least allow for water to be used in high-value activities instead of being wasted.

POLLUTION FROM PESTICIDES, FERTILIZER, AND ANIMAL WASTE

When environmentalists get engaged in agricultural issues, it is often the air and water pollution from farming that captures the most attention, with pesticides front and center. This is unsurprising given the health effects of pesticide residues in our food, the direct harm suffered by farm workers, and the widespread ecological impacts. Before discussing pesticide policy, it is worth noting two other very serious pollution issues associated with agriculture that tend to garner less attention.

The first is fertilizer use, which results in massive damage to underground aquifers, and perhaps more important, to rivers and coastal areas. The nitrogen content of fertilizers in particular can starve water systems of oxygen, leading to huge algae blooms that choke off all other forms of life. This phenomenon has resulted in large "dead zones" in coastal regions throughout the world.[19] One of the largest dead zones is off the Gulf Coast of the United States, fueled by the massive quantities of fertilizers used in fields of the Midwest, which makes its way down the rivers and empties into the sea. On its way, many river systems are also damaged and groundwater is polluted.

No one suggests banning these types of fertilizers since they are essential to industrial agricultural production. However, it is clear that too much is entering the environment.

One potential policy fix is to tax fertilizers based on their capacity to pollute, with the most water-soluble forms being taxed the most. Faced with a significant cost for highly polluting nitrogen fertilizers, farmers would have the option of switching to less damaging methods of fertilization, such as the use of nitrogen-fixing cover crops, developing new seed varieties that require less fertilizer, creating larger buffer zones between their crops and waterways, or switching to less nitrogen-demanding crops. With a high enough tax it is likely that nitrogen pollution could be curtailed.

Another policy option is set a national, regional, or statewide cap on the use of nitrogen fertilizer and let farmers buy and sell permits. This policy is already at work in Connecticut.[20] Monitoring and enforcement is costly because analyses have to be routinely conducted in the waterways near farms to gauge individual runoff rates. This is technically feasible, but requires not only significant capital investment, but also a new bureaucracy to administer the program effectively. Farmers must also be penalized severely for noncompliance or the system breaks down.

Unfortunately, up until now attempts to deal with agricultural dead zones have been limited, and the ecological damage continues to expand year after year. Again, the power of the agricultural industry has hampered serious efforts, and it is not for lack of options that the problem remains unaddressed.

The same can be said for the growing problem of animal waste. As livestock production continues to become industrialized and concentrated, it is not uncommon for operations to boast 100,000-plus animals on a single gigantic lot.[21] While there are no doubt efficiencies gained from containing so many animals in one place (aside from the serious ethical implications of doing so), this also greatly concentrates the animal waste. In fact, waste from factory farms is now orders of magnitude greater than all of the waste generated by the human population. Most of it ends up piled in gigantic mountains or in artificial lagoons.[22] The problem is that it's virtually impossible to keep all of this waste from seeping into the environment, especially during periods of rain and storms. In the United States there have been horrific examples of massive lagoons of pig waste bursting their seams and flooding nearby rivers, killing everything in their wake.[23]

Again, the polluters, in this case the factory farm operators (and indirectly the consumers of animal products), are not paying the true cost for the pollution they create. A waste surcharge levied per animal or a limit on the total quantity of waste that can be kept in a certain area are policy options.

In the above examples, the government could dictate that any revenue generated by agricultural pollution taxes or permit trading be allocated toward efforts to reduce those problems. For example, the revenue from taxes levied on nitrogen fertilizer could be used to buy land adjacent to waterways, create additional buffer zones, improve water-quality monitoring, or fund ecological restoration efforts in dead zones and other waterways impaired by agricultural runoff. Taxes on animal production could be used to develop better ways to recycle animal waste into energy and fertilizer or to create more effective means of disposal.

The issue of agricultural pesticides is much more complicated because the current state of our scientific knowledge with respect to toxins is extremely poor. Most economic policy responses are reasonably straightforward when it is possible to make sound estimates of damages. But when we know very little about which chemicals have which effects, and how they act in combination, we are left with little in our economic toolbox that can provide anything approaching precise solutions.

The central problem is one of risk management. How should we weigh improving the productivity of agriculture, and thereby lowering the price of food, against the increased exposure to toxic risks, both for ourselves and the plants and animals that come in contact with pesticides?

The organic agriculture industry has demonstrated that many people are prepared to pay a price premium for foods with much lower quantities of toxic residues. It is possible to argue that the emergence of the organic market is proof of the market's effectiveness, in that individuals can choose their level of risk based on their own priorities.[24] Banning pesticides or dramatically increasing their price would likely lead to higher food prices and deny people the option of which food to purchase based on their own perceived risk preferences. But perhaps this is the right thing to do.

It all comes down to whether the larger impacts on ecosystems and farm workers are great enough to warrant such an intervention, as well as whether people are truly informed about the risks they face from pesticide residues, which, again, are poorly understood. Undoubtedly, there are some pesticides, for example methyl bromide, that are known to be highly toxic and damaging to the environment, that have rightly been banned (although exceptions have been made and they remain on the market).[25] There are also some pesticides that are universally thought to be benign that have proved very useful for farmers and have demonstrably improved agricultural productivity.[26]

It is the pesticides that we are less sure of, both with respect to their impacts and their overall effectiveness, where decisions get trickier. Should the onus be on producers to prove that not only is a pesticide safe but also greatly needed for the industry? Or should the onus be on those who want to prevent the use of chemicals to prove that they are damaging and that substitutes exist?

There is no precise answer to this question; it comes down to society's collective appetite for risk. In some countries, the regulatory apparatus strongly favors precaution (the EU), while in others (notably the United States) the rights of industry to experiment with new chemicals are greater.

GENETICALLY MODIFIED ORGANISMS (GMOS)

The issue of whether to allow the use of genetically modified organisms (GMOs) in agricultural production is a topic for which the environmental community is essentially split. Some contend that GMOs represent such an extreme deviation from what is "natural" and pose such great environmental and health risks that the process should be banned. This is what the organic industry has done; in fact, virtually the only way to obtain food that is free (in principle)[27] of GMOs is to buy organic. The European Union has been the most adamantly opposed to GMOs, going so far as to ban their importation from the United States until their recent loss in the WTO court.[28]

Putting aside issues of what is natural (which includes the argument that most uses of genetic engineering are little more than the acceleration of plant-breeding techniques that have been practiced for millennia),[29] the fundamental argument against GMOs once again revolves around notions of risk. Those opposed to GMOs believe that the introduction of new organisms into the environment has not been studied sufficiently and presents an unacceptable environmental hazard. There are also concerns that people with allergies to certain foods may be unaware that the genes of one food are contained in another, thus leading to medical risks.

Those in favor of GMOs cite their potential to actually decrease the environmental impact of agriculture through the development of pest-resistant crops or crops that require less water and fertilizer. There is also the potential to modify crops to increase their nutrient content, which is being done with rice, bananas, and potatoes, and could be very beneficial in countries where the populace suffers from malnutrition.[30]

The consensus view, based on the available evidence so far, is that GMO crops do not represent a grave threat to ecosystems.[31] GMOs have been in production on a large scale for more than ten years and there is as of yet no reported incidences of major ecological disruptions due to the propagation of GMO crops.[32] This is not to suggest that there aren't potential negative effects or effects that have yet to be discovered, only that little to no evidence currently exists.

However, there is a significant consumer-rights movement that believes individuals have a right to know whether they are eating GMO food that is pushing for mandatory labeling.[33] From a market-based perspective this seems reasonable since consumers can make informed decisions only if they have sufficient information.

But if we are going to require mandatory GMO labeling, the question arises as to what other information should be mandatory. Foods do not list the pesticides and fertilizers used in their production, or the miles the food traveled, or the country of origin, or the wages of the workers. It is difficult to make the case that this information is any less important. And mandatory labeling of GMO foods is costly, requiring sorting by seed type throughout the production process, along with expensive monitoring.

Is it worth it?

Without clear evidence that GMOs represent new and significant risks to the environment it is not clear that the mandatory labeling is warranted. There are already plenty of companies that voluntarily advertise GMO-free food, and organic is by default GMO-free. Certainly, in the case of foods with a high allergen potential mandatory labeling is needed—for example, if peanut genes were injected into almonds.

If the evidence continues to point to the relative benign nature of GMOs, it seems appropriate to let the market choose the winners and losers in this new realm of agricultural technology. In the instances where GMOs can cut costs and minimize environmental impacts, they should be embraced. When they are used for little more than cosmetic improvements, this may appear wasteful, but if the products are competitive and there is significant demand from farmers they shouldn't be opposed strictly on ideological grounds. Remember, it is not the government's job to regulate people's tastes, but to protect the public interest.

If in fact GMOs do develop the potential to greatly reduce environmental impacts, this may pose a challenge to the organic industry, which may be compelled to revisit its opposition. It is certainly permissible for any industry to determine its own standards, but an industry that prides itself on environmental stewardship should be open to the possibility that GMO technology could be an ally in the future. And developing countries that suffer from very low yields and contain large swaths of unproductive lands would be well advised to consider GMOs as one potentially beneficial tool to employ.

The ultimate fate of GMO crops should be determined by their effectiveness and their cost.

SUMMARY

The environmental impacts of agricultural are truly astounding. While industrial food production has created the foundation upon which much of modern prosperity is based, it has come with significant costs. Many of these costs, however, are the result of bad policies that distort agricultural practices and reward mostly large farmers at the expense of small growers, taxpayers, and environmental quality.

Fixing these problems requires taking on powerful and entrenched agricultural interests. One of the greatest allies for agricultural reform is the WTO, whose mission is to create a level playing field internationally in agriculture, which requires eliminating all forms of agricultural subsidies.

Although the agricultural landscape both within and across countries is extremely varied, the essential economic logic for good policy remains consistent: don't subsidize farmers (but if you do, decouple the subsidies from production) and create incentives for farmers to take into consideration their pollution when making their production decisions.

CHAPTER 11

CHEMICAL POLLUTION

One of the defining moments in the environmental movement was the 1962 publication of Rachel Carson's book *Silent Spring,* which awakened the United States (and the world) to the potential hazard that toxic chemicals could wreak on the environment. Carson's work led to a major public outcry, which gave rise to many of the organizations that comprise the modern environmental movement. In 1972 the United States banned the chemical DDT, which Carson had linked to reductions in bird populations, including the nation's symbol—the bald eagle—and the peregrine falcon.[1]

Like many of the other landmark pieces of environmental legislation that were passed during this era in the United States (the Endangered Species Act, Clean Water Act, and Clean Air Act), there was no explicit use of benefit-cost analysis employed to enact the ban. No economists were asked to determine the "value" of the bald eagles and falcons and weigh this against the benefits to agriculture (mostly the cotton industry) of the use of DDT. It was determined that it was simply unacceptable to risk the extinction of these birds and the larger environmental and human costs associated with the use of DDT.

Almost forty years have passed and there is virtually no one in the United States who believes that the ban was the wrong decision. There has been some controversy regarding attempts to ban or greatly diminish the use of DDT in developing countries, particularly those in the tropics, because DDT can be effective against the mosquitoes that carry malaria, which unfortunately still kills tens of thousands of people a year.[2]

Still, most people today would be surprised to learn that the majority of chemicals that they are routinely exposed to have barely been studied at all. Those that have are usually tested in animal studies, which do not necessarily provide accurate information regarding human health effects (putting aside the ethical implications of subjecting millions of animals to often painful procedures). There is virtually no scientific data that analyzes the synergistic effect of the thousands of chemicals working in concert in our bodies and the environment every day.[3]

In addition, many chemicals that have been banned or phased out long ago still persist in the environment, and their toxic legacy continues. In fact, DDT is a persistent organic pollutant that has shown up in relatively high concentrations in Arctic ecosystems, negatively affecting many forms of Arctic wildlife decades after it was banned and thousands of miles away from where it was used.[4]

It is not an exaggeration to suggest that we are all, more than ever, human "guinea pigs" when it comes to the toxic legacy we have both inherited and continue to promulgate. Hundreds of new chemicals are produced every year and brought to market, transmitted through everything from plastics, electronics, pesticides, shampoos, processed food, cosmetics, and industrial processes. In addition, the new and exciting world of nanotechnology is introducing ever smaller particles into our environment that pose new risks and challenges.[5]

While in most parts of the world longevity is increasing—a testament to one measure of improved health—cancer deaths remain extremely high. The persistent high incidence of cancer may very well turn out to be a product of our chemical burden, given that the bloodstream of the average person can contains more than ninety different chemicals, many of them known to be toxic.[6] It is safe to say that whatever damage we are inflicting on ourselves is multiplied many times over on nonhuman creatures, who do not have the benefit of advanced medicine, detection, filtration, or the ability to switch food sources based on a knowledge of their toxicity.

Faced with the prospect that our current levels of chemical pollution are subjecting us and our surrounding ecosystems to elevated levels of risk, which we don't fully understand, conventional economic analysis does not suffice. We simply do not have the information with which to even begin making a fully informed benefit-cost analysis, even if it was deemed an ethically appropriate method to assess which chemicals should be restricted or not.

This presents a much more difficult policy situation than some of the other environmental problems that we face. We are dealing with probabilities of risk, with large gaps in our knowledge, and a great degree of uncertainty.

Comparing how the United States approaches the issue of controlling toxic substances with the approach currently being undertaken by the European Union is instructive. In the United States, industry has much more power to limit restrictions on chemicals, which must be proven to be harmful before they can be regulated. The EU, on the other hand, invokes the "precautionary principle" and the bar for banning or restricting chemicals is much lower; chemicals are restricted if there is even a reasonable chance that they can cause significant harm.[7] This difference in regulatory approach is creating a widening gulf between the types of chemicals that are permitted within the United States and the EU. This shift marks a contrast to the era when the United States set one of the highest standards for chemical safety in the world.

The family of chemicals known as phthalates, which are used to make plastic toys more pliant, has now been banned in the EU due to fears that children will chew on them and face a toxic risk, whereas in most of the United States the chemical is still widely used (some states, including California, have recently banned it).[8]

Although the EU has not undertaken explicit benefit-cost analyses in its rulings prohibiting many chemicals, there is an underlying benefit-cost logic below the surface. In cases where relatively cheap substitutes exist that are known to be less toxic, the EU has ruled in favor of bans or limitations on the more toxic materials. In areas where a chemical is crucial to a production process and the overall competitiveness of European industry, the precautionary approach has not always prevailed; for example, despite a growing volume of evidence that bisphenol A (BPA) mimics estrogen in the body and causes cancer and developmental disabilities, it has not been banned in the EU (Goodman, 2008).[9]

The lessons on how best to approach the issue of chemical pollution by the environmental community (which can be applied to all forms of chemicals, including industrial, residential, and agricultural) can be summarized as follows:

1. Changing the regulatory paradigm is probably the most important step in reducing toxic chemicals. With woefully incomplete scientific information on the majority of chemicals in everyday use, a regulatory system that requires definitive proof of toxicity will almost always favor industry over public health and the environment. Stressing that the burden of toxic chemicals often falls on the most vulnerable—pregnant women, infants, the elderly—is a big part of changing this paradigm. The crux of the argument is not so much about economic efficiency, but about the distributional effects of chemical pollution.

2. Policies that encourage the development of nontoxic or "green" substitutes for common chemicals represent one of the best long-term strategies for dramatically reducing the use of toxic chemicals. Such policies include subsidies for "green" chemical research,[10] as well as more money for research that demonstrates the ill effects of the chemicals currently in use.[11]

3. Given the tens of thousands of chemicals currently in use, it is best to focus on classes of chemicals, such as PCBs.[12] This way the unintended consequence of banning one chemical, only to have industry switch to another related chemical that is equally or potentially more toxic, can be avoided.

4. Focus on the chemicals that are most likely contributing
    to the worst effects; that is, choose priorities. This may
    seem like stating the obvious, but there have been notable
    examples of environmental groups expending significant
    resources to oppose the use of chemicals that are not be-
    lieved to be acutely toxic. For example, the opposition to
    Alar in the United States in 1989, or the more recent cam-
    paigns against fluoride in drinking water.[13] This is not to
    suggest that these chemicals are entirely benign, only that
    given limited political capital and resources, priorities are
    essential; campaigns against elevated levels of mercury or
    lead offer a much better public and environmental health
    return for every ounce of organizational investment.[14]

5. Finally, the most controversial of my recommendations:
    in most cases eschew market-based mechanisms in favor
    of "command and control" policies such as limits or bans.
    Command and control regulation is often inefficient, but
    in the area of toxic chemicals it may be the best regula-
    tory approach we have. The problem with market-based
    mechanisms—especially cap and trade—is that they
    can lead to the creation of "toxic hot spots"—areas with
    disproportionately elevated levels of toxic pollution.[15]
    Sometimes it is better to simply limit the levels of certain
    chemicals across the board or ban them altogether.

Plans have been discussed in the United States to extend the cap
and trade system for sulfur pollution to mercury.[16] The policy would
set a cap on the total levels of mercury emitted by coal-fired power
plants and then issue permits to be traded. From an efficiency standpoint the policy would most likely "work" in that it would reduce
total mercury pollution at the lowest cost (i.e., it would be efficient);
unfortunately, some segments of the population might be exposed to
unacceptably high risks in the process.

It is entirely conceivable that the older plants with high mitigation costs would purchase the bulk of the permits, thereby leading to
much *higher* concentrations of mercury in the surrounding areas. In

this case a limit on mercury emissions across *all* power plants, while not the most cost-effective, is preferable. Equity concerns sometimes must trump efficiency concerns. This logic can be applied to the majority of situations in which the goal is to curtail the use of acutely toxic chemicals, especially those that disproportionately harm the most vulnerable populations.

REGULATING TOXIC CHEMICALS INTERNATIONALLY

Because chemicals emitted into the air and water don't respect political boundaries, and through international trade they are transported to every corner of the world, there is a great need for international cooperation, especially for the most toxic substances.

Most countries are signatories to a host of international agreements that ban or severely limit the use of many highly toxic chemicals, and the International Organization for Standardization (ISO), which publishes standards for thousands of products and is the premier global standardization body, includes chemical and other environmental safety standards in much of its work.

Despite these efforts, which have succeeded in partially leveling the international playing field and reducing some of the worst uses of toxic chemicals, there is a wide gap between the institutional and enforcement capacity between developed and developing countries. Not only do many developing countries lack the regulatory infrastructure—scientists, labs, detection equipment, auditors and other staff—necessary to adequately address the problem, but also the laws governing chemical pollution in many developing countries are significantly weaker to begin with.

This disparity is largely what motivated the international agreement that has come to be known as the Basel Convention, which governs the trade in hazardous waste.[17] The agreement came into force in 1992; it severely restricts the quantities and types of waste that can be shipped from one country to the next. It was motivated by the desire to prevent wealthy nations from dumping their toxic waste in the developing countries, which was viewed both as unethical and an impediment to the development of cleaner production processes; the ability to outsource pollution diminishes the incentive for home countries to produce more efficient and environmentally benign technology.

One consequence of the Basel Convention is that the toxic waste industry in developing countries—everything from disposing of medical waste, e-waste, and nuclear waste to ship breaking—has declined, which is considered a success by most environmentalists. However, these industries employ millions of people, often the least educated and the poorest, and it is unclear if they are now actually better off. Despite the hazards they were exposed to in the toxic waste industry, their employment options are severely limited.[18]

These types of trade-offs are extremely difficult for people in wealthy countries to grapple with and for good reason: we are at a stage of development where the types of environmental health and safety risks that are routine in many developing countries are considered unacceptable. And through the Basel Convention we have exported these values to the poorest nations of the world, with good intentions no doubt, but also perhaps with unintended consequences.

SUMMARY

For many types of toxic substances, benefit-cost analysis is not plausible because we have insufficient information with which to assign monetary values to the pros and cons of using particular chemicals. Traditional market-based strategies, such as environmental taxes or cap and trade, can be appropriate policy responses for chemicals that are well studied and not acutely toxic (e.g., CO_2 or SO_x), but do not make sense for persistent organic pollutants, heavy metals, and highly carcinogenic compounds.

A command and control approach that bans or severely limits the use of highly toxic chemicals is the most sensible approach, especially when many of the worst chemicals disproportionately affect the most vulnerable segments of society—children, pregnant women, and the elderly. These regulations should be coupled with government efforts to promote research into less toxic alternatives, greater scientific information about the effects of the chemicals already in use, and strong international cooperation to ensure that all countries severely limit the worst classes of chemicals.

CHAPTER 12

FISHERIES AND THE MARINE ENVIRONMENT

The oceans are in serious trouble; this is not hyperbole or more "doom and gloom" prognosticating. Multiple assessments of the state of the oceans show that the majority of fisheries are declining and face complete collapse.[1]

In areas where unsustainable rates of fishing have already led to the collapse of large fisheries, such as the cod fishery off the coast of New England and Canada in the 1990s, tens of thousands of jobs have been lost and entire local communities devastated. Even in areas where fisheries have yet to collapse, the toll of overfishing has created serious economic hardship.

This decline of the world's fisheries is easy to explain: virtually all of the oceans are "open access" resources, and fishermen, fueled by a surge in demand for seafood,[2] harvest as much fish as they can resulting in unsustainable rates of fishing. Not only has demand for seafood skyrocketed, but also technology for catching fish has improved dramatically; many large commercial fleets employ sophisticated sonar systems costing hundreds of thousands of dollars and nets hundreds of meters long.

INDIVIDUAL FISHING QUOTAS (IFQS)

Theoretically, the solution to the problem of overfishing is relatively straightforward: limit the quantity of fish that can be caught. This necessitates creating property rights to fishery resources and assigning them to different parties (or finding some other way to distribute them, such as an auction), essentially creating a cap and trade–style system over these natural resources.

In countries such as New Zealand, Norway, Iceland, Canada, and the United States, systems have been put in place that create property rights for fisheries and limit the total catch. These are referred to as Individual Fishing Quota (IFQ) or Individual Tradable Quota (ITQ) systems (and sometimes also as "catch shares").[3] In almost all of the regions where they have been implemented they have been successful at helping to create sustainable fisheries. In all of these programs, fisherman can freely buy and sell permits among themselves.

The mechanics of setting up these programs are complex, and they are not simple to manage. IFQs are only possible in areas where the government or some other legal entity has clear property rights over the ocean resources with which they can exercise authority. The Law of the Sea Convention grants nations the rights to all ocean resources within two hundred miles of their coastlines.[4] These regions are where all of the current IFQ systems exist. Within these boundaries nations are entitled to utilize their ocean resources as they see fit, which includes creating property rights systems over particular resources.

The scientific data requirements of IFQ systems are very strong; to determine the sustainable levels of fishing, detailed information about historic fish stocks must be available. This is complicated by the fact that fish species intermingle; while fishing for one species, other species are often caught as well. This typically results in conservative estimates for the "maximum allowable catch." Another reason in support of more conservative estimates is that when faced with fishing quotas, fishermen are apt to "high-grade"—only bringing to shore the best catches and dumping the others back into the ocean—which increases the total impact of a given fish quota. Since the science of fisheries is imperfect, fisheries must be constantly monitored, and if it turns out that the original quotas were set too high, adjustments must be made in future allotments.

An IFQ system, like all cap and trade systems, works only if there is reliable and consistent enforcement. In the case of fishing, fishermen are required to present their quotas at the docks when they bring in their hauls. Inspectors must be present to identify the species, weigh them, and check that the fishermen have sufficient quotas. If they do not, this must be met with stiff penalties to deter breaking the rules. Fisheries with a small number of docks where fishermen can bring their catches to shore make the system much more manageable.

While the general distrust of government among fishermen is even greater than in the general population, there is a grudging acceptance that IFQs may be one of the best ways to ensure the long-term sustainability of fisheries, which is certainly in the long-term interests of the fishing industry. The major complaints against IFQs are that they generally raise the cost of fishing and that more often than not they lead to a decrease in current fishing employment (even if they ensure long-term survivability of the fishing industry).

This simply reflects the reality that currently there is too much fishing in most parts of the world, and that the fisheries cannot support the current levels of employment. This, of course, raises equity concerns since some people must lose their jobs. Quotas are typically allotted to those who have historically been active in the fishery, and the greater degree of overfishing the lower the total amount of allowable quotas to get the fishery back on a sustainable path.

Compensating those who are unable to continue fishing can come in the form of "buyouts" from the government; some governments have chosen to auction a limited number of the fishing quotas and use this revenue to pay the fishermen who exit the industry. The bottom line is that the pressure on most fisheries is excessive and there needs to be some pullback if the fisheries are going to survive.

An added benefit of IFQs is that they allow fishermen to spread their work out over the entire year or fishing season. In many fisheries, instead of quantity limits on fish extraction, fishing is limited to short windows of operation, sometimes as little as a few days. The resulting rush to get as much fish as quickly as possible is referred to as a fish "derby" or "rodeo." These affairs are often extremely danger-ous since, in the crowded frenzy to catch as much fish as they can, injuries are commonplace. In addition, fish buyers have dispropor-tionate power in these arrangements, knowing that the fishermen must unload all of their fish very quickly. Since much of the excessive fish must be frozen, this further decreases the price. In an IFQ system fishermen can sell at the higher fresh-fish prices all year long and can bring fish to market when prices are most favorable.

IFQ systems may still entail significant negative externalities to marine resources. Millions of animals, including seals, otters, sea lions, turtles, dolphins, whales, and sharks, are caught (as bycatch) in fishermen's nets every year, and most die horrible deaths.[5] In addi-tion, practices such as "bottom trawling," in which large nets literally scrape the ocean floor in search of fish, often destroy everything in their wake, including slow-growing coral. This practice is banned in parts of the world, but it is still widely practiced; efforts are currently underway for a global ban.[6]

Commercial fishing, even if technically "sustainable," entails serious damage to marine life; there is no way around it. Regulations can (and should) be enacted to mandate modifications to nets or improved monitoring so that fewer animals are inadvertently killed, but the numbers will always be high in large-scale fishing operations.

It is important to emphasize that IFQ systems can only work in areas where nations have legal jurisdiction over the territory. In the international waters of the open ocean entirely new legal regimes and agreements have to be developed that can create mutually agreed upon and enforceable rules and norms over fisheries that multiple countries currently access.

Such an agreement is in the works between eight of the Pacific Island nations that fish for lucrative tuna in the nearby oceans. The agreement calls for the establishment of an "OPEC-style" cartel that will help them coordinate to better conserve the tuna and earn a greater proportion of the profits from the industry, which is currently dominated by larger players.[7]

In addition, as promising as the IFQ systems are, many scientists think that they are not sufficient to the task given the catastrophic damage that has already been done to marine ecosystems.

MARINE PROTECTED AREAS

A growing movement supports the creation of Marine Protected Areas (MPAs)—the marine equivalent of terrestrial protected areas—in which all consumptive activity in a given region of ocean is severely restricted or prohibited. Currently, less than 1 percent of the world's ocean resources are under legal protections that would qualify them for designation as MPAs.[8] MPA systems are currently being developed in the United States,[9] Kiribati,[10] Australia, Canada, Chile, Colombia, Easter Island, Fiji, Grenada, Italy, Federated States of Micronesia, New Zealand, Samoa, Solomon Islands, South Africa, Spain, Vanuatu, and Vietnam, among others. For MPAs to make a significant impact in stemming the oceans' decline, the hope is for upwards of 10 to 20 percent of the world's marine ecosystems to eventually come under some type of MPA protection.

Because MPAs ban virtually all forms of consumptive use, they are typically more controversial than IFQ systems and require strong political leadership. However, there is already evidence that the fisheries adjacent to MPAs improve over time,[11] which bolsters the case for MPAs. Organizations like the National Ocean Economics Program (NOEP), which have developed detailed accounting systems and databases for the dissemination of the economic impacts of ocean activities, including recreation, tourism, and wildlife viewing, can also help build the economic case for conservation of marine resources.[12]

But winning the battle for ocean conservation will also rely heavily on changing public attitudes about the oceans. For most of history, the oceans have been considered too massive to be susceptible to large-scale degradation by human activities, and most people never get to see ocean resources up close, as they do with natural wonders like Yosemite National Park. Raising awareness about the plight of the oceans and bringing their beauty to the public through documentaries, web videos,[13] and popular culture will go a long way toward affording them similar protection as our land resources.

DIRECTLY TARGETING THE CONSUMER

Ecolabels for "sustainably caught" fish are on the rise, with many organizations touting their particular brand. The Marine Stewardship Council (MSC) has a popular international label, while others include Friends of the Sea, Fair Fish, Fish 4 Future, Dolphin-Safe, and Fish Forever.

The Monterey Bay Aquarium, a global leader in ocean conservation, is very involved in consumer information about sustainable fisheries through its Seafood Watch program, which distributes millions of pocket-size cards that rate commonly bought fish species according to a three-tier color-coded rating system: green for "best choices," yellow for "good choices," and red for "avoid." Consumers can download cards specific to their regions from the website[14] and find detailed information about the program's conservation efforts worldwide. Much of this information can now be accessed by cell phones and other mobile devices.

MSC, Seafood Watch, and other organizations are also trying to influence the seafood industry at the supply side by urging large seafood buyers to restrict their purchases to seafood caught in sustainable fisheries. Walmart has already agreed to buy all of its fish from MSC-certified fisheries,[15] and other large chain stores are considering following their lead.

To date, there have been no large-scale systematic efforts to gauge the effectiveness of these campaigns, but the sheer scope of the labeling programs and the commitments already made by some of the world's largest seafood retailers demonstrate that they are clearly having an impact. Many restaurants[16] and stores are advertising that they serve only sustainable products, and consumers are becoming more assertive in their demands for sustainable seafood.

As with all labeling programs, they are ultimately only as good as the science behind them and the degree to which they are verified and enforced. Anytime there is a significant price premium between a sustainable and nonsustainable food product (or any type of product for that matter) there is an incentive for cheating in the industry; it is extremely profitable to sell unsustainable products as sustainable ones.

Unfortunately, this situation is rampant in the seafood industry. An article in the December 2008 issue of *Conservation* (Fox, 2008)[17] describes how much of the seafood sold in stores and restaurants is mislabeled, and often purposefully so.[18] Until the situation markedly improves consumers cannot be guaranteed that fish identified as sustainably caught truly are.

THE WTO AND FISHERIES SUBSIDIES

A very positive development on the international front is the WTO's increasing recognition that global fisheries' subsidies, which total tens of billions a year, arc significant trade distortions that need to be eliminated. The WTO is slated to address this issue in the current round of Doha negotiations.[19]

The problem of fisheries subsidies underscores the potentially very constructive role that the WTO can play in helping the world move away from some of the more egregious forms of "perverse subsidies"—paying people for bad behavior—that wreak havoc on the environment around the world.[20]

Environmentalists have often been at odds with the WTO, believing that it unfairly favors corporate interests over environmental concerns,[21] but this is one area (in addition to eliminating agricultural subsidies) where they should be in strong agreement.

It will be a great day when environmentalists are touting the WTO's success at eliminating fisheries (and agricultural, energy, forestry, and water) subsidies as evidence of a new global consensus on the benefits of well-functioning markets. The WTO is one of the only international bodies with significant enforcement power that even powerful countries heed; it is past time that environmentalists recognize that the WTO's mandate to eliminate trade-distorting subsidies would be a huge boon to many dimensions of the environmental cause. A stronger and more consistent WTO would be better for the global environmental than a world without the WTO.

SUMMARY

Overfishing and the threats it poses to the health of marine ecosystems is a serious problem that is only getting worse as population grows and people become wealthier, increasing the demand for seafood. The problems are exacerbated because most of the oceans are "open access" resources that face unlimited exploitation from fleets of powerful fishing vessels, many of which are subsidized by their respective governments.

Creating property rights systems over ocean resources and limiting the total allowable catches is the best way to promote fisheries sustainability, and it has a long history in many countries. But these efforts must be coupled with additional restrictions on fishing equipment to limit bycatch and protect fragile ocean habitats, as well as the development of Marine Protected Areas, which can allow severely degraded ocean ecosystems the opportunity to regenerate.

Consumers also have a role to play, and many types of ecolabels and product information can help individuals choose sustainably caught fish. However, the success of these programs is tempered by the fact that a large portion of the fish sold in stores and restaurants is mislabeled, and better enforcement mechanisms are urgently needed.

CHAPTER 13

POPULATION GROWTH AND TECHNOLOGICAL CHANGE

Population growth and its impact on the environment has been a hot topic for decades, ever since Paul Ehrlich's *The Population Bomb* was published in 1968. Extending many of the arguments first put forth by Thomas Malthus in the eighteenth century,[1] Ehrlich predicted an exponential increase in global population coupled with massive starvation, given that growth in the food supply wouldn't be able to keep pace.

The world's population has essentially doubled in the past forty years, from 3.3 billion to 6.8 billion,[2] but there has not been widespread famine. In fact, where there have been regional food crises (e.g., Ethiopia in 1983–1985),[3] they have not been caused by a global food shortage but by unfavorable changes in local climatic conditions coupled with ineffective and unresponsive governments.

Global food production continues to keep pace with population growth, and given that vast quantities of food are used inefficiently in the production of livestock, there is plenty of food available to feed a much greater world population (raising grain crops such as soy and corn and feeding them to cows, pigs, and chickens wastes about

90 percent of the energy content of the primary food crop).[4] As Nobel Laureate Amartya Sen has convincingly demonstrated, the issue of famine, starvation, and malnutrition is dictated more by economic opportunity and the presence of a democratic government accountable to the people than by natural resource constraints.[5]

The question arises whether at present a focus on population growth, and policies to limit it, should be priorities for environmentalists. There are those who argue that increases in population are the root cause of many of our present environmental problems, and that these will only be exacerbated by billions more people.

There is no doubt that *all else equal*, if we were simply to add more people to the world, environmental problems would grow worse. But population growth rates interact with many important social and economic variables and require a more nuanced perspective. It is not accurate to claim that population growth is the root cause of environmental problems—*it is specific types of consumption that drive environmental degradation.*

SUSTAINABLE CAPITALISM?

Some environmentalists point out that there is a fundamental flaw in the capitalist model: modern industrial economies are dependent upon exponential growth in GDP to keep up with population growth and to continually raise living standards. But with finite natural resources, exponential economic growth will eventually confront limits and the system will break down. This, the critics argue, points to the need for a new economic model not predicated on constant growth rates—an alternative to modern capitalism.*

This argument is flawed because economic growth does not necessarily mean growth in material throughput. Growth is generated through value, and this can come from the development of new technologies and ideas that actually decrease our ecological footprint. While it is true that much of the world's GDP is composed of products and services that entail natural resource consumption, this doesn't have to be the case. In fact, it is possible to envision a world of extremely high material standards of living but with much lower environmental impacts than today.

There is nothing intrinsic in the capitalist system that necessitates using more land, water, energy, copper, or steel every year. Growth can be in solar panels, or new nanomachines, or in living architecture that recycles materials and produces food. Capitalism is in effect only limited by the limits of human creativity and ingenuity.**

* Herman Daly is probably the most famous economist to formally question the fundamental assumptions of capitalism with respect to natural resource limits; many environmentalists have been inspired by his work, and he helped to create the field of "ecological economics." While his contributions have been important, many of his critiques are more a matter of semantics than a true challenge to the foundations of economic theory and market systems.

** Julian Simon was a business professor who noted that the "ultimate resource" (the title of his most famous book, first published in 1981) was the human mind, and that throughout history human ingenuity always wins out against natural resource constraints. He won a bet against Paul Ehrlich in which he predicted that the price of commodities would decrease (in real terms) over the course of the next decade, contrary to Ehrlich's dire warnings that they would dramatically increase in price.

A U.S. citizen who owns two sports utility vehicles (SUVs) and a 2,000-square-foot home, both of which are air-conditioned, and eats factory-raised meat multiple times a day has an environmental footprint hundreds of times larger than a rice farmer in Vietnam. A focus exclusively on population is misplaced because it does not account for these differences in consumption. Most of the world's population growth is taking place in the developing countries of the world, while most of the consumption takes place in the developed world.[6]

This is starting to change; consumption is rising in the developing world as income rises, but at the same time population growth rates are declining.[7] This is because population growth rates are highly correlated with income. As people become wealthier, the opportunity cost of having an additional child grows (think college tuition and less time spent working at a higher salary) and people tend to prefer to invest more resources in few number of children (conversely, those who are desperately poor have large numbers of kids because many of them die prematurely and children act as a form of social insurance for their old age).

This presents environmentalists with somewhat of a conundrum: the wealthy are driving the high rates of consumption, and yet as people become wealthier they have fewer children. If limiting total global population were truly the goal, the surest way to achieve this would be to help countries develop and become wealthy as quickly as possible. However, if we were simply to duplicate current patterns of consumption with billions of new people, the results would be disastrous.

This is why *the population issue is largely a distraction.* The key issue is how to transition to much more resource efficient modes of production that allow for high levels of material well-being, with a projected stable population of potentially nine billion people later this century.[8]

Efforts to improve women's health and empowerment, which are also highly correlated with decreases in population growth, should also be supported. But from a strictly environmental perspective, it is the transition to a less resource-intensive economy that should be the top priority.

There are some encouraging signs that this is already on the way.

As economies grow they tend to become much more energy efficient and the ratio of additional resource use for every dollar of additional GDP declines.[9] We have yet, however, to reach a point where the absolute amount of resource use declines as countries grow; while countries do become better at utilizing resources, they still consume more in raw quantities.

Creating a society where we can become richer while using less absolute quantities of natural resources is the great environmental challenge that we face. Getting there will require enacting many of the policies already outlined in this volume, but it will also necessitate major new incentives for technological innovation.

Environmental economists have long argued that if prices reflected the "full" costs of production—including all of the external costs and free of government subsidies—this would raise the price of commodities such as oil, gas, forest products, and minerals sufficiently to create new incentives for the creation of renewable and less polluting substitutes.

There is no doubt a large degree of truth to this.

For example, once greenhouse gases are assigned a price, we will likely see a move away from coal as a power source and a greater move toward alternatives such as wind and solar, which will be able to more effectively compete. The same goes for the full range of other products and services that currently enjoy an artificially low price, due to either direct government subsidies or the lack of accounting for the environmental damage they generate.

But "getting the prices right" alone is unlikely to provide sufficient incentives for the type of major environmental innovations, and their quick adoption, that many scientists think is key to averting environmental crises. Therefore, further government action is warranted. Economic analysis can help environmentalists differentiate between the types of interventions that will likely support these efforts versus those that will hamper them.

Case in point: Subsidies for corn ethanol production.

Over the past few years, with global warming and energy security major topics in the news, the U.S. government dramatically increased subsidies for ethanol production to the tune of billions of dollars;[10] this is on top of the already lavish subsidies that corn farmers receive. Predictably, this led to a surge in domestic ethanol production. The problem is that ethanol is a terrible substitute for oil. Not only does corn production result in a host of significant externalities (such as the "dead zone" in the Gulf of Mexico), but it also turns out that once we account for all of the energy that goes into ethanol production, it represents a net increase in greenhouse gas emissions per unit of fuel.[11] This means that the end result of this expensive government program is more environmental degradation, more greenhouse gases, and less incentive for truly "green" energy alternatives, which are at an economic disadvantage since they do not receive subsidies.

For the next decade the example of ethanol subsidies should be environmentalists' "Exhibit A" of how *not* to craft government policy.

Why did this policy fail so miserably—and more important, how can this be avoided in the future?

For starters, farm politics in the United States has more to do with the electoral map than with sound economics. But more fundamentally, this policy was premised on the notion that the government should be in the business of picking "winning" technology and actively supporting it. This is not something that governments are particularly good at it. What governments can and should do is create an economic climate where an entire host of technologies can vie and compete for dominance on an even playing field.

Renewable portfolio standards, which mandate that a certain percentage of energy in a region be produced using renewable technology, don't state *which* technology. They leave the playing field wide open and don't distort the market in favor of one technology over the other (as long as the definition of "renewable" is based on sound principles and not specific technologies).

Generous research grants for R&D in renewable energy, whose findings are subsequently made part of the public domain, would also support the entire renewable sector and not privilege one technology over the other. Grants are particularly good at encouraging risk-taking behavior, which is often the key to the development of new "breakout" technologies.

The use of economic prizes can also generate innovation without distorting incentives against any subset of nascent technologies. For example, a prize for the first commercially viable carbon sequestration technology would leave the field open to a host of initiatives, including clean coal, underwater sequestration, or other forms of geoengineering. Already, the government, as well as some private foundations, has sponsored (relatively minor) prizes in the areas of fuel efficiency, robotics, and medicine, which have been reasonably successful.[12] To have a major impact and draw significant new talent to environmental projects, these prizes would have to be large and prestigious.

There may come a time when specific new technologies have proven themselves worthy of significant government support, especially if major infrastructure changes are required. For example, if car battery technology improves dramatically such that it would be possible to transition to 100 percent battery-powered vehicles, it may be justified for the government to invest in the new types of power grids that would be required to support such an effort.

But again, extreme caution would have to be exercised so that we don't repeat the corn ethanol debacle. Switching to an electric transportation sector makes sense only if the new vehicles are extremely energy efficient and if we generate electricity from predominantly renewable sources. Switching from gasoline-powered vehicles to electricity generated from coal wouldn't be an improvement; it might actually make matters worse.

This is why all major environmental initiatives must pass a "life cycle test"; all of the impacts across the board must be incorporated into the final assessment. If this had been done with respect to ethanol, the subsidy program would never have been passed. If Congress had insisted on finding a way to financially support farmers in the pursuit of new energy policy, support for research into better forms of cellulosic ethanol or the conversion of agricultural land to wind and solar energy could have been explored, both of which would have been significantly better policy.

The more a policy allows for a wide range of potential solutions and focuses on the root causes of problems, the more efficient it will be and the lower probability that it will lead to environmentally harmful unintended consequences.

SUMMARY

Population growth is not the driving force behind the world's most pressing environmental problems; it is the high rates of consumption, particularly those that entail massive inputs of natural resources and produce massive quantities of toxic pollution.

A world with nine billion people will only be sustainable if we dramatically improve our resource efficiency and dramatically incorporate new technology into our economies. The government has a role to play to promote this transition, but it must be very careful how it does so if it is not to make the problems worse. Policies that focus on the root causes of problems and don't privilege particular technologies over others—thus keeping our options as wide as possible—offer our best hope.

CHAPTER 14

DEMAND-SIDE INTERVENTIONS

The majority of this book has focused on supply-side solutions—policies that influence the behavior of farmers, landowners, timber companies, fisherman, and corporations. Many of these policies, by influencing the prices and quantities of goods produced, end up influencing demand. But there are many interesting and effective policy interventions that directly address the demand side of the equation.

The following are descriptions of some of the latest and potentially most effective demand-side interventions for improving environmental quality (in no particular order):

REAL-TIME ELECTRICITY PRICING

Virtually everywhere the price of electricity is constant throughout both the months of the year and the hours of the day; for example, electricity always costs $.115 per kilowatt hour where I live, whether at noon in the middle of the summer or at night in the dead of winter. This is extremely inefficient because the cost of producing energy, as well as the associated pollution, varies greatly at different times.

During peak energy demand times, which are typically during the day in the hot summer months (mainly due to air-conditioning demand), energy can be up to 300 percent more costly to produce.[1] Since so many power plants need to be on line to meet demand, the pollution created is also worse (due to the warm weather and the dirtiest plants coming on line).

Economists have long recommended charging customers different electricity prices at different times to match the true cost of producing electricity. If both consumers and businesses had to pay a premium for electricity in the hot daytime hours, this would help shift production toward less intensive periods and decrease pollution.

Setting up such a system requires special metering and billing and making sure that customers understand the differential pricing system. Real-time pricing experiments are already underway in Italy, Canada, the United States (especially California), Turkey, Australia, New Zealand, the Netherlands, and the Nordic countries, with positive results ("Smart Meter," 2008). This policy is consistent with the economic maxim that prices should reflect the true costs of production as accurately as possible.

BLOCK WATER PRICING

Water prices for piped water throughout much of the world are relatively minor with respect to personal income. The result is that very few people pay much attention to the amount of water they use unless there is a serious drought situation. While businesses pay more for water, the same basic scenario applies in most cases: the price of water often isn't high enough to lead to major changes in usage.

But water is a precious commodity that is becoming increasingly scarce and is required for many environmental uses, such as rivers, wetlands, and lakes. Reducing water demand is a priority in areas with rapid population growth and limited rainfall, particularly with climate change threatening future supplies.

One way to reduce water demand is to employ block pricing, which is essentially a tiered pricing schedule. For residential use, prices remain low for an amount of water that covers average usage (with a little leeway built in for larger families), and then prices rise sharply for usage that exceeds this monthly amount. This has the desired effect of creating a significant disincentive to use more water than is needed for essential uses such as washing, bathing, and cooking, such as for watering lawns or washing cars.

The same system can be put in place for industry, with rates held constant for normal use patterns and then sharp increases levied for producers that use water inefficiently. Block water pricing is in use in Albuquerque, New Mexico; Goleta and Irvine Ranch Water District, California; Massachusetts; Phoenix, Arizona; and Seattle, Washington.[2]

SOUTH KOREA'S "LAW OF ONE USE" FOR DISPOSAL ITEMS

In 2005, South Korea passed a groundbreaking law requiring all retailers to charge customers for "one-use" disposable items, such as paper cups and plastic bags. The result has been a sea change in behavior in South Korea; for example, the use of paper bags has decreased by 24 percent.[3]

Predictably, many Koreans now bring their own cups to cafes and their own shopping bags to stores to avoid the charges, which can add up quickly. By putting a price on waste, the South Korean government was able to create incentives for environmentally friendly behavior.

CONGESTION PRICING FOR AUTOMOBILES

Similar to real-time pricing for electricity, congestion pricing refers to a system where automobiles are charged a premium for driving during peak hours (usually within crowded city limits) to decrease rush-hour traffic and the associated pollution.

London was the first major city to institute congestion pricing and the results so far indicate that congestion pricing is working.[4] New York City has floated an idea similar to London's, but it has yet to be enacted.

One of the concerns is that these programs hurt small businesses, especially those dependent on ground transportation. Since individual commuters have many public transportation options, this isn't a major problem.

STATUS QUO BIAS AND DEFAULT OPTIONS:
GREEN POWER AND BEYOND

As discussed in Chapter 6, one of the most fascinating findings within the field of behavioral economics is what is called "status quo bias," which refers to the tendency for people to stick with default options even if they are not economically optimal.

There has been surprisingly little investigation into how default options influence decisions in the environmental realm, but it is likely a major factor in some very important areas; it is hoped that it will eventually garner the attention it deserves within the environmental community.

Besides the example of "green power," just imagine how consumer choice would change if the default position for produce in the supermarket was pesticide-free—that is, fruits and vegetables without pesticides would remain unlabeled—while what is now considered "conventional" and devoid of labels was instead labeled "grown with pesticides." It is likely that the demand for the produce grown with pesticides would decrease significantly even though nothing at all had changed besides the labeling. The way products are presented to the public, especially when contrasted with similar products produced in a different way, is instrumental in framing how they are perceived.

HARNESSING INSTITUTIONAL AND GOVERNMENT
PURCHASING POWER

This policy prescription is straightforward: pressuring major institutions, including the government, to procure products from green sources. For example, the U.S. government is the biggest purchaser of paper in the world, so if it chooses to buy recycled paper or paper without bleach, this has both a dramatic impact on pollution from paper products and on the composition of the entire industry.[5] In fact, some institutions are so large that they can create new markets almost overnight.

Amazing environmental benefits could be reaped if institutions decided to use nontoxic products or to buy power from renewable sources. These institutions can include nonprofits, foundations, educational establishments, and well as businesses. For example, when Walmart decides to significantly reduce packaging, this has dramatic implications for entire upstream industries;[6] when the City of San Francisco decides to replace bottled water with water filters at sinks, this can lead to major reductions in energy use and garbage;[7] when Home Depot decides to carry Forest Stewardship Council (FSC) certified wood products, this can create huge new markets for sustainable wood that didn't yet exist.[8]

Even small institutions can have relatively large impacts. Where I work we have begun a policy where 50 percent of the food served at campus-wide events must be plant-based, all new appliances must be Energy Star certified, all campus landscaping plants should be drought-resistant native varieties, and all cleaning products should be nontoxic.

SUMMARY

Changing behavior and consumption patterns of the end user is crucial for influencing the industrial composition of our economies in a more sustainable direction. The cumulative effects of billions of people bringing their own bags to the grocery store, turning off the lights when they leave a room, or buying fruits and vegetables without toxic chemicals has a tremendous impact.

But environmentalists must remember that some of the biggest challenges we face require government action, such as putting a price on greenhouse gases or figuring out how to manage the open oceans.

FINAL THOUGHTS AND ADDITIONAL RESOURCES

Because environmental problems are immensely complex, solving them requires creative thinking and the ability to juggle and digest huge quantities of information. I hope this book has demonstrated how economic thinking and analysis can help better understand the root causes of environmental problems and the types of policies that can ameliorate them.

But these pages represent only a small taste of what economics has to offer the environmental community. In this increasingly interconnected and fast-paced world, new information and insights are continually being added to the body of information that we have to draw on for policy ideas and inspiration. Economic tools can always use refinement, and as our scientific understanding of ecosystems grows we will always face new surprises.

Due to the dynamic nature of the environmental movement, the chapters in this book will be updated periodically. Be sure to check the book's website to receive these updates, as well as links to new case studies and additional commentary.

The following is a list of other online resources for those who want to stay current:

BLOGS AND WEBSITES

Grist: http://grist.org/
Environmental Economics: http://www.env-econ.net/
Mongabay: http://www.mongabay.com/
Environmental Defense Fund: http://www.edf.org/page.cfm?tagID=
42078
China Environmental Law: http://www.chinaenvironmentallaw.com/
Climate Progress: http://climateprogress.org/
The Energy Collective: http://theenergycollective.com/TheEnergy
Collective/
REDD-Monitor: http://www.redd-monitor.org/

PERIODICALS

Review of Environmental Economics and Policy (requires subscription for
e-journal access): http://reep.oxfordjournals.org/
Yale Environment 360: http://e360.yale.edu/
OnEarth: http://www.onearth.org/
World Watch Magazine: http://www.worldwatch.org/taxonomy/term/41
World Conservation Magazine: http://www.iucn.org/knowledge/
publications_doc/world_conservation/
The Economist (always has something interesting on the environment):
http://www.economist.com/

*   *   *

Before I sign off, I'd also like to reiterate that economics can go only
so far in solving environmental problems.

Some extremely important environmental issues will require
more than good policies and political will. They will require a step
forward in our moral evolution. Economics alone can't stop commercial whaling, factory farming, the demand for exotic endangered
pets, or the massacring of dolphins[1]—these issues require a universal
ethic that respects all sentient beings.

In the hopes of a greener and more peaceful world....

NOTES

1 THE ROOT CAUSES OF ENVIRONMENTAL PROBLEMS

1. In 1848, John Stuart Mill was the first economist to break from classical economics and recognize positive social externalities such as education and public utilities. In 1901, Henry Sidgwick further developed the theory of externalities through examples of the overuse of natural resources. Sidgwick found that one of the reasons for overusing natural resources stems from a failure to take all the positive and negative social costs into account (Medema, 2004).

2. For information on mountaintop-removal see: http://www.epa.gov/region3/mtntop/#what).

3. The original jury found the ship's master liable for $5,000 in punitive damages, and the owners (Exxon Shipping Company, owned by Exxon Mobile Corporation) liable for $5 billion in punitive damages. These damages were reduced to $2.5 billion after three appeals. On June 25, 2008, the U.S. Supreme Court ruled that for cases such as this with no "exceptional blameworthiness," under maritime law, the upper limit of appropriate punitive damages should be set by a 1:1 ratio with the amount of compensatory damages. The Court accepted the district court's calculation of $507.5 million in total relevant compensatory damages (*Exxon v. Baker*, 2008).

4. Hardin, Garrett. (1968). "The Tragedy of the Commons," *Science*, 162(3859):1243–1248.

5. Sixty-four percent of the world's oceans are international waters and not under the jurisdiction of a sovereign state (IUCN, 2007).

6. There are a few large national and international emissions trading schemes, as well as several statewide and regional schemes that attempt to control the atmosphere. The United States as a nation controls SOx emissions (Schmalensee et al., 1998), while several individual states, such as California with Assembly Bill 32 (AB32), have plans for significantly limiting carbon emissions (Royden-Bloom, 2007). The European Union Emissions Trading Scheme (EU ETS) was created to meet the goals of the Kyoto Protocol and controls carbon emissions through mandatory international carbon emissions trading. In Australia, the New South Wales state

government has implemented mandatory reductions in carbon emissions for the electricity sector ("Greenhouse Gas Reduction Scheme," n.d.).

7. Forty years ago, Garret Hardin referred to what are now called open access resources as the "commons," but as several prominent anthropologists, such as Elinor Ostrom (who won the 2009 Nobel Prize in Economics) have shown, many natural resources that were once thought to be open access rely on high levels of management, and the number of people who can use them, as well as the ways they can be used, are restricted. Therefore, the term "commons" now refers to natural resources that are held and managed by communal organizations, distinguishing them from pure open access resources, which anyone can exploit.

8. A recent study concluded that as of 2003, 29 percent of international-water fisheries had reached the level of collapse, and that by 2050, 100 percent of international-water fisheries will reach this level. The study defined "level of collapse" as less than 10 percent of the original population remaining (Worm et al., 2006).

9. In 2002, Tuvalu, Kiribati, and the Maldives threatened to sue major polluting nations and corporations for damages in an international court. In 2005, the Inuit Circumpolar Conference published a petition to the Inter-American Human Rights Commission arguing that the United States is infringing on their livelihood by failing to regulate greenhouse gas emissions (Hsu, forthcoming).

10. Economist Frank Ackerman and law professor Lisa Heinzerling makes this case in *Priceless: On Knowing the Price of Everything and the Value of Nothing* (2004).

11. Property rights in Brazil are written such that landowners maintain ownership of their land as long as a certain percentage of land is in production, with production referring to farming or ranching. In order for landowners to avoid having their land seized and redistributed, they must clear the forest in preparation for crops or cattle (Alston et al., 1999). By 2004, around 590,000 square kilometers (more than 14 percent) of closed forest in the Brazilian Amazon basin had been removed, and continues to be removed at rates of 10,000 square kilometers to 20,000 square kilometers per year (Walker, 2004). An empirical study on land use and property rights in Panama found that less deforestation occurs when effective property rights are in place than in locations without those rights (Nelson et al., 2001).

Worldwide increase in demand for soybean meal (used as animal feed in industrial farming) has presented Brazil with the opportunity to export soybeans (Ortega et al., 2005). However, the level of production of soybeans in Brazil does not take into account many of the externalities associated with production. The Brazilian savanna is not well suited to growing only soybeans, causing the farmers to clear more and more forest in order to find suitable farmland. If the long-term results of such deforestation and industrial farming, including soil and nutrient erosion, carbon dioxide, methane, and nitrous oxide emissions, health risks from pesticide use, effluent treatment, and savanna destruction, were factored in, the price of Brazilian soybeans would increase, and demand decrease (Lopez and Galinato, 2005).

2 DETERMINING THE "OPTIMUM" AMOUNT OF POLLUTION

1. In economic terms, this is the point at which the marginal cost of abating pollution is equal to the marginal benefit of pollution abatement.
2. The United Nations Universal Declaration of Human Rights named clean air as a fundamental human right in 1948 (UN General Assembly, 1948), and the Committee on Economic, Social, and Cultural Rights added clean water to the list in 2002 (UN Committee on Economic, Social, and Cultural Rights, 2002).
3. In economic terms, this translates to a situation where some costs are deemed appropriate to derive benefits that are not as great (construed in pure economic terms), leading to a net economic loss.
4. I use the term benefit-cost instead of the more common term cost-benefit based on the rationale provided by Arrow et al. (1996).
5. A report published by the Organization for Economic Co-operation and Development (OECD) in 2006 discussing recent developments in benefit-cost analysis theory suggests that environmental benefits (goods and services) generally have no market, and therefore are given a value of $0. While conducting research for this book, the author surveyed European Union benefit-cost analyses and found that health benefits account for one-third to 100 percent of the benefits used to create a positive CBA outcome. This trend is also seen in the United States (Pearce et al., 2006). For example, the Clean Air Interstate Rule (CAIR) CBA mentions air quality and environmental benefits along with the health benefits, but is only able to monetize the health benefits, effectively discrediting the environmental benefits (U.S.-China Joint Economic Research Group, 2007).
6. Consistent with the report mentioned in the previous note, an earlier OECD report found that environmental benefits are underestimated when monetary values are applied (Barde and Pearce, 1991). In 2005, in response to a draft report to Congress on "Costs and Benefits of Federal Regulations," a coalition of health and environmental groups commented that the CBA guidelines in the draft report failed to correct for the fact that environmental benefits tend to be underestimated due to the difficult nature of applying monetary values to these benefits (Warren, 2005).
7. A 2000 review of regulatory cost estimates compared *ex ante* cost estimates of twenty-eight regulations with their respective *ex post* estimates (Harrington et al., 2000). These regulations were chosen based on the existence of both an *ex ante* cost estimate prepared by a regulatory agency experienced in cost analysis and a detailed *ex post* estimate; twenty-one of the regulations are federal, four are from California, and three are international. Overall,

ex ante estimates overestimated the total costs of regulation in fifteen cases, and only underestimated the costs in three relatively small regulations. Per-unit costs were overestimated slightly less frequently, with fourteen cases overestimated and six underestimated. The quantity of pollution reduced was overestimated in nine cases and underestimated in four cases. Some of the overestimations, such as regulating the pesticide Mancozeb and phase I of SO_2 regulation, were due to failing to recognize the presence of a substitute. Other overestimations, such as OSHA regulations of asbestos and cotton dust, were related to inaccurate baseline estimates. Other causes of cost overestimation include a less than predicted level of compliance (EPA's regulated gas regulation) and overestimated direct costs (OSHA's vinyl chloride regulation), to name a few.

8. In general the EPA determines the safety of a pesticide or other toxic chemical based on tests of individual chemicals. In reality, we are exposed to many of these chemicals at the same time, and even when the physical exposure occurs at different times, many of these chemicals remain in the body for long periods. We have no knowledge of the synergistic effects of these chemicals in any combinations, but researchers are beginning to see indications that these effects are harmful to our health even in small doses (Washington Toxics Coalition, 2004). In 1996, after many studies (the first in 1957) suggested the existence of synergistic effects, the EPA was required to include cumulative effects of pesticides when setting tolerance levels for pesticides that have the same mechanism of toxicity (i.e., cause liver cancer after being ingested) (Kepner, 2004).

9. One opinion is that we should worry less about further reductions from current levels in dietary exposure of pesticides and more about workplace exposures, persistent environmental chemical contaminants, and synthetic hormones and hormone-mimicking chemicals in food and other consumer products. (Hoffmann, Sandy, personal communication, May 2, 2008.)

3 VALUING ECOSYSTEMS

1. In his 1864 book *Man in Nature*, George Marsh first brought up the idea that ecosystems perform services beneficial to humans. Marsh described the elements—water, soil, animals, and plants—as gifts from God, and refuted the idea that natural resources are infinite. However, in the context of the high levels of industrial production taking place at the time, Marsh's ideas received little following. In the 1970s, ecologists and economists began studying ecosystems from various perspectives, and ecosystem services became an important concept (Bao et al., 2007).

2. In 1999, the 3.5 million acres of wetlands along the Louisiana coast were estimated to have the capacity to prevent $728 million to $3.1 billion worth of storm damage (LaCoast, 1999). A study on restoring the one hundred–year flood zone associated with the Upper Mississippi Watershed indicates that restoration to this level will save more than $16 billion in projected flood costs.

The Charles River in Massachusetts is estimated to protect the area from an average $17 million of property damage annually (U.S. EPA, 2006).

3. For excellent overview of the methodologies involved in valuing ecosystems, see the report, "How Much Is an Ecosystem Worth: Assessing the Economic Value of Conservation" (World Bank, 2004), which in my view is the gold standard for thinking about ecosystem valuation. Other work by the World Resources Institute, the United Nations Environmental Program (UNEP), the United Nations Development Program (UNDP) (World Resources Institute, 1998), and the Global Environment Facility (GEF) (UNEP 2006) are worth looking at as well. Also see the Natural Capital Project at http://www.naturalcapital.org.

4. Contingent valuation is sometimes referred to by the letters CV or CVM (contingent valuation method). While the exact number of CV studies is difficult to quantify due to the high volume of papers published by non-economic journals in recent years, more than six thousand contingent valuation studies have been published since the early 1960s. The number of studies published annually grew exponentially throughout the late 1970s, 1980s, and early 1990s. Since then, the number has remained steady at about four hundred to five hundred studies per year. Studies have been produced in all thirty-two OECD countries and more than ninety developing countries. As of November 19, 2007, the Environmental Valuation Resource Inventory, an international online project spearheaded by Environment Canada, lists 1,178 studies conducted in North America, 849 in Europe, 308 in Asia, 75 in Africa, and 43 in South America. (This website is not complete and is continuously updated.) Studies are most commonly conducted to value air and water safety standards, as well as to protect natural and cultural resources, improve public utilities and schools, and study transportation issues (Carson, in press). An online database has been designed to allow policymakers, scientists, and economists to match CV study sites with current policy sites to estimate the value of policy changes under consideration (Environmental Valuation Reference Inventory, 2007).

5. If a CV survey persuades the interviewee that their decision is consequential, this is referred to as "incentive compatible."

6. The use of contingent valuation to estimate the lost passive-use values from the spill was a major source of controversy, especially given the huge stakes involved. The arguments pitted top economists against each other, some arguing that contingent valuation does not measure what it purports to and is an unreliable tool, and others arguing that the estimates derived are defensible. One of the offshoots of these arguments was the convening of a prestigious panel to review the contingent valuation method and make recommendations to the government as to whether it is admissible in courts and under what criteria. The panel found that under strict conditions, contingent valuation can provide reasonable estimates of passive-use values, although these conditions have been rarely met in practice, and

the controversy continues. For a description of the panel's recommendations, see the paper by Arrow et al. (1993).
7. For more information on how CV was used in the *Exxon Valdez* case, see the paper by Carson et al. (2003).

4 PUTTING MONETARY VALUES ON THE ENVIRONMENT AND LIVING THINGS

1. Peter Singer, the Princeton philosophy professor, has written extensively about the demands on individual behavior and lifestyle if one takes extremely seriously the needs of others, including nonhuman beings.
2. According to the Insurance Safety Institute, the higher speed limit led to an approximately 15 percent increase in deaths between 1995 and 1999 ("Insurance Safety Institute Finds," 1999).
3. Based on studying the results of negligence trials where the defendant is accused of driving under the influence, juries value the loss of life at $2.3 million to $4.9 million (net value after subtracting punitive, property, and medical damages). Most states do not allow the value of life to be recovered when the injured party has died; however, since most states allow "loss of enjoyment of life" awards, this study modeled awards based on a percentage of permanent disability and estimated the value of life as the value for 100 percent permanent disability (Smith, 2000).
4. In 1988, a survey of jury awards found that pain and suffering payments are dependent on the total economic loss, and have average awards (in 1988 dollars) of $9,000 to $270,000 (Rodgers, 2003). In more recent cases, a New York trial lawyer has published damages in the range of $0 to $2 million for injury to appendages, and up to $10 million for head, neck, and back injuries (Hochfelder, 2006).
5. Starting out with a target and figuring out the cheapest way to achieve it is referred to as "cost-effectiveness analysis."
6. Sulfur dioxide is to be reduced to 50 percent of 1980 levels (Schmalensee et al., 1998); the Kyoto Protocol mandates a 5 percent reduction from 1990 levels ("The Kyoto Protocol," 2007); California is planning to reduce greenhouse gas emissions to 80 percent of 1990 levels by 2050, and the states involved in the Regional Greenhouse Gas Initiative (RGGI) will reach their first goal by reducing greenhouse gas emissions by 10 percent of 1990 levels by 2010 (Royden-Bloom, 2007); twenty-eight eastern states are reducing SO_2 by 70 percent and NO_x by 50 percent, according to the Clean Air Interstate Rule ("Clean Air Interstate Rule" 2007); the 33/50 program in the United States met and exceeded its goals to reduce seventeen chemicals by 33 percent by 1992, and by 50 percent by 1995 (U.S. EPA, 1999).
7. Although in fairness the program did call for continual cuts. In the first phase, the original 1995 allocation of 8.7 million tons of emissions

allowances were gradually reduced to approximately 7.4 million tons in 1999. During this time, companies banked their unused allowances, creating the overall effect of 16.6 million tons of usable allowances in 1999. In the second phase, the annual allocation jumped to around 10 million tons in 2000 and then remained steady. However, as companies used up their banked allowances, the total allowances available decreased from 21.6 million tons in 2000 to 16.4 million tons in 2005 (U.S. EPA, 2006). Overall, the effect of these emissions allocations is that the level of SO_2 emissions in 2005 was 57.9 percent of the 1980 level (15 million tons emitted in 2005, compared with 25.9 million tons emitted in 1980) ("Air Emissions Summary Through 2005," 2007).

8. Recently, the U.S. Supreme Court agreed to hear arguments in a case (*Entergy Corporation v. Environmental Protection Agency (EPA)*, No. 07-588) regarding proposed guidelines (published in 2004) to regulate under the Clean Water Act "cooling water" intake and outflow mechanisms according to best available technology. The issue in question is that the EPA regulations offer individual operators the ability to request a waiver if costs would be significantly higher than the environmental benefits. The U.S. Court of Appeals for the Second Circuit ruled in 2007 that the EPA did not have the right to participate in the type of benefit-cost analysis proposed. Since cost considerations in the proposed guidelines were unclear, the regulation was sent back to the EPA for reconsideration. Entergy Corporation is now challenging this ruling (Greenhouse, 2008). In 2001, the U.S. Supreme Court upheld prior precedent that the EPA was not to consider cost to industry when setting national ambient and air quality standards. The constitutional mandate of the Clean Air Act is that the EPA is to consider human health risks and factor in a margin of safety when setting the standards (*EPA v. American Trucking*, 2001).

9. Ecosystem services are increasingly recognized as essential to human health and well being; these services are divided into four categories by the 2005 Millennium Ecosystem Assessment report: provisioning (food, fresh water, wood and fiber, fuel); regulating (climate regulation, flood regulation, water purification, disease regulation); cultural (spiritual, aesthetic, recreation, education); and supporting (primary production, soil formation, nutrient cycling) (Millennium Ecosystem Assessment, 2005).

With respect to the effects of industrial pollutants, one study found that on average adults in the industrialized nations carry a toxic load of ninety-one chemicals each, representing 167 different chemicals (Environmental Working Group, 2003).

5 VALUING FUTURE GENERATIONS

1. If worst-case scenarios come to pass, our generation may be dooming future generations to a much lower overall standard of living, including the decimation of many ecosystems and species (Parry et al., 2007).

2. And certainly we would want to strongly implore the early settlers against massacring the Native Americans and practicing slavery.

3. In 2004, 980 million people worldwide lived on less than $1 per day (Millennium Development Goals 2007 Report, 2007).

4. The Stern Review estimates the costs of sufficiently reducing the risks of climate change at 1 percent of annual global GDP by 2050 (Stern, 2006). The World Bank estimates global GDP in 2050 at $135 trillion (World Bank, 2006), 1 percent of which is $1.35 trillion.

5. See Dasgupta (2006) and Nordhaus (2007) for critiques on the discount rate used in the Stern Review.

6. Based on S&P 500 raw data (adjusted for inflation), the arithmetic average rates of return for stocks and ten-year bonds are as follows (geometric means in parentheses) (Damodaran 2008):

   1928–2007: stocks = 11.69 percent (9.81 percent), bonds = 5.26 percent (5.01 percent)

   1967–2007: stocks = 11.98 percent (10.77 percent), bonds = 7.66 percent (8.81 percent)

   1997–2007: stocks = 9.39 percent (8.81 percent), bonds = 6.71 percent (6.47 percent)

7. According to the UN, the risk-free rate of return from 1997 to 2006 ranged from 4 percent to 6.35 percent, averaging 5.02 percent (UN Statistics, n.d.).

6   TOOLS TO ADDRESS ENVIRONMENTAL PROBLEMS: TAXES, PROPERTY RIGHTS, INFORMATION, PSYCHOLOGICAL INSIGHTS, AND COMMAND AND CONTROL REGULATION

1. Pigou discovered that by implementing a per-unit tax equal to the external costs on the source of an environmental problem, the level of supply will shift upward, bringing the equilibrium point to the socially optimum point (Pigou, 1932).

2. Elasticity is the absolute value of the percent change in quantity divided by the percent change in price: $E = \left| \frac{\%\Delta Q}{\%\Delta P} \right|$. For a good with inelastic demand, such as gasoline, food, water, or medicine—things with few substitutes—$E < 1$; the demand for the good is not very sensitive to price, meaning that consumers will purchase the good largely regardless of the price. Elastic goods typically have lots of substitutes (such as magazines, sodas, clothes), and therefore the demand will be relatively sensitive to price—if the price goes up significantly, then demand will drop off as a result.

3. Approximately 61 percent of transportation greenhouse gas emissions in the United States are from passenger cars and light-duty trucks. The transportation sector as a whole is responsible for about a third of all U.S. greenhouse gas emissions (U.S. EPA, 2007).

4. "Global warming potentials" are standardized comparisons of greenhouse gasses to carbon dioxide, based on the ability of the gas to absorb heat and the rate of decay of the gas. According to the IPCC's third assessment report, carbon dioxide is the least damaging greenhouse gas; for example, methane is twenty-three times worse than carbon dioxide, and nitrous oxide is 296 times worse (U.S. Energy Information Administration, 2002).

5. As of 2001, eight European nations—Denmark, Finland, Germany, Italy, the Netherlands, Norway, Sweden, and the United Kingdom—have implemented environmental tax reform (ETR), and two others—Austria and Belgium—have implemented elements of ETR. These countries are taxing environmentally damaging activities and explicitly folding the revenues back into society through reductions in other taxes such as labor taxes and nontax labor costs such as social security.

Through ETR, European countries are successfully internalizing the negative externalities by charging the full cost for environmental resources, as well as encouraging economic growth by reducing taxes on useful activities such as employment and investment (Hoerner and Bosquet, 2001).

The blog http://gregmankiw.blogspot.com, by Gregory Mankiw, Harvard economist and former chair of the President's Council of Economic Advisors, includes many posts about the benefits of Pigouvian taxes (ETR is an example of a Pigouvian tax). In one post, he points out that no taxation is favorable, but if the government has to implement them, it is best to select the taxes that do the least harm or the most good. Pigouvian taxes are good because they correct the market failures associated with the negative externalities of environmental resources (Mankiw, 2006).

6. Chart of Taxes on Income, Profits, and Capital Gains as a Percentage of Revenue (International Monetary Fund, 2006): General Government.

Country	Data year	Income tax as % of Revenue	Country	Data year	Income tax as % of Revenue
Denmark*	2004	52.28	Korea*†	2005	28.87
New Zealand*	2005	50.71	Germany	2005	25.86
Australia	2005	48.54	Austria*	2005	25.23
Canada*	2005	39.08	Czech Republic	2005	24.47
PR China: Hong Kong	2004	38.76	Russian Federation*	2005	23.86
United States*	2005	38.41	Japan	2004	23.81

Continued

Country	Data year	Income tax as % of Revenue	Country	Data year	Income tax as % of Revenue
Continued					
Norway*	2005	37.90	Netherlands*	2005	22.30
Iceland	2002	36.96	Greece*	2005	21.09
Mexico[†]	2000	34.15	Brazil[†]	1998	20.79
United Kingdom	2005	34.10	Hungary*	2005	20.58
Ireland*	2005	34.01	France	2005	20.57
Switzerland	2002	33.87	Poland	2005	15.89
Sweden*	2005	32.97	Slovak Republic*	2005	14.71
Belgium*	2005	32.74	General Government is the average of local, state, and central governments *Data are preliminary or provisional [†]Data are for Central Government only		
Finland*	2005	32.03			
India*[†]	2003	31.06			
Luxembourg	2005	30.59			
Italy*	2005	29.37			

7. Some environmentalists compare pollution permits to the indulgences offered by the Catholic Church in the Middle Ages. The Church allowed believers to purchase indulgences in exchange for reduced penance for their sins ("Indulgence," 2008). Transnational Institute's report "The Carbon Neutral Myth" (Smith, 2007), and George Monbiot's article in the *Guardian* are two examples of environmentalists comparing offsets to indulgences (2006). Similarly, Michael Sandel (1997) of Harvard argues that tradable permits are immoral because they remove the negative stigma associated with pollution.

8. Most of the initial sulfur dioxide permits were distributed to firms based on historical data. Every year, a small percentage of permits are auctioned to new entrants and anybody needing extra permits (Joint Economic Committee Study, 1997). In the European Union Emissions Trading System (EU ETS), each country was allowed to auction up to 5 percent of all permits in phase one and up to 10 percent in phase two; the rest were given away without charge. The European Commission has proposed that

in phase three, beginning in 2014, 100 percent power-sector allocations will be auctioned (Point Carbon, 2008).

Absent federal carbon dioxide legislation in the United States, several northeastern states joined together to develop a trading system known as the Regional Greenhouse Gas Initiative (RGGI); each state determines the percentage of their permits to auction, and most have committed to eventual 100 percent auction systems (Regional Greenhouse Gas Initiative, 2007). The first auction took place on September 25, 2008, where 100 percent of the 12,565,387 permits offered were sold for $3.07 each (Regional Greenhouse Gas Initiative, n.d.).

9. 226,384 allowances were sold on the private market between April 1993 and March 1994. A single market value of these trades is difficult to quantify due to companies not sharing the price of the transaction and due to reported prices varying widely. The Emission Exchange Corporation began reporting sale values in July 1993, and the trade price remained at approximately $170 until May 1994; this number is a conservative estimate of the private trading value. At least one sale of unknown size took place in November 1993 for $205 per ton (Joskow et al., 1998).

10. A few examples of this are an environmental group in Canada buying out a whole outfitting company in 2005 ("Environmentalists Buy Out Bella," 2005), and supporters of Friends of the McNeil River (Alaska) won and purchased six of the eight brown bear permits offered in 1995 (About Friends of McNeil River, n.d.).

11. Any interested party can register with EU ETS and participate in the carbon exchange market (Szabo 2006). A British company, Carbon Retirement, sells EU permits to private individuals wishing to offset their carbon emissions. Each permit sold reduces the amount of industry-allowed carbon dioxide emissions by one ton (Szabo, 2008).

12. The expected penalty for noncompliance of a regulatory statue is the probability of being caught multiplied by the penalty. This means that the government has two ways to maximize compliance—either by increasing the likelihood of being caught or the size of the fine. High probabilities and high penalties are obviously the most effective. However, since monitoring is very expensive and time consuming, a relatively low chance of being caught can be compensated for by a very high penalty.

13. The Clean Air Act and the Clean Water Act are examples of environmental legislation that include the possibility of serving time in prison for noncompliance. For example, a U.S. District Court sentenced Derrik Hagerman to sixty months in jail for altering documents required by the Clean Water Act (*United States v. Derrik Hagerman*, 2007), and Sheon DiMaio was sentenced to forty-two months in jail for acts violating the Clean Air Act (*United States v. Sheon DiMaio*, 2007).

14. For more information on this act, see this page on the EPA's website, http://www.epa.gov/lawsregs/laws/epcra.html.

15. Noted environmental economist Tom Titenberg (1998) has called the establishment of right-to-know programs the "third wave of

environmentalism"; command and control policies and market-based instruments are considered waves one and two.

16. In 2000, the European Pollutant Emission Register (EPER) was the first to report CO_2 emissions at the facility level; more information about the program can be found at http://www.eper.cec.eu.int/.

17. More information about these and other right-to-know programs:

    Global Right-to-Know Resource: http://www.mapcruzin.com/globalchem.htm

    Canada: National Pollutant Release Inventory (1999), http://www.ec.gc.ca/pdb/npri/

    Chile: Registro de Emisiones y Transferencia de Contaminantes (RETC) (2002), http://www.conama.cl/especiales/1305/propertyvalue-14774.html

    Mexico: Registro de Emisiones y Transferencia de Contaminantes (2004), http://www.semarnat.gob.mx/gestionambiental/cali daddelaire/Pages/retc.aspx

    Australia: National Pollutant Inventory (1998), http://www.npi.gov.au/ index.html

    China: Emergency Response Law (2007), http://www.china-em bassy.org/eng/xw/t357027.htm

    India: Freedom of Information Bill (2002), http:// timesofindia.indiatimes.com/cms.dll/html/uncomp/ articleshow?artid=31500188ands Type=1

18. http://scorecard.org/

19. Important Eco-labeling programs include:

    Forest Stewardship Council: http://www.fsc.org

    Marine Stewardship Council: http://www.msc.org

    Dolphin Safe Tuna: http://www.earthisland.org/dolphinSafeTuna/consumer/

    Green Seal: http://www.greenseal.org/index.cfm

    EU Flower: http://ec.europa.eu/environment/ecolabel/index_en.htm

    United States: Energy Star, http://www.energystar.gov/

    Germany: Blue Angel, http://www.blauer-engel.de/index.php (English site under construction)

    The Nordic Swan: http://www.svanen.nu/Default.aspx?tabName=StartPage

    Japan's Eco Mark: http://www.ecomark.jp/english/

20. In 2005, organic and Alaskan wild salmon labels were found to be false in surveys of New York City fish markets (Burros, 2005; *Consumer Reports*, 2006).

21. Examples of government oversight include the USDA overseeing the organic label (http://www.sciencedaily.com/releases/2005/06/050607005738.htm), and the U.S. EPA overseeing the Energy Star label (http://www.epa.gov/oig/reports/2007/20070801-2007-P-00028_glance.pdf).

22. In 2007, the Forest Stewardship Council (FSC) partnered with the European Space Agency to study the applicability of using remote sensing technology to monitor forest management ("Satellite Imagery to Be Used," 2006). The Nature Conservancy and Surnalindo Lestari Jaya, an Indonesian corporation, have been experimenting with using barcodes to track wood from forests to U.S. customers in order to meet the qualifications for FSC certification (Colchester, 2006).

23. GoodGuide is led by a group of academics and technology experts; http://GoodGuide.com.

24. Over the years, there have been several attempts at quantifying the level of information that triggers overload reactions in the consumer. A recent study of online product information found that the overload threshold is dependent on the number of alternatives, number of attributes for each alternative, and the distribution of attribute levels (Lee and Lee, 2004).

25. The first U.S. governmental effort to monitor and control the chemicals being introduced to the marketplace was the Toxic Substances Control Act (TSCA), which was passed by Congress in 1976. The TSCA, however, exempted all 62,000 chemicals already on the market from toxicity review. In 2006, the equivalent of about 623,000 tanker truckloads of chemicals entered the American market daily. Of these chemicals, fewer than two hundred have undergone testing by the EPA (Schapiro, 2007).

26. Venture capital is going to clean technology at a very high rate—the Cleantech Venture Network invested 52.9 percent more in clean technology in 2006 than in 2005. Cleantech Capital Group invested approximately $8.8 billion between 1999 and 2006, and expects to invest another $8.7 billion between 2006 and 2009 (Worrell, 2006). Kleiner Perkins (of which Al Gore is a partner) recently announced a $700 million fund to invest in green-tech start-up companies over the next three years, and a $500 million Green Growth fund to invest in later-stage companies (Gage, 2008). Overall, venture capital investments in clean-tech firms quadrupled between 2000 and 2007; during the same time frame, clean-tech investments increased from 0.6 percent of all venture capital investments in 2000 to 9.1 percent in 2007 (Gage, 2008).

27. The field of behavioral economics has entered the mainstream with popular books such as *Freakonomics*. For more serious treatments, see work by Matthew Rabin, Richard Thaler, Cass Sunstein, and Daniel Kahneman, among others.

28. In California, 1.9 percent of eligible residential customers had switched providers by April 2000, and mostly to green providers. Through March 2000, approximately 1.6 percent of eligible customers in Pennsylvania had chosen a new green provider. Massachusetts and Rhode Island report negligible customer switching to green power, and Maine and New Jersey had not been open to retail competition very long. Overall, by 2000, approximately 1.2 percent of eligible customers nationwide had switched to green power (Wiser et al., 2000). By 2005, the U.S. average had improved to 1.5 percent participation, with 4.6 percent to 13.6 percent participation in the top ten programs (Bird and Swezey, 2006).

29. Throughout the 1990s, professors Stephen DeCanio and Richard B. Howarth each published several papers on barriers to energy efficiency in corporations. Citations for these papers can be found on their respective websites: http://www.stephendecanio.com/Stephen_DeCanio_Site/published_works.html and http://www.dartmouth.edu/~rhowarth/files/Howarth-CV.pdf.

30. In 2009, the California state legislature passed a law mandating energy-efficiency standards for the large-screen televisions that are becoming increasingly popular; it goes into effect at the end of 2010. See http://articles.latimes.com/2009/nov/19/business/fi-big-screen-tvs19.

31. For a discussion of this result and a summary of other recent developments in this field, see the working paper "Behavioral Science and Energy Policy" by Alcott and Mullainathan (2010), which is an extended version of their March 5, 2010, article in *Science* and can be accessed at http://web.mit.edu/allcott/www/Allcott%20and%20Mullainathan%20 2010%20-%20Behavioral%20Science%20and%20Energy%20Policy.pdf.

32. For EPA's analysis of the costs and benefits of the Clean Air Act, see http://www.epa.gov/air/sect812/; for analysis of the economics of the Clean Water Act, see http://www.epa.gov/waterscience/economics/.

33. When examining any type of government intervention in the market, it is useful to look at whether the policy is aimed at correcting a market failure. If it is not, many times it will make matters worse. Take the housing market: here we have close-to-perfect information (prospective buyers can get detailed evaluations of the property they want to buy, as well as detailed information about the neighborhoods), there is close-to-perfect competition (there are hundreds of real estate agents for consumers to choose from), the transaction costs are relatively low (closing costs are a few percentage points), and when buying a property there is no significant externality on anyone else (my choosing to buy a house versus renting one doesn't fundamentally affect my neighbors). And yet, the U.S. government (and other governments around the world) greatly subsidizes housing by giving huge tax breaks to homeowners and providing lower interest rates to low- and middle-income buyers. This distortion in the market has existed for decades simply because politicians believe that home ownership is a key component of the "American Dream." The government should not be in the business of favoring home ownership over renting since all this does is create situations where people buy homes that they ultimately can't afford, and tens of billions of tax revenues are forfeited to distort a market that would work just fine without any government intervention. These policies are one of the reasons we experienced the huge housing bubble of the mid-2000s. One can make the case, however, that once foreclosures reach very high levels, the government has a role to play in minimizing the negative externalities these foreclosures have on the surrounding neighborhoods. But even here the solution is tricky, because if all the government does is once again prop up an artificially inflated housing market, the problem will resurface in the future.

34. The U.S. Minerals Management Service, which oversees offshore oil drilling, and gave an exemption from environmental review to BP's Deepwater Horizon oil rig, is a classic example of regulatory capture with disastrous consequences (For details see http://www.nytimes.com/2008/09/11/washington/11royalty.html?_r=3 and http://www.rollingstone.com/politics/news/17390/111965?RS_show_page=0#). Regulatory capture is also prevalent in many of the governmental bodies that oversee fishing quotas, regulate forestry companies, energy firms, and agribusiness (authority for banning pesticides was given to the U.S. EPA instead of the U.S. Department of Agriculture (USDA) because the USDA is known to be friendly to agribusiness). Regulatory capture goes well beyond the environmental realm; the worst forms are probably linked to the financial industry, which uses its tremendous might to block oversight and preserve its huge profits.

35. For much of its history the discipline of economics has been referred to as "political economy."

7 ENVIRONMENT VS. ECONOMY: GROWTH RATES, JOBS, AND INTERNATIONAL TRADE

1. For U.S. Industrial Production Index data, see http://www.federalreserve.gov/releases/g17/Current/default.htm. For an excellent blog post on the subject, see http://www.fivethirtyeight.com/2010/02/us-manufacturing-is-not-dead.html.

2. For data on global agricultural production, see http://www.pecad.fas.usda.gov/ and http://faostat.fao.org/.

3. Harvard business professor Michael Porter developed a theory (referred to as the "Porter Hypothesis") that posits that environmental regulation can spur innovation and therefore offset any additional regulatory costs. See Porter and van der Linde (1995).

4. For a good discussion on the limitations and flaws in the GDP, see Cobb et al. (1995).

5. For an alternative to the GDP that tries to capture a wider range of societal values, see the Genuine Progress Indicator (GPI) at http://www.rprogress.org/sustainability_indicators/genuine_progress_indicator.htm.

6. Measurements of so-called "green GDP" try to capture the values of these types of ecosystem services and also to subtract environmental degradation from traditional GDP figures. Despite its appeal, there is no firmly established methodology for calculating green GDP, and no consistent annual accounting is done to estimate it for the major economies of the world.

7. For a discussion of Simon Kuznets' views, see Rowe (2008).

8. A relationship referred to as the "Environmental Kuznets Curve (EKC)" posits an inverted U-shaped relationship between environmental quality and wealth. As countries develop, they start polluting more up until a point where various factors lead to a gradual diminishment in pollution.

For more information on the EKC, see http://www.eoearth.org/article/Environmental_kuznets_curve.

9. According to the CIA World Factbook, the GDP for the EU was $16.01 trillion in 2009, ranking it number one (https://www.cia.gov/library/publications/the-world-factbook/geos/ee.html), whereas the U.S. 2009 GDP was $14.27 trillion (https://www.cia.gov/library/publications/the-world-factbook/geos/us.html), ranking it number two.

10. Another intriguing metric is the Environmental Sustainability Index (ESI) (http://www.yale.edu/esi/). The Human Development Index (HDI) also has its strong points (http://hdr.undp.org/en/statistics/).

8 CLIMATE CHANGE

1. For an outstanding paper on the economics and politics of the Montreal Protocol, see DeCanio (2003).

2. According to the Fourth IPCC report, if all greenhouse gas and aerosol emissions had remained at their 2000 levels, the best estimate for average global temperature change is a rise of 0.1° C per decade until 2030, and a total increase of 0.6o C by the end of the twenty-first century (IPCC, 2007).

3. A *USA Today*/Gallup poll from February 8–10, 2008, found that while the environment, including global warming, ranks as extremely or very important for 62 percent of Americans, it falls at the bottom of a long list of priorities including the economy, Iraq, education, health care, energy and gas prices, terrorism, social security, etc. An NBC News/*Wall Street Journal* poll conducted January 20–22, 2008, found that when asked to identify (from a list) the top governmental priority, only 6 percent of respondents chose the environment and global warming. A CNN/Opinion Research Corporation poll from mid-January 2008 found that respondents considered global warming extremely or very important in the 2008 presidential election only 48 percent of the time, compared to over 75 percent for the economy, Iraq, terrorism, and health care (Polling Report, 2008b). These already low numbers went down further as economic conditions deteriorated in 2009.

A 2006 report surveyed residents of Australia, South Korea, India, China, and the United States about critical threats facing their country. Global warming ranked third out of twelve in Australia, first out of sixteen in South Korea, sixth out of thirteen in India, third out of eleven in China, and sixth out of thirteen in the United States (Bouton et al., 2006).

4. Hansen suggests that since significant changes are occurring at the current atmospheric CO2 level of 383, we have already overshot a safe pollution level and should aim to reduce concentrations to 350 parts per million (McKibben, 2007).

5. The OECD Environmental Outlook Baseline projects global annual GDP growth at 3.4 percent for 2005–10; 2.7 percent for 2010–20; 2.5 percent for 2020–30; and 2.8 percent overall for 2005–30 (2008). Cisco's Foresight

2020 (2006) projects annual global GDP growth for the period 2006–20 at 3.5 percent, and Global Insight (2005) projects global annual GDP growth of 3.1 percent between 2005 and 2025.

6. The IPCC SRES scenario, with peak global population of nine billion around midcentury, and with continuing fossil-heavy energy sources estimates approximately 125 Gt (billion tons) CO_2-equivalent emissions in 2050. This represents an approximate increase of 400 percent from 1990 levels (Barker et al., 2007).

7. For details on how Exxon continues to fund groups that deny the science of climate change, see http://www.guardian.co.uk/environment/2009/jul/01/exxon-mobil-climate-change-sceptics-funding. Meanwhile, the U.S. coal industry lobby, the American Coalition for Clean Coal Electricity (ACCE), has spent tens of millions to lobby members of the U.S. Congress against climate change legislation.

8. The Carbon Tax Center recommends beginning with a $37 per ton carbon ($0.10 per gallon gasoline) tax and increasing the tax annually at a rate equal to 5 to 10 percent of the baseline cost of fossil fuels. They assume that these increases will decrease CO2 emissions by 4 percent each year (Carbon Tax Center, 2008).

9. A paper analyzing the set of carbon tax bills under consideration by the U.S. Congress in spring 2008 concludes that the regressive nature of a carbon tax can be offset with carefully structured rebate programs (Metcalf et al., 2008). Economist William Nordhaus (2001), in a paper comparing alternative methods for controlling greenhouse gas emissions, concludes that a pricing method such as taxation is preferred to cap and trade. One reason for this preference is because of the ability to rebate the taxed funds to the consumer and avoid any changes in the efficiency losses from taxation.

10. A CNN/*USA Today* poll in September 2003 found that 51 percent of respondents felt that China was an unfair trade partner because of "unfair tactics, such as the Chinese government's manipulation of its currency." A Chicago Council on Foreign Relations (CCFR) poll in 2004 found that 51 percent of respondents felt that China trades unfairly; only 36 percent felt that China trades fairly (Americans and the World, n.d.). In February 2004, a *Newsweek* poll found that respondents believe that other countries' lower environmental and worker health standards are a reason Americans lose jobs to foreign countries 81 percent of the time, compared to 11 percent who disagree (Polling Report, 2008a). The 2006 CCFR poll found that 49 percent, 47 percent, and 58 percent of Americans think that Mexico, India, and China, respectively, trade unfairly (Bouton et al., 2006).

11. Through its oil imports, the United States (both directly and indirectly) sends hundreds of billions of dollars each year to Iran, Saudi Arabia, Venezuela, and Russia. These regimes are not only opposed to many U.S. interests, but also actively support policies that weaken American security.

12. The conventional wisdom is that in order for this to happen, the United States has to first sign into law its own national cap and trade system to

show that it is serious about making significant greenhouse gas reductions, after which it is likely that India and China will also agree to reduction targets, and combined with the signatories to the Kyoto Protocol a multilateral cap and trade system can be established. Without the United States, China, and India, which are the world's largest emitters, taking part, any international cap and trade system would fail to reduce emissions by the amount needed to mitigate catastrophic climate change.

13. In 2004, industrialized countries produced 40 percent of the global greenhouse gas emissions and accounted for only 20 percent of the population; they produced sixteen tons CO_2-equivalent per person compared to the four tons CO_2-equivalent per person produced by developing countries (Union of Concerned Scientists, 2007).

14. For more information on issues relating to climate change equity, see http://www.ecoequity.org/.

15. The Environmental Defense Fund, Nature Conservancy, National Wildlife Federation, Natural Resources Defense Council, Pew Center on Global Climate Change, and World Resources Institute are members of the United States Climate Action Partnership, which promotes cap and trade policies as essential to mitigating global climate change (United States Climate Action Partnership, 2007).

16. In an international cap and trade system that included all the countries of the world, the act of paying people to reduce their own emissions would be subsumed within the permitting system since all nations would face greenhouse gas caps; i.e., there would be no entities outside of the permit system that companies could contract with to offset emissions.

17. There is no reason that carbon offsets couldn't be built into tax systems as well; faced with a tax on its greenhouse gas emissions, a firm would be allowed to instead purchase offsets of an equivalent amount (and would do so if it were cheaper than the tax). While theoretically equivalent in a tax or cap and trade system, offsets have only been discussed in policy circles in the context of cap and trade legislation.

18. For the regional distribution of CDM projects, see http://cdm.unfccc.int/Statistics/Registration/RegisteredProjByRegionPieChart.html.

19. See http://articles.sfgate.com/2009–09-18/news/17205678_1_carbon-flight-purchase.

20. For more information on additionality, see the Clean Development Mechanism Rulebook at http://cdmrulebook.org/pageid/84.

21. For more on critiques of the CDM, see papers by Stanford law professor Michael Wara at http://www.law.stanford.edu/directory/profile/308/Michael%20Wara/#publications_cases.

22. Carbon offsets in forestry (under the proposed Reduced Emissions from Deforestation and Degradation-REDD system) have their own unique set of potential challenges and benefits that are discussed in Chapter 8.

23. In the European Union Emissions Trading System (EU ETS), each country was allowed to auction up to 5 percent of all permits in phase one and up to 10 percent in phase two, while the rest were given away

without charge; the European Commission has proposed that in phase three, beginning in 2014, 100 percent power sector allocations will be auctioned (Point Carbon, 2008).

24. For details of the bill, see http://cantwell.senate.gov/issues/CLEARAct. cfm.

25. For a discussion among prominent environmentalists and economists on what is better, a tax or cap and trade, see http://e360.yale.edu/content/feature.msp?id=2148.

26. See these two articles that are only months apart: http://www.cnn. com/2008/US/05/26/gas.driving/index.html and http://www.nytimes. com/2008/10/30/business/30gasoline.html.

27. For an overview of the CAFE program, see http://www.nhtsa.dot.gov/portal/site/nhtsa/menuitem.43ac99aefa80569eea57529cdba046a0/.

28. For details on the Energy Star program, see http://www.energystar.gov/.

29. For an assessment of the EU's feed-in tariffs (and other policies to support renewable energy), see the Commission of the European Communities report, "The Support of Electricity from Renewable Energy Sources," which can be downloaded at http://ec.europa.eu/energy/climate_actions/doc/2008_res_working_document_en.pdf.

30. In addition, if not applied properly, feed-in tariffs can lead to excessive capacity in uneconomic types of renewable power, as the following case with solar power in Spain exemplifies: http://www.nytimes. com/2010/03/09/business/energy-environment/09solar.html?hp.

9   FOREST AND BIODIVERSITY CONSERVATION

1. For background information on the utilitarian doctrine, read the original thesis by John Stuart Mill (1879), and visit the *Encyclopedia Britannica* online (West, 2008).

2. Conservation International identifies twenty-five hot spots utilizing the definition put forth by Myers et al. (2000). A hot spot must contain at least 1,500 endemic species of vascular plants (greater than 0.5 percent of the world's total), and have lost at least 70 percent of the original habitat (Conservation International, 2008).

   World Wildlife Fund (2006) has identified 238 ecoregions in order to conserve the most comprehensive selection of the world's flora and fauna. These regions were selected to represent the twenty-six habitat types and seven biogeographic realms, and where further selections were necessary ecoregions were compared and selected based on species richness, endemism, higher taxonomic uniqueness, extraordinary ecological or evolutionary phenomena, and global rarity of the dominant habitat type.

   BirdLife International (2008) targets areas termed Endemic Bird Areas. These areas are identified as the locations where the restricted habitats (larger than 50,000 square kilometers) of two or more endemic species overlap.

3. Even though their share of global land area has decreased by half (from about half of global land cover to about a quarter), forests continue to provide habitat to more than 50 percent of the world's species (Groombridge and Jenkins, 2000). Forests are found on all six inhabited continents, especially in the tropical and temperate zones. Good maps of global forest cover and overall terrestrial ecological zones can be found at http://www.fao.org/DOCREP/004/Y1997E/y1997e1g.htm, figures 47-1 and 47-2, respectively.

4. Illegal logging constitutes 90 percent of all logging activity in Cambodia, 80 percent in Bolivia and Peru, 70 to 80 percent in Indonesia, and 70 percent in Ecuador, Gabon, and Papua New Guinea (World Bank, 2006).

5. For example, the U.S. Forest Service loses around $40 million annually in subsidizing the logging industry in the Tongass National Forest, and inexpensive logging fees for Canadian timber companies are disputed as unfair subsidies by the U.S. logging industry (Taxpayers for Common Sense, n.d.; Cushman, 2006).

6. See http://www.un-redd.org/ for details of the proposed program, and http://www.redd-monitor.org/about/ for a collection of commentary on REDD.

7. David Fogarty (2007) provides background information about the debate in his article published by Reuters. Delegates at the Bali convention agreed to include the Reducing Emissions from Deforestation and Degradation (REDD) program in future talks on the post-Kyoto global warming treaty. By the end of the Bali talks, they had agreed that the REDD program is important and should be strengthened, but left it at voluntary action ("Bali Delegates," 2007). At about the same time, the World Bank announced the formation of the Forest Carbon Partnership Facility as a fund to pay countries to not cut down their forests as proposed in the REDD program. As of December 11, 2007, developed countries (not including the United States) and one NGO had already pledged US$160 million ("World Bank Fund," 2007).

8. For free REDD modeling software and discussions of different REDD scenarios, explore this site: http://www.conservation.org/osiris/Pages/overview.aspx.

9. For a great overview of efforts around the world to link biodiversity preservation to incentive programs, see the report by Ecosystem Marketplace, "State of Biodiversity Markets: Offset and Compensation Programs Worldwide," which can be downloaded at http://www.ecosystemmarketplace.com/documents/acrobat/sbdmr.pdf.

The Natural Capital Project is a joint effort of the Woods Institute for the Environment at Stanford University, the Nature Conservancy, and the World Wildlife Fund to define the economic value of ecosystem services at locations around the world; http://www.naturalcapitalproject.org/about.html.

10. A review of the program by Sierra and Russman (2006) suggests that payments are not directly contributing to forest conservation and that the funds would be better spent in restoration activities. A study by Brian

Steed (2007) concludes that while the program is theoretically good, areas of caution/concern include ensuring that incentives are adequate for the targeted participants, and that sound payment mechanisms are established to ensure continuity of the program over time.

11. The Terra Nova Rainforest reserve, which was deeded to the Belize Association of Traditional Healers in 1993, was designed for three purposes: use by traditional healers and their students, use by U.S. scientists for ethnobotanical and ecological research, and ecotourism (Balick et al., 1994). Bioprospecting may, however, have limited viability as a force for forest preservation (Simpson et al., 1996).

12. Using 145 Willingness to Pay (WTP) estimates from forty-six contingent valuation studies on six continents, Jacobsen and Hanley (2008) found that demand for biodiversity conservation increases with rising income.

13. Debt-for-nature swaps generally fall in two major categories: bilateral debt-for-environment swaps by a creditor (one country buys back the debt of a lesser-developed country), and commercial debt-for-nature swaps (a private organization buys the debt of a lesser-developed country). In both cases, the debt is purchased at a discount and then converted to the local currency and used to fund environmental programs or to set aside protected areas (World Wildlife Fund, 2008). Between 1998 and 2002, more than $1.1 billion had been generated in conservation funds in more than thirteen countries (WWF Center for Conservation Finance 2003b; 2003a). A large swap occurred in 2007 when the U.S. government, the Nature Conservancy, and Conservation International came together to purchase $26 million of Costa Rica's foreign debt at a discounted price of $12.6 million ("Costa Rica," 2007).

14. The first recorded swap took place in 1987 between Bolivia and Conservation International (Resor, 1997).

15. Conservation International and The Nature Conservancy, in conjunction with the United States and Guatemalan governments, worked out a debt for nature swap in 2006 to provide Guatemala with more than $24 million for forest protection ("Historic Debt-for-Nature Swap," 2006).

16. Conservation International (n.d.) estimates the human population within biodiversity hot spots at approximately two billion.

17. There has been much criticism of the environmental movement by those who believe that local people and indigenous groups have been treated unfairly. For examples, see Mathews (2005) and Melosi (2000).

18. Initial responses to Chapin's article were published in the January/February 2005 World Watch magazine and are available for download at http://www.worldwatch.org/system/files/EP181C.pdf. Additional responses that were not published in print are available at http://www.worldwatch.org/node/1832.

19. Mr. Hotelling (1947) found that by dividing the area around a park into concentric zones and then comparing the cost of traveling from a particular zone to the percentage of inhabitants of a particular zone who actually travel to the park, the park officials could plot a point for each

zone on a demand curve for the service of the park, and thus determine the economic value of a visit to the national park.

20. For more information on Lancaster's bundles of attributes theories, see http://www.blackwellreference.com/public/tocnode?id= g9780631233176_chunk_g978140510066319_ss1-13.

21. Two examples of highly valued natural resources are Polish forests and the Hawaiian coral reefs. Using the travel cost methodology, the annual recreational value of Polish forests in 2005 was approximately 5 billion to 8.5 billion euros, or 570 to 970 euros per hectare (Bartczak et al., 2008). Hawaii's coral reefs are estimated to contribute $360 million annually to the Hawaiian economy and have an overall asset value of approximately $10 billion (Cesar and van Beukering, 2004).

22. For a description of the differences between nature-based and ecotourism, see http://www.gdrc.org/uem/eco-tour/eco-sust.html.

23. This area is famous for close encounters with whales. For photos, see http://www.nrdc.org/wildlife/marine/baja/bajainx.asp.

24. In the 1990s, Merck entered into an agreement with Costa Rica's National Biodiversity Institute (INBio) to pay $1.1 million up front for the right to sample plant, animal, and insect species from within protected areas of Costa Rica. The Costa Rican government agreed to invest 10 percent of the upfront fee and 50 percent of the royalties back into conservation and biodiversity protection. ("Agreement Between Merck and Costa Rica," n.d.).

    Initial funding for the 2,400-hectare Terra Nova Rainforest Reserve in Belize came from Shaman Pharmaceuticals (Spiro, 1998). The park was deeded to the Belize Association of Traditional Healers in June 1993 for four purposes: extraction of traditional medicinal plants, a location for traditional healing education and apprenticeship, ethnobotanical and ecological research, and ecological tourism (Balick et al., 1994). Shaman Pharmaceuticals formed and funded the Healing Forest Conservancy as a nonprofit organization through which they could send product profits back to the indigenous communities in the form of specific programs (King and Carlson, 1995).

25. Beyond the more than 800,000 metric tons of shark that were harvested for meat, up to an additional 260,000 metric tons were slaughtered for their fins and thrown back into the ocean. Many shark populations are currently at around 80 percent of their preindustrial fishing population levels. Without the top predator, many ecosystems become unbalanced and cannot survive (WildAid, 2007).

    In addition to the large quantities of African bush meat hunted for subsistence, 13,000 pounds of bush meat are exported to Western countries annually (*Newsweek*, 2007). Surveys conducted between 1998 and 2000 found that due to hunting and disease, ape populations had been reduced by more than half since 1983 (Weiss, 2003).

26. More than eighty celebrities have filmed public service announcements that have reached more than one billion viewers globally per week. These

PSAs can be viewed on the WildAid website: http://www.wildaid.org/index.asp?CID=7andPID=507.

27. For an excellent paper on this topic, see Metrick and Weitzman (1998).

10 AGRICULTURE

1. While ubiquitous in discussions about agriculture, the term "family farm" doesn't have a precise meaning, and family owned operations can include gigantic agricultural empires.

2. For a contrarian view, see Jared Diamond's "The Invention of Agriculture: The Worst Mistake in the History of the Human Race" (1987).

3. Through selective breeding of mutant wheat strains in Mexico, Dr. Borlaug developed strains of wheat with yields three times as large as previous strains. Exporting these strains to India in the late 1960s increased India's food production such that the country shifted from the brink of starvation to food self-sufficiency ("Ears of Plenty," 2005). In 2005, Dr. Borlaug and former president Jimmy Carter defended the use of genetically modified crops to improve crop yields and alleviate hunger in areas where the farmers must cultivate marginal lands (Borlaug and Carter, 2005).

4. Countries with agriculture production subsidies: producer support estimate per cent of gross farm receipts.

	2003–2005**	2004–2006*		2003–2005**	2004–2006*
Iceland		66%	Russia	17%	
Norway		66%	United States		14%
Switzerland		66%	Mexico		14%
Korea		63%	Bulgaria	8%	
Japan		55%	China	8%	
EU		34%	South Africa	8%	
OECD		29%	Australia		5%
Romania	27%		Brazil	5%	
Turkey		24%	Ukraine	3%	
Canada	22%	22%	New Zealand		1%

Notes: * Organization for Economic Co-operation and Development, 2007b.
** Organization for Economic Co-operation and Development, 2007a.

5. Globally, the top ten subsidized crops (by percentage of total value), from most to least heavily subsidized, are: milk, beef and veal, rice, wheat, pig meat, maize, other grains, oilseeds, poultry, and sugar (Organization for Economic Co-operation and Development, 2004a).

6. The persistent strength of the U.S. agricultural lobby is a classic case of political economy in which the potential losses from a change in the status quo are highly concentrated among a relatively small group, and the revenue that would be saved would be dispersed over the entire population or absorbed into the general budget. Those who stand to lose are very vocal and invest significant sums in lobbying, while the general public remains relatively apathetic and business as usual continues.

7. Each state is allowed two senators; however, on a per capita basis, the main agricultural-state senators (except California) represent fewer people than many nonagricultural-state senators.

8. For information on the Environmental Working Group's (EWG) farm subsidy database and related news, see http://www.ewg.org/farmsubsidies.

9. Agricultural subsidies overall have gone down in OECD countries, but they persist at extremely high levels.

10. Even the developed countries suffer from artificially depressed food prices. In 1991, it was estimated that the developed market economies would gain $35 billion annually by the removal of agricultural subsidies (above and beyond the savings in government revenue) (Council of Economic Advisers, 1991).

11. For example, see the U.S.–Florida Excise Tax case and the U.S.–Upland Cotton case (World Trade Organization, 2008a and 2008b).

12. In May 2008, Congress finally passed the 2007 Farm Bill legislation, which was immediately vetoed by President George W. Bush. Both houses then voted to override the veto and enact the Farm Bill (Walsh and Barrett, 2008). The USDA page with information about the bill is at http://www.usda.gov/wps/portal/usdafarmbill?navtype=SUandnavid=FARM_BILL_FORUMS.

13. Like the Europeans, the proposed U.S. Farm Bill includes provisions such as the Conservation Reserve Program (CRP) and the Environmental Quality Improvement Program (EQIP) that pay farmers for environmental measures, but the overwhelming bulk of U.S. farm payments remain in the form of direct production subsidy payments. Approximately 14 percent of the $290 billion Farm Bill is marked for crop subsidies; more than 65 percent of the bill goes toward food stamps and emergency food aid programs, and 1 percent is for foreign food aid (Woodruff, 2008).

14. For more information about the program, read articles published by the Frontier Center for Public Policy (Federated Farmers of New Zealand, 2002) and the UN Environmental Programme (1999).

15. A reference to the dominant role that oil plays in the world economy, along with the strife that accompanies it.

16. According to the most recent Food and Agriculture Organization of the United Nations data (2000–2006, depending on the country),

approximately 70 percent of global water use is by the agricultural sector (Food and Agriculture Organization, 2008).

17. The history of how California farmers were able to establish rights to such vast quantities of water at such highly subsidized rates is extremely complicated and the subject of many articles and books. The legendary battles over California water rights have been popularized in such movies as *Chinatown* and Marc Reisner's highly entertaining book *Cadillac Desert.*

18. Australia has been grappling with a terrible drought and has enacted many new policies to try to create a more efficient and just water system. For information on these efforts, see http://www.environment.gov.au/water/.

19. In 2003, the UNEP identified 146 dead zones. Major dead zones include the Gulf of Mexico, the Baltic Sea, the Northern Adriatic Sea, the Gulf of Thailand, the Yellow Sea, and Chesapeake Bay. A map of all dead zones and more information can be found in the UNEP Global Environment Outlook Yearbook 2003 (United Nations Environment Program, 2003).

20. A nitrogen credit exchange was developed in Connecticut in 2002 to reduce the state's total maximum daily emissions of nitrogen into Long Island Sound (Connecticut Department of Environmental Protection, 2007).

21. The U.S. Department of Agriculture does not publish the size of individual farms, but they do publish the number of farms over a certain size and the total number of animals on those farms. The data below is taken from the 2002 Census of Agriculture (National Agricultural Statistics Service, 2004).

Animal	Farm size	# Farms	# Head	Average head/ farm
cattle and calves	>=5,000	905	12,936,108	14,294
hogs and pigs	>=5,000	2206	31,715,604	14,377
poultry-layers	>=100,000	498	252,712,220	507,454
chickens-meat	n/a	37,937	1,389,279,047	36,621

22. Based on information from a 1997 report compiled by the minority staff of the U.S. Senate Committee on Agriculture, Nutrition, and Forestry for Senator Tom Harkin of Iowa (Dem.), the U.S. meat industry generates 1.4 billion tons of animal waste annually, 130 times as much as annual human waste production (Silverstein, 1999).

23. According to the Natural Resources Defense Council (NRDC), an eight-acre hog-waste lagoon burst in North Carolina in 1995, spilling 25 million gallons of manure into the New River and killing about 10 million fish. Between 1995 and 1998, 13 million fish died due to 200 manure-related

incidents and 1,000 spills occurred at livestock feedlots in ten states. At least five manure lagoons burst in North Carolina in 1995 due to damage from Hurricane Floyd. Outbreaks of *Pfiesteria piscicida* in Maryland and North Carolina have been linked to chicken and hog-waste runoff, killing millions of fish and causing health problems for the local human populations (Natural Resources Defense Council, 2005).

24. The counterargument that because of its price organic is by definition elitist is becoming less of an issue as the price premium declines, especially in developed countries where even many low-income people purchase luxury items such as big-screen televisions, cell phones, and cars.

25. For a list of EPA- and UN-banned or severely restricted pesticides, visit http://www.epa.gov/oppfead1/international/piclist.htm.

    Critical-use exemptions exist for those situations where the applicant can show that significant market disruption will happen without an exemption and that no technically or economically feasible alternatives exist. For methyl bromide, independent advisory panels to the Parties of the Montreal Protocol review each country's exemption applications and determine the final allocation of exemptions (U.S. Environmental Protection Agency, 2007). The U.S. 2008 exemptions are published for public record at http://www.epa.gov/ozone/mbr/2008CUEFinalRule12-19-07.pdf.

26. Examples of relatively benign pesticides include sulfur, petroleum oil, mineral oil, copper sulfate, and copper hydroxide. In California, these pesticides make up 50 percent of total use (Gan, 2001).

27. Even organic foods might be contaminated with GMOs because drifting pollen from GMO crop fields can contaminate organic fields (Gillam, 2008).

28. The Dispute Settlement Board found that by implementing a moratorium on genetically modified products, the European Commission was in violation of trade agreements. One of the reasons the EU lost this case is that its own scientists admitted that there was no proof that importing GMO food posed a significant risk to the EU environment. The WTO court ruled that the GMO ban was a form of protectionism.

29. GMO crops can sometimes include the transfer of genes across species, which makes these GMO crops qualitatively different from the products of regular plant breeding. Proponents of GMOs have sometimes been disingenuous when they have claimed that GMO technology is simply an acceleration of natural plant breeding techniques; taking a fish gene and injecting it into a plant is something that could never be accomplished naturally.

30. According to a report by Friends of the Earth, no crops with enhanced nutrition have been introduced commercially (Villar and Freese, 2008). Experimentally, bananas are being engineered to carry vaccines for hepatitis B, cholera, jaundice, polio, measles, and diarrhea, as well as resistant to fungus. "Golden rice" was developed at Texas A&M with excess beta-carotene. Potatoes with the hepatitis B vaccine and high-protein sweet potatoes are also being developed (Baden-Wurttemberg, n.d.).

31. The GM Science Review Panel, commissioned as part of the United Kingdom's investigation into the safety of genetically modified crops, concluded that the currently available GM crops are unlikely to cause additional threats to UK ecosystems (GM Science Review Panel, 2003).

32. The UN reports that large-scale growth of genetically modified crops first began in the United States around 1996 (Dargie, 2001).

33. Organizations and groups backing this approach include a grassroots campaign promoting GMO labeling with the support of several politicians and food companies (http://www.thecampaign.org/), Friends of the Earth (http://www.foe.org/), RecipeforAmerica (http://www.recipeforamerica. org/), Greenpeace Canada (http://www.greenpeace.org/canada/en/), and Consumers International (http://www.consumersinternational.org/).

11 CHEMICAL POLLUTION

1. After World War II, DDT was used extensively to control mosquitoes and agricultural pests. Due to runoff, the chemical made its way into the coastal ecosystems and into the fish that were subsequently eaten by the eagles and other raptors. The bird populations quickly declined because they were unable to reproduce. DDE, the primary component of DDT, builds up in the fatty tissue and inhibits female birds from producing the calcium necessary to create strong eggshells. When nobody else would expose the situation, Rachel Carson published her book *Silent Spring*, leading to congressional hearings about DDT and the eventual banning of DDT by the Environmental Protection Agency on December 31, 1972 (U.S. Fish and Wildlife Service, 2007).

2. Malaria killed 65,510 people around the world in 2003: total confirmed malarial deaths equaled 5,308 and total probable or clinically diagnosed malarial deaths equaled 60,202 (World Health Organization, 2007). Some argue that small-scale and largely indoor spraying of DDT against malaria provides benefits to human health that outweigh any potential environmental or other human health risks.

3. The published EPA review process does not include testing synergistic effects of chemicals (U.S. Environmental Protection Agency, 2007).

4. For information on DDT's effects in the Arctic, see http://www.arctic. noaa.gov/essay_calder.html.

5. For articles on the science and developments in nanotechnology, see http://www.scientificamerican.com/topic.cfm?id=nanotechnology; for information on some of the recently discovered risks of nanotechnology, see http://www.sciencedaily.com/releases/2009/06/090610192431.htm and http://www.sciencedaily.com/releases/2009/09/090913134026.htm.

6. A study by the Environmental Working Group (EWG), in conjunction with the Mount Sinai School of Medicine, found an average of ninety-one chemicals in nine participants. In total, they found 167 different

chemicals in the participants; seventy-six of the found chemicals are carcinogens, seventy-nine cause birth defects or affect development, and ninety-four are neurotoxins (Environmental Working Group, 2003).

7. Rogers (2003) and Schapiro (2007) discuss the EU's use of the precautionary principle in chemical regulation.

8. The U.S. Centers for Disease Control and Prevention (CDC) reports that the effect of phthalates on humans is not entirely known, but some studies suggest that it affects semen quality and genital development in boys, and shortens pregnancies and leads to premature breast development in adolescent girls (Center for Disease Control, 2007). Phthalates have been banned in the European Union and California ("California Bans Plastic Toy Chemical," 2007).

9. The decision not to ban BPA is probably due in part to strong industry pressure and the pervasiveness of the chemical in plastic bottles and containers; however, it is difficult to know whether continuing to allow BPA is primarily because of industry pressure or primarily due to lingering questions about the scientific evidence of health effects (Schapiro, Mark, personal communication, December 9, 2008).

10. The Environmentally Responsible Solvents and Processes Program of the National Science Foundation Science and Technology Center publishes a list of related research groups at http://www.nsfstc.unc.edu/research. htm. Other U.S. schools involved in "green" chemical research include the University of Tennessee (http://eerc.ra.utk.edu/ccpct/index.html) and Yale University (http://www.greenchemistry.yale.edu/).

11. In 2001, the European Commission published a white paper entitled "Strategy for a Future Chemical Policy," in which it described a single system to record the names, properties, and risks of all chemicals produced or imported at a rate greater than one metric ton per year (Ahrens, 2002). The Registration, Evaluation, Authorization, and Restriction of Chemical substances (REACH) program entered into law on June 1, 2007, and shifts the burden of proof from the countries' authorities to the chemical producers and includes existing chemicals in the regulatory scheme. The central database will be run by a new organization, the European Chemicals Agency (ECHA), in Helsinki; REACH provisions will be phased in over the next eleven years (European Commission, 2008).

12. Polychlorinated biphenyl (PCB) is a family of compounds previously used commonly as a lubricant, heat-transfer fluid, and plasticizer. PCBs are known to be a skin irritant and suspected to cause birth defects and cancer. They are especially deadly to fish and invertebrates, and stay within the food chain for several years.

13. Chemistry Daily publishes information about the campaign to ban Alar at http://www.chemistrydaily.com/chemistry/Alar. The Fluoride Action Network's campaign against fluoride is at http://www.fluoridealert.org/.

14. Economist Rick Nevin's research shows a direct relationship between lead exposure levels in children and the violent crime rate two decades

later. This relationship is consistent across nine countries and a century of data (Vedantam, 2007). Another recently published study provides a biological explanation of the variation of crime rates with lead exposure. Using MRI scans, scientists found that adolescents who were exposed to lead as children have less brain matter in the parts of the prefrontal cortex associated with judgment and reasoning (Marshall, 2008).

15. This occurred in the cap and trade program for sulfur dioxide in the United States; while nationally acid rain decreased substantially, because of a shift to greater coal use in the upper midwestern states, the state of New York experienced increased levels of sulfur pollution and acid rain. This could have been prevented by creating regional caps instead of one national cap. This way no one region could become too concentrated with polluting sources. This is a classic example of the trade-off between efficiency and equity: the most efficient system is a national cap, but to deal with distributional concerns some efficiency would have to be traded for greater equity.

16. On March 15, 2005, the EPA issued a rule to permanently cap and control mercury emissions from coal-fired power plants. The Clean Air Mercury Rule (CARM) extends the Clean Air Interstate Rule (CAIR) to address SO_2, NO_x, and mercury simultaneously (U.S. Environmental Protection Agency, 2008). However, a ruling by the D.C. Circuit Court of Appeals vacated the CARM rule (State of New Jersey, 2008) and there are currently no plans for a cap and trade in the United States for mercury emissions.

17. For an overview of the agreement, see http://www.basel.int/.

18. For a fascinating news clip on ship-breaking in Bangladesh see http://www.cbsnews.com/video/watch/?id=3228443nandtag=related; photovideo.

12   FISHERIES AND THE MARINE ENVIRONMENT

1. After studying four continental shelf systems and nine oceanic systems, Myers and Worm (2003) found that 90 percent of predatory fish stocks have been depleted since the start of industrialized fishing in the 1950s. A later study found that the loss of ocean biodiversity results in increasing rates of fishery collapse and exponential decrease in recovery potential, stability, and water quality, meaning that as we remove key pieces of oceanic systems, the ocean becomes increasingly unable to provide us with food or maintain quality water, and the chance for recovery decreases (Worm et al., 2006).

2. World demand for seafood increased from around 20 million tons in 1950 to around 140 million tons in 2004, and is expected to grow to about 179 million tons by 2015 (Food and Agriculture Organization, 2006).

3. New Zealand, Iceland, Canada, United States, Australia, Greenland, Norway, Portugal, the Netherlands, United Kingdom, and South Africa all utilize IFQ systems (Florida Fish and Wildlife, 2005).

4. The United Nations Convention on the Law of the Sea (UNCLOS) came into force on November 16, 1994. It addresses topics such as territorial sea limits and areas of economic jurisdiction, legal status of resources on the sea floor beyond national jurisdiction, navigational rights, conservation and management of marine resources, and marine research regimes. UNCLOS grants coastal countries with a twelve-mile territorial sea limit, within which a country can enforce any law and regulate and exploit any resources. The countries are also granted a contiguous zone extending twenty-four nautical miles from shore, within which they can implement certain rights to pursue drug smugglers, illegal immigrants, and tax evaders. Beyond the contiguous zone, coastal countries have the right and obligation to exploit, develop, manage, and conserve all resources within a two hundred–mile radius of shore. Globally, these exclusive economic zones ensure that 99 percent of all fisheries fall within at least one country's jurisdiction (United Nations Division for Ocean Affairs, 1998).

5. Forty-four billion pounds of bycatch are recorded annually (Dobrzynski et al., 2002).

6. In 2006, Iceland and Russia led other fishing nations to block UN negotiators from gaining unanimous support for a global ban on bottom trawling (Heilprin, 2006). Since then, annual UN Generally Assembly resolutions have called on fishing nations to protect bottom fisheries on the high seas and other vulnerable marine ecosystems. The UN Food and Agriculture Organization (FAO) helps fisheries management organizations develop guidelines to protect these ecosystems.

7. For information on this new agreement, see http://www.businessweek. com/ap/financialnews/D9E356H00.htm.

8. For this and other statistics about Marine Protected Areas, see http:// www.wdpa-marine.org/#/countries/about.

9. Marine Protected Areas of the United States: http://www.mpa.gov.

10. The world's largest Marine Protected Area was created in the Phoenix Islands of Kiribati (Conservation International, 2008).

11. Gell and Roberts (2003) compiled many studies showing the improvement of fisheries inside Marine Protected Areas. For example, inside the Tsitsikamma National Park in South Africa (one of the oldest Marine Protected Areas), fish species are found in numbers five to forty-two times greater than outside the protected area boundaries. In reserves around New Zealand, snapper are fourteen times more likely to be larger than the legal catch size in Marine Protected Areas than in unprotected areas. Lingcod in protected areas off the Washington coast produce twenty times more eggs than those outside the protected areas.

12. Access NOEP's databases at http://www.oceaneconomics.org/.

13. View an excellent short video on ocean acidification sponsored by the Natural Resources Defense Council at http://www.youtube.com/watch?v=5cqCvcX7buo.

14. The Monterey Bay Aquarium Seafood Watch Program: http://www.montereybayaquarium.org/cr/cr_seafoodwatch/sfw_recommendations.aspx.

15. For information about Walmart's MSC-only policy, see http://walmartstores.com/pressroom/news/5638.aspx.

16. The first sustainable sushi restaurant in the world was started by one of my students in San Francisco: http://www.tatakisushibar.com/. Check it out.

17. The article can be accessed at http://www.conservationmagazine.org/articles/v9n4/impostor-fish/.

18. This type of mislabeling also occurs in the organic food industry.

19. At the ministerial meetings in Doha in 2001 World Trade Organization (WTO) member nations agreed to address the issue of fisheries subsidies in the next round of talks, with the goal of helping developing countries capitalize on their own small-scale fishing economies (Capella, 2004). In December 2005, the United States, EU, Brazil, Chile, New Zealand, Senegal, and the Philippines called on the WTO to ban the subsidies contributing to overfishing. Iceland and Norway agreed to limit subsidies, and Japan, South Korea, and Taiwan have agreed to support bans on the subsidies that lead to harmful overfishing as long as there is not a blanket ban on all fisheries subsidies. Unfortunately, any agreement on fisheries subsidies will not come into effect until all other issues are resolved and a final document is agreed upon by all parties to the WTO talks (Bradsher, 2005).

20. Norman Myers has written extensively on the underreported subject of perverse subsidies. See his article in *Nature* (1998), and his book cowritten with Jennifer Kent (2001).

21. Two high-profile WTO cases involving the protection of dolphins and sea turtles soured many environmental groups to the WTO because its judicial body ruled against enforcement of trade restrictions enacted by the United States that would have protected these species. But a close reading of these cases demonstrates that there is ample room within the WTO framework for countries to exercise environmental protection as long as it is not done in a discriminatory manner. For an excellent overview of these two cases, see http://www1.american.edu/TED/tuna3.htm and http://gurukul.ucc.american.edu/ted/SHRIMP2.HTM.

13   POPULATION GROWTH AND TECHNOLOGICAL CHANGE

1. Copies of Malthus's writings can be found at http://www.faculty.rsu.edu/~felwell/Theorists/Malthus/Index.htm.

2. For current U.S. and global population estimates, see http://www.census. gov/main/www/popclock.html.
3. Ethiopia has suffered multiple famines, the most severe of which lasted from 1983 to 1985 ("1984–1985 Famine in Ethiopia," 2008).
4. Animals convert 5 to 15 percent of the energy content embodied in plants into cellular material (Decrausaz, 2005).
5. For more information, see Amartya Sen's work on this subject (Dr'eze and Sen, 1987).
6. Consumer Spending and Population by Region, 2000 (Worldwatch Institute, 2004):

Region	Share of world private consumption expenditures (%)	Share of world population (%)
United States and Canada	31.5	5.2
Western Europe	28.7	6.4
East Asia and Pacific	21.4	32.9
Latin America and the Caribbean	6.7	8.5
Eastern Europe and Central Asia	3.3	7.9
South Asia	2	22.4
Australia and New Zealand	1.5	0.4
Middle East and North Africa	1.4	4.1
Sub-Saharan Africa	1.2	10.9

7. Due in large part to economic growth, birth rates (and consequently population growth rates) have been declining in developing countries (except for parts of Sub-Saharan Africa and the Middle East) since the mid-1960s (Soubbotina, 2004).
8. The medium projection is for the population to rise to 9.2 billion people by 2075, declining to 8.3 billion by 2175, and then increasing back up to 9 billion by 2300 (United Nations, 2003).
9. For an excellent overview of efforts around the world to link biodiversity preservation to incentive programs, see the report by Ecosystem Marketplace, "State of Biodiversity Markets: Offset and Compensation Programs Worldwide," which can be downloaded at http://www.ecosystemmarketplace.com/documents/acrobat/sbdmr.pdf.

    The Natural Capital Project is a joint effort of the Woods Institute for the Environment at Stanford University, the Nature Conservancy, and the World Wildlife Fund to define the economic value of ecosystem services at locations around the world; http://www.naturalcapitalproj-ect.org/about.html.

Chart 1   Energy Intensity by Religion, 1980–2030

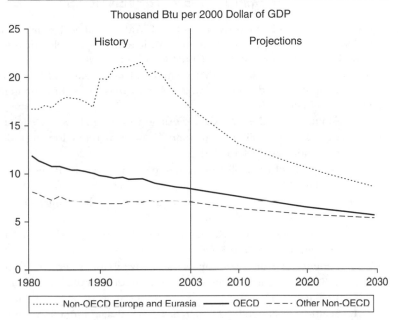

Sources: History derived from Energy Information Administration (EIA), International Energy Annual 2003 (May–June 2005), Web site www.eia.doe.gov/iea/. Projections: EIA, System for the Analysis of Global Energy Markets (2006).

10. Between 1979 and 1986, total subsidies for ethanol jumped from $86 million to $2 billion (in 2006 dollars). U.S. government support of ethanol grew to $5.8 billion to $7 billion in 2006 and is expected to continue rising (Koplow, 2007).

11. The production of ethanol results in a net 25 percent increase in energy; however, most of that energy is embodied in the animal feed by-product (Hill et al., 2006).

12. The X Prize Foundation's first award, the Ansari X Prize, went to Burt Rotan in October 2004 for completing the first private flight to space. Other X Prizes include the Progressive Automotive X Prize to develop a production-capable 100 mpg vehicle, the Archon X Prize for Genomics to develop a breakthrough in genome sequencing, the Google Lunar X Prize to send a robot to the moon. Soon to come are several energy X Prizes. While a private company sponsors each X Prize, the Progressive Automotive X Prize, for example, is offered in partnership with the U.S.

Department of Energy. For more information, visit http://www.xprize.org/.

14 DEMAND-SIDE INTERVENTIONS

1. From a study to estimate costs in New South Wales, total peak-time electricity load costs $89.59 per megawatt hour, while total off-peak electricity load costs $22.66 per megawatt hour (Intelligent Energy Systems, 2004).
2. A demand-reducing strategy that includes block pricing (among other incentives) produced the following water savings (U.S. Environmental Protection Agency, 2002):
   1. Albuquerque, New Mexico: reduction of 45 gallons per capita per day from 1995 to 2001, and 14 percent reduction in peak demand from 1990 to 2001.
   2. Goleta, California: 50 percent decrease in per capita usage from 1989 to 1991.
   3. Irvine Ranch Water District, California: water savings of 19 percent from 1990 to 1992.
   4. Massachusetts Water Resources Authority: water savings of 24 percent from 1987 to 1988.
   5. Phoenix, Arizona: per capita water savings of 6 percent from 1982 to 1987, and 14 percent total decrease in water usage from 1990 to 1995.
   6. Seattle, Washington: 2.3 percent water-usage reduction from 1990 to 1998 contributed to pricing structure alone.
3. The Resource Conservation and Recycling Facilitation Act, originally signed in 1992 and amended in 2002, requires stores to charge 100 won for paper bags and 50 won for plastic bags regardless of the value of the purchase. Fast food establishments and restaurants are required to recycle at least 90 percent of their used paper containers, and a voluntary program has to-go establishments charging a deposit on their paper containers, refundable when the item is returned for recycling (Sang, 2003). The purchase of paper bags has decreased from 48.6 percent in 2001 to 24.0 percent in 2004, and 30 percent of disposable cups were returned for recycling (Ministry of Environment, 2005).
4. In 2003, London became the first city to charge private vehicles (with some exceptions) a fee to enter the city center on weekdays between 7 a.m. and 6 p.m. to reduce congestion and pollution. Video cameras around the city record license plates, which are then matched to a list of all vehicles that have paid for the right to drive in the city. By 2006, average traffic speed within the fee zone had increased 37 percent, peak-period congestion delays decreased by approximately 30 percent, bus congestion delays

decreased 50 percent, bus ridership increased 14 percent, and subway ridership increased by approximately 1 percent (Litman, 2006).

5. The U.S. government purchases more than 20 billion sheets of copier paper each year. Due to President Clinton's recycled-paper mandates in 1993 and 1998, 98 percent of all paper purchases are compliant with the 30 percent recycled content requirement, saving 400,000 trees annually, and spending over $350 million on recycled products every year (Government Purchasing Project, n.d.).

6. In September 2006, Walmart announced that beginning in 2008 it would make purchasing decisions based on suppliers' ability to cut down on packaging. Walmart is expected to save $3.4 billion annually from this policy, and the entire supply chain is expected to save around $11 billion annually ("Walmart Goes Green," 2005). Packaging should be reduced by 5 percent and 667,000 metric tons of carbon dioxide should be kept from entering the atmosphere ("Walmart Packaging," 2006).

7. By July 1, 2007, all city offices were prohibited from buying single-serving water bottles, and by December 1, 2007, all city offices were to have switched from bottled dispensers to dispensers of Hetch Hetchy water. The new dispensers will cost about $400 each, but this cost is minimal in comparison to the $500,000 the city of San Francisco used to spend each year on bottled water (Vega, 2007). Forty-seven million gallons of oil are used and one billion pounds of carbon dioxide are released to produce the bottles consumed annually by Americans (Newsom, 2007).

8. In 1999, Home Depot announced a new policy of preferential treatment for FSC-certified wood (Home Depot, 2003). Between 1999 and 2003, sales of FSC certified wood at Home Depot increased from $15 million to $350 million (Standley, 2005).

FINAL THOUGHTS AND ADDITIONAL RESOURCES

1. The Academy Award–winning documentary *The Cove* has brought attention to the incredible annual dolphin slaughter in Japan, but an even more gruesome tradition takes place in Denmark every year: http://www.examiner.com/x-37619-Environmental-Policy-Examiner~y2010m2d12-Denmark-teen-passage-to-manhood-kill-innocent-dolphins-for-sport.

REFERENCES

1984–1985 famine in Ethiopia (2008). *Wikipedia.* Retrieved March 23, 2008, from http://en.wikipedia.org/wiki/1984%E2%80%931985_famine_in_Ethiopia.

About Friends of McNeil River (n.d.). Retrieved September 27, 2008, from http://www.mcneilbears.org/index.cfm?section=About.

Agreement between Merck and Costa Rica's National Biodiversity Institute, The (n.d.). *Intellectual property right and the environment.* Retrieved October 12, 2008, from http://www.american.edu/TED/hpages/ipr/misa.htm.

Ahrens, R (2002, September 27). *European chemicals policy reform—from paralysis to action* (EEB Pub. No. 2002/016). Brussels: European Environmental Bureau. Retrieved March 19, 2008, from http://www.eeb.org/activities/chemicals/Publication-EEB-013_02.pdf.

Air emissions summary through 2005 (2007). *Air Trends.* Retrieved November 4, 2007, from Environmental Protection Agency: http://epa.gov/airtrends/2006/emissions_summary_2005.html.

Alcott, H and S. Mullainathan (2010). *Behavioral Science and Energy Policy.* MIT Working Paper. Retrieved March 11, 2010 from http://web.mit.edu/allcott/www/Allcott%20and%20Mullainathan%202010%20-%20Behavioral%20Science%20and%20Energy%20Policy.pdf.

Alston, L. J., G. D. Libecap, and B. Mueller (1999). *Titles, conflict, and land use: The development of property rights and land reform on the Brazilian Amazon frontier.* Ann Arbor: University of Michigan Press. Preview obtained December 12, 2007, from Google Books: http://books.google.com/books?id=IuYrOK3Re04C.

Americans and the World (n.d.). Trade with China. *World Public Opinion. org.* Retrieved February 19, 2008, from http://www.americans-world.org/digest/regional_issues/china/china5.cfm.

Are you being served? Environmental economics (2005, April 23). *Economist.* Retrieved March 23, 2008, from LexisNexis Academic.

Arrow, K. J., M. L. Cropper, G. C. Eads, R. W. Hahn, L. B. Lave, R. G. Noll et al. (1996, April 12). Is there a role for benefit-cost analysis in environmental, health, and safety regulation? *Science, 272,* 221–222.

Arrow, K., R. Solow, P. R. Portney, E. E. Leamer, R. Radner, and H. Schuman (1993). Report of the NOAA panel on contingent valuation. *Federal Register, 58*(10), 4601–4614.

Azzi, C. F. and J. C. Cox (1973). Equity and efficiency in evaluation of public programs. *The Quarterly Journal of Economics, 87*(3), 495–502. Retrieved December 26, 2007, from JSTOR database.

Baden-Wurttemberg (n.d.). Vaccination with bananas—the use of green gene technology. *The Biotech/Life Sciences Portal.* Retrieved March 17, 2008, from http://www.bio-pro.de/en/life/magazin/00386/index.html.

Bali delegates agree to support forests-for-climate (REDD) plan (2007, December 16). *Mongabay.com.* Retrieved February 21, 2008, from http://news.mongabay.com/2007/1215-redd.html.

Balick, M. J., R. Arvigo, and L. Romero (1994). The development of an ethnobiomedical forest reserve in Belize: Its role in the preservation of biological and cultural diversity. *Conservation Biology, 8*(1), 316–317. Retrieved March 23, 2008, from JSTOR.

Bao, Y., W. Wu, M. Wang, W. Liu (2007). Disadvantages and future research directions in valuation of ecosystem services in China. *International Journal of Sustainable Development and World Ecology, 14*(4), 372–381. Retrieved November 17, 2007, from ProQuest database.

Barde, J. and D. Pearce (1991). *Valuing the environment: Six case studies.* London: Earthscan. Referenced in Mazurek, Janice V. (1996). The role of health risk assessment and benefit-cost analysis in environmental decision making in selected countries: An initial survey. *Resources for the Future Discussion Paper 96–36.* Retrieved September 8, 2008, from http://www.rff.org/rff/Documents/RFF-DP-96–36.pdf.

Barker T., I. Bashmakov, L. Bernstein, J. E. Bogner, P. R. Bosch, R. Daveet al. (2007). Technical summary. In: *Climate change 2007: Mitigation. Contribution of Working Group III to the Fourth Assessment Report of the Intergovernmental Panel on Climate Change* [B. Metz, O. R. Davidson, P. R. Bosch, R. Dave, L. A. Meyer (eds.)], Cambridge University Press, Cambridge, United Kingdom and New York, NY, USA.

Bartczak, A., H. Lindhjem, S. Navrud, M. Zandersen, and T. Zylicz (2008). *Valuing forest recreation on the national level in a transition economy: The case of Poland. Forest Policy and Economics, 10*(7–8), 467–472. Retrieved November 18, 2008, from http://mpra.ub.uni-muenchen.de/11483/.

Bird, L. and B. Swezey (2006.) *Green power marketing in the United States: A status report* (Ninth ed.) (NREL/TP-620–40904). Golden, CO: National Renewable Energy Laboratory. Retrieved March 29, 2008, from http://www.eere.energy.gov/greenpower/resources/pub_chrono.shtml.

BirdLife International (2008). EBA Programme. *BirdLife International Data Zone.* Retrieved February 20, 2008, from http://www.birdlife.org/datazone/ebas/eba_programme.html.

Birrell, K (2007). Kiwi fruit for America. *Frontier Centre for Public Policy.* Retrieved March 11, 2008, from http://www.fcpp.org/main/publication_detail.php?PubID=2005.

Borlaug, N. and J. Carter (2005, October 14). Food for thought. *The Wall Street Journal.* Retrieved May 31, 2008, from AgBioWorld: http://www.agbioworld. org/biotech-info/topics/borlaug/WSJ-2005-Foodthought.html.

Bouton, M. M., C. Hug, S. Kull, M. Kulma, B. I. Page, T. C. Schaffer et al. (2006). *The United States and rise of China and India.* The Chicago Council on Global Affairs. Retrieved on February 19, 2008, from http://www. thechicagocouncil.org/curr_pos.php.

Bradsher, K (2005, December 15). New consensus on WTO fishing policy. *The International Herald Tribune,* p. 15. Retrieved October 25, 2008, from LexisNexis Academic database.

Burros, M (2005, April 10). Stores say wild salmon, but tests say farm bred. *The New York Times.* Retrieved January 29, 2008, from *New York Times* online: http://www.nytimes.com/2005/04/10/dining/10salmon.html.

California bans plastic toy chemical (2007, October 17). *CBS News online.* Retrieved March 18, 2008, from http://www.cbsnews.com/stories/ 2007/10/15/health/main3366238.shtml.

Capella, P (2004, April 27). Momentum builds in global talks on fisheries subsidies. *Agence France Presse,* Financial Pages. Retrieved October 25, 2008, from LexisNexis Academic database.

Carbon Tax Center (2008, February 26). *FAQs.* Retrieved May 25, 2008, from http://www.carbontax.org/faq/.

Carson, R (1962). *Silent spring.* Boston: Houghton Mifflin.

Carson, R. T., R. C. Mitchell, M. Hanemann, R. J. Kopp, S. Presser, and P. A. Ruud (2003). Contingent valuation and lost passive use: Damages from the Exxon Valdez oil spill. *Environmental and Resource Economics, 25,* 257–286.

Carson, R.T (in press). Introduction. In *Contingent Valuation: A Comprehensive Bibliography and History.* Northampton, MA: Edward Elgar Publishing.

Center for Disease Control (2007). Spotlight on phthalates. *CDC's Third National Report on Human Exposure to Environmental Chemicals* (NCEH Pub 05–0664). Atlanta: Center for Disease Control. Retrieved March 18, 2008, from http://www.cdc.gov/exposurereport/pdf/factsheet_phthalates.pdf.

Cesar, H. S. J. and P. J. H. van Beukering (2004). Economic valuation of the coral reefs of Hawaii. *Pacific Science, 58*(2), 231–242. Abstract retrieved December 9, 2008, from http://www.cababstractsplus.org/google/abstract. asp?AcNo=20043090540.

Chapin, M (2004, November/December). A challenge to conservationists. *World Watch Magazine, 17*(6), 17–31. Retrieved November 4, 2008, from World Watch: http://www.worldwatch.org/system/files/EP176A.pdf.

Chen, D. W (2004a, June 16). Special master steered a program through its many curves. *New York Times* Online. Retrieved October 28, 2007, from www. nytimes.com: http://query.nytimes.com/gst/fullpage.html?res=9500E5D9 1E30F935A25755C0A9629C8B63&n=Top/Reference/Times%20Topics/ People/F/Feinberg,%20Kenneth%20R.

Chen, D. W (2004b, November 18). $7 billion for the grief of Sept. 11. *New York Times* Online. Retrieved October 28, 2007, from www.nytimes.com: http://

www.nytimes.com/2004/11/18/nyregion/18fund.html?_r=1&n=Top/
Reference/Times%20Topics/People/F/Feinberg,%20Kenneth%20R.&
oref=slogin.

Chomitz, K. M., E. Brenes, and L. Constantino (1998). *Financing environmental services: The Costa Rican experience and its implications.* Washington, DC: World Bank.

Christine Todd Whitman, Administrator of Environmental Protection Agency, et al. v. American Trucking Associations, Inc. et al., 531 U.S. 457 (2001). Retrieved September 15, 2008, from LexisNexis Academic database.

Cisco (2006, June 22). China to contribute 27% to global economic growth by 2020. *Press Release.* Hong Kong: Author. Retrieved September 28, 2008, from http://newsroom.cisco.com/dlls/global/asiapac/news/2006/pr_06–22.html.

Clean Air Interstate Rule (2007). Retrieved November 4, 2007, from Environmental Protection Agency: http://www.epa.gov/cair/index.html.

Cobb, C., Halstead, T., and Rowe, J (1995). If the GDP is up, why is America so down? *The Atlantic Monthly,* October, 59–77.

Colchester, M (2006, April). FSC dilemmas in the heart of Borneo: Step-wise sand bag or sell out? *World Rainforest Movement Bulletin, 105.* Retrieved September 27, 2008, from http://www.wrm.org.uy/bulletin/105/Borneo.html.

Confessore, N (2008, April 7). Congestion pricing plan dies in Albany. *New York Times* Online. Retrieved November 6, 2008, from http://cityroom.blogs.nytimes.com/2008/04/07/congestion-pricing-plan-is-dead-assembly-speaker-says/?hp.

Connecticut Department of Environmental Protection (2007). *Nitrogen control program for Long Island Sound.* Retrieved March 15, 2008, from http://www.ct.gov/dep/cwp/view.asp?a=2719&q=325572&depNav_GID=1654.

Conservation International (2005). Map of Hotspots. *Biodiversity Hotspots.* Retrieved February 20, 2008, from http://biodiversityhotspots.org/xp/hotspots/resources/Pages/maps.aspx.

Conservation International (2008). Hotspots Defined. *Hotspots Science.* Retrieved February 20, 2008, from http://www.biodiversityhotspots.org/xp/hotspots/hotspotsscience/Pages/hotspots_defined.aspx.

Conservation International (2008, February 14). World's largest marine protected area created in Pacific Ocean. *Conservation International.* Retrieved March 22, 2008, from http://www.conservation.org/newsroom/pressreleases/Pages/PIPA-largest-protected-area-in-pacific.aspx.

Conservation International (n.d.). Human Population. *Biodiversity Hotspots.* Retrieved February 27, 2008, from http://www.biodiversityhotspots.org/xp/hotspots/hotspotsscience/hotspots_in_peril/Pages/human_population.aspx.

Consumer Reports (2006). The salmon scam: "Wild" often isn't. *Consumer Reports.org.* Retrieved January 29, 2008, from http://www.consumerreports.

org/cro/food/food-shopping/meats-fish-protein-foods/mislabeled-salmon/salmon-8–06/overview/0608_salmon_ov.htm.

Costa Rica gets largest debt-for-nature swap (2007, October 17). *World News— World Environment.* Retrieved February 27, 2008, from http://www.msnbc. msn.com/id/21345405/.

Council of Economic Advisers (U.S.) (1991). Trade liberalization and economic growth. In *Economic report of the President* (pp. 233–263). Washington, DC: Author. Retrieved October 5, 2008, from http://fraser. stlouisfed.org/publications/ERP/issue/1515/.

Cushman, T (2006, February 1). Import taxes on Canadian softwood raises the price by 20 percent. Do US sawmills really need the protection? *Builder.* Retrieved March 23, 2008, from LexisNexis Academic.

Damodaran, A (2008). Historical returns on stocks, bonds, and bills—United States. *The Data Page.* Retrieved January 23, 2008, from http://pages.stern. nyu.edu/~adamodar/New_Home_Page/data.html.

Dargie, J (2001). *Biotechnology, GMOs, ethics and food production.* Stockholm: Food and Agriculture Organization of the United Nations. Retrieved March 15, 2008, from http://www.fao.org/news/2001/stockholm/biotech.pdf.

Dasgupta, P. (2006). Comments on the Stern review's economics of climate change. University of Cambridge. Retrieved November 4, 2007, from http://www.econ.cam.ac.uk/faculty/dasgupta/STERN.pdf.

DeCanio, S. J (2003). Economic analysis, environmental policy, and intergenerational justice in the Reagan administration: The case of the Montreal Protocol. *International Environmental Agreement: Politics, Law and Economics, 3*(4), 299–321. Retrieved February 6, 2008, from ABI/INFORM Global database.

Decrausaz, B (2005). Virtual water and agriculture in the context of sustainable development. Adelaide: OECD Workshop on agriculture and water. Retrieved March 23, 2008, from http://www.oecd.org/secure/ pdfDocument/0,2834,en_21571361_34281952_35590094_1_1_1_1,00.pdf.

Diamond, J (1987, May). The worst mistake in the history of the human race. *Discover Magazine,* 64–66.

Dobrzynski, T., C. Gray, and M. Hirshfield (2002). *Oceans at risk: Wasted catch and the destruction of ocean life.* Washington, DC: Oceana. Retrieved March 22, 2008, from http://www.oceana.org/uploads/bycatch_final.pdf.

Dr'eze, J. and A. Sen (1987) *Hunger and public action.* Oxford: Clarendon Press. Referenced in Sen, A (1999). Democracy as a universal value. *Journal of Democracy, 10*(3), 3–17.

Ears of plenty (Electronic version) (2005, December 20). *The Economist.* Retrieved May 31, 2008, from http://nue.okstate.edu/crop_information/ The_Story_of_Wheat.htm.

Easterly, W (2006). *The white man's burden: Why the West's efforts to aid the rest have done so much ill and so little good.* New York: Penguin Press. Citation retrieved May 26, 2008, from http://www.amazon.com.

Ellerman, D. and B. K. Buchner (2007, Winter). The European Union emissions trading scheme: Origins, allocation, and early results. *Review of Environmental Economics and Policy, 1*(1), 68–87.

Energy Information Administration (2002). Comparison of global warming potentials from the second and third assessment reports of the Intergovernmental Panel on Climate Change (IPCC). *IPCC Global Warming Potential.* Retrieved November 23, 2007, from http://www.eia.doe.gov/oiaf/1605/gwp.html.

Energy Information Administration (2007). Chapter 1—World energy and economic outlook. *International Energy Outlook 2007.* Washington, DC: Author. Retrieved March 23, 2008, from http://www.eia.doe.gov/oiaf/ieo/world.html.

Engler, M. and R. Parry-Jones (2007). *Opportunity or threat: The role of the European Union in global wildlife trade.* Brussels: TRAFFIC. Retrieved November 5, 2008, from http://www.traffic.org/general-topics/.

Environmental Valuation Reference Inventory (2007). Geographic characteristics. Retrieved November 19, 2007, from Tour EVRI: http://www.evri.ec.gc.ca/.

Environmental Working Group (2003). *BodyBurden: The pollution in people* (Executive summary). Oakland, CA: Author. Retrieved June 1, 2008, from http://archive.ewg.org/reports/bodyburden1/es.php.

Environmentalists buy out Bella Coola Outfitters in BC (2005). *The Hunting Report.* Retrieved January 28, 2008, from HuntingReport.com: http://www.huntingreport.com/worldupdate.cfm?articleid=239.

European Commission (2008). *REACH.* Retrieved March 22, 2008, from http://ec.europa.eu/environment/chemicals/reach/reach_intro.htm.

Evans, W. N., S. J. Berardi, M. M. Ducla-Soares, and P. R. Portney (1992). The determinants of pesticide regulation: A statistical analysis of EPA decision making. *Journal of Political Economy, 100*(1), 175–197.

Exxon Shipping Company, et al., Petitioners v. Grant Baker et al., 128 S. Ct. 2605 (2008). Retrieved September 6, 2008, from LexisNexis Academic database.

Federated Farmers of New Zealand, Inc (2002). Life after subsidies. *Frontier Centre for Public Policy.* Retrieved March 10, 2008, from http://www.fcpp.org/main/publication_detail.php?PubID=171.

Florida Fish and Wildlife Conservation Commission (2005). *Individual fishing quota (IFQs).* Retrieved March 22, 2008, from http://myfwc.com/commission/2005/Nov/RD_ITQ_Dec2005_2.pdf.

Fogarty, D (2007, December 5). Saving rainforests a thorny issue at Bali talks. *Reuters.* Retrieved February 21, 2008, from http://www.reuters.com/article/environmentNews/idUSSP15328520071205?sp=true.

Food and Agriculture Organization of the United Nations (2004). Table A.4 Land use. *FAO Statistical Yearbook, 2*(1). Retrieved March 10, 2008, from http://www.fao.org/es/ess/yearbook/vol_1_1/site_en.asp?page=resources.

Food and Agriculture Organization of the United Nations (2007). State of the world fisheries and aquaculture 2006 (ISSN 1020–5489). Rome: Author. Retrieved March 22, 2008, from http://www.fao.org/docrep/009/A0699e/A0699e00.htm.

Food and Agriculture Organization of the United Nations (2008). Online database query. *Aquastat.* Retrieved March 13, 2008, from http://www.fao.org/nr/water/aquastat/dbase/index.stm.

Gage, D (2008, May 2). Kleiner Perkins bets big on green tech firms. *San Francisco Chronicle.* Retrieved May 25, 2008, from SFGate: http://www.sfgate.com/cgi-bin/article.cgi?f=/c/a/2008/05/01/BUTH10F8I3.DTL.

Gan, J (2001, Fall). Pesticide use trend in California. *PesticideWise, 1.* Retrieved March 15, 2008, from http://www.pw.ucr.edu/PesticdeWise.asp.

Gell, F. R. and C. M. Roberts (2003). Benefits beyond boundaries: The fishery effects of marine reserves. *Trends in Ecology & Evolution, 18*(9), 448–455. Retrieved June 1, 2008, from http://assets.panda.org/downloads/benefitsbeyondbound2003.pdf.

Gillam, C (2008, March 12). U.S. organic food industry fears GMO contamination. *Reuters.* Retrieved March 15, 2008, from http://www.reuters.com/article/domesticNews/idUSN1216250820080312.

Global Insight, Inc (2005, August). Global macroeconomic scenarios and world trade statistics and forecast (Contract No. 146531). Retrieved September 28, 2008, from http://www.pancanal.com/csp/plan/cstudios/0303-cxcc.pdf.

GM Science Review Panel, The (2003). *GM science review (first report): An open review of the science relevant to GM crops and food based on interests and concerns of the public.* London: Department of Trade and Industry. Retrieved June 1, 2008, from http://www.gmsciencedebate.org.uk/.

Goodman, S (2008, July 24). Bisphenol A poses no human health risk, E.U. agency says. *Greenwire.* Retrieved December 13, 2008, from http://www.factsonplastic.com/bisphenol-a-poses-no-human-health-risk-eu-agency-says/.

Government Purchasing Project (n.d.). *Government purchasing factsheet.* Washington, DC: Resource Conservation Alliance & Author. Retrieved March 29, 2008, from http://www.gpp.org/pub.html.

Greenhouse gas reduction scheme. *New South Wales State Government.* Retrieved October 13, 2007, from http://greenhousegas.nsw.gov.au/.

Greenhouse, L (2008, April 15). Court sets fall debate on standards of water act. *New York Times* Online. Retrieved September 15, 2008, from www.nytimes.com: http://www.nytimes.com/2008/04/15/washington/15scotus.html?_r=1&oref=slogin.

Groombridge, B. and M. D. Jenkins (2000). *Global biodiversity: Earth's living resources in the 21st century.* Cambridge: World Conservation Press.

Hamilton, J P (2005). *Regulation through revelation: The origin, politics, and impacts of the toxics release inventory program.* New York: Cambridge University Press. Preview obtained January 29, 2008, from http://www.amazon.com/Regulation-through-Revelation-Politics-Inventory/dp/0521855306.

Harrington, W., R. D. Morgenstern, and P. Nelson (2000). On the accuracy of regulatory cost estimates. *Journal of Policy Analysis and Management, 19*(2), 297–322.

Heilprin, J (2006, November 24). Moves to impose trawling ban stymied. *Washington Post online.* Retrieved March 22, 2008, from http://www.washingtonpost.com/wp-dyn/content/article/2006/11/24/AR2006112400766.html.

Hendrickson, J (2006, February 1). The economics of fairness. Message posted to The Everyday Economist Blog: http://everydayecon.wordpress.com/2006/02/01/the-economics-of-fairness/.

Hill, J., E. Nelson, D. Tilman, S. Polasky, and D. Tiffany (2006, July 25). Environmental, economic, and energetic costs and benefits of biodiesel and ethanol biofuels. *Proceedings of the National Academy of Sciences, 103*(30), 11206–11210. Retrieved March 24, 2008, from http://www.pnas.org/cgi/reprint/0604600103v1.

Historic debt-for-nature swap protects Guatemala's tropical forests (2006, October 2). *The Nature Conservancy.* Retrieved March 22, 2008, from http://www.nature.org/pressroom/press/press2641.html.

Hochfelder, J (2006–2007). *The Hochfelder Report.* Retrieved September 14, 2008, from http://www.newyorkinjurycases.com/personal-injury-article.asp?id=19408.

Hoerner, J. A. and B. Bosquet (2001). *Environmental tax reform: The European experience.* Washington, DC: Center for a Sustainable Economy. Retrieved November 20, 2007, from http://www.rprogress.org/publications/2001/eurosurvey_2001.pdf.

Home Depot, The (2003, December 3). The Home Depot® and Tembec team up to offer environmentally friendly lumber to consumers. *The Home Depot.* Retrieved March 29, 2008, from http://ir.homedepot.com/ReleaseDetail.cfm?ReleaseID=123833.

Hotelling, H (1947). *Letter to the National Park Service.* Published in Prewitt (1949). *The Economics of Public Recreation. The Prewitt Report.* Washington, DC: Department of the Interior. Retrieved February 27, 2008, from http://selene.uab.es/prieram/carta.htm.

Hsu, S (Forthcoming). A realistic evaluation of climate change litigation through the lens of a hypothetical lawsuit. *University of Colorado Law Review.* Retrieved September 6, 2008, from SSRN: http://ssrn.com/abstract=1014870.

Indulgence (2008). *Wikipedia.* Retrieved May 24, 2008, from Wikipedia: http://en.wikipedia.org/wiki/Indulgences.

Insurance safety institute finds higher speeds lead to increase in mortalities [Fifth ed.] (1999, January 19). *Journal of Commerce.* Retrieved November 2, 2007, from ProQuest.

Intelligent Energy Systems (2004). *The long run marginal cost of electricity generation in New South Wales.* Sydney: Author. Retrieved March 25, 2008,

from   http://www.ipart.nsw.gov.au/documents/Pubvers_Rev_Reg_Ret_
IES010304.pdf.
International Monetary Fund (2006). *Government finance statistics yearbook*, pp.
12–23.
International Monetary Fund (2007, October). World economic and financial
surveys. *World Economic Outlook Database*. Retrieved February 18, 2008, from
http://www.imf.org/external/pubs/ft/weo/2007/02/weodata/index.
aspx.
International Monetary Fund (2008, January 29). An update of the key WEO
projections. *World Economic Outlook*. Retrieved February 20, 2008, from
http://www.imf.org/external/pubs/ft/weo/2008/update/01/index.htm.
International Union for Conservation of Nature (IUCN) (2007, April 18–20).
Countdown 2010 for marine ecosystems. Retrieved October 12, 2007, from www.
countdown2010.net/file_download/78.
IPCC (2007). Summary for policymakers. In: *Climate change 2007: The physical
science basis. Contribution of Working Group I to the Fourth Assessment Report of the
Intergovernmental Panel on Climate Change* [Solomon, S., D. Qin, M. Manning,
Z. Chen, M. Marquis, K. B. Averyt et al. (eds.)]. Cambridge University Press,
Cambridge, United Kingdom and New York, NY, USA.
Jacobsen, J. B. and N. Hanley (2008, August 8). Are there income effects
on global willingness to pay for biodiversity conservation? [Electronic
version]. *Environmental and Natural Resource Economics*. Abstract retrieved
October 12, 2008, from SpringerLink: http://www.springerlink.com/
content/mn20014x2473736u/. Submitted manuscript available at http://
www.economics.stir.ac.uk/People/staff/Hanley/jacobsen%20and%20
hanley%20revised.pdf.
Joint Economic Committee Study (1997). Tradable emissions. *United States
Congress*. Retrieved November 24, 2007, from http://www.house.gov/jec/
cost-gov/regs/cost/emission.htm.
Joskow, P. L., R. Schmalensee, and E. M. Bailey (1998). The market for
sulfur dioxide emissions. *The American Economic Review*, *88*(4), 669–685.
Retrieved November 24, 2007, from EbscoHost: http://web.ebscohost.
com/ehost/pdf?vid=3&hid=22&sid=999b41f2–26ee-46fa-9051–
84176932d6a6%40SRCSM1.
Kepner, J (2004). Synergy: The big unknowns of pesticide exposure. *Pesticides
and You, 23*(4), 17–20. Retrieved September 7, 2008, from Beyond Pesticides:
http://www.beyondpesticides.org/infoservices/pesticidesandyou/
Winter%2003–04/Synergy.pdf.
Kindest cut of all, The (2002, November 16). *The Economist*. Retrieved March
2, 2008, from Lexis-Nexis.
King, S. R. and T. J. Carlson (1995). Biocultural diversity, biomedicine, and
ethnobotany: The experience of Shaman Pharmaceuticals. *Interciencia*,
19(3), 134–139. Retrieved November 11, 2008, from http://interciencia.
org/v20_03/art03/index.html.

Koplow, D (2007). *Biofuels—At what cost? Government support for ethanol and biodiesel in the United States: 2007 update.* Geneva: International Institute for Sustainable Development. Retrieved March 24, 2008, from http://www.earthtrack.net/earthtrack/library/BiofuelsUSupdate2007.pdf.

Koretz, G (1997). Hit the gas—And save lives: The paradox of higher speed limits. *Business Week, 3548,* 20. Retrieved November 2, 2007, from ProQuest.

LaCoast (1999, Summer). *Other impacts from coastal wetlands.* Retrieved November 19, 2007, from http://www.lacoast.gov/watermarks/1999c-summer/4other/.

Lee, B. and W. Lee (2004). The effect of information overload on consumer choice quality in an on-line environment. *Psychology & Marketing, 21*(3), 159–183. Retrieved September 28, 2008, from ABI/INFORM Global database (Document ID: 573032131).

Levinson, A (2010). Offshoring pollution: Is the United States increasingly importing polluting goods? *Review of Environmental Economics and Policy, 4*(1), 63–83.

Litman, T (2006). *London congestion pricing: Implications for other cities.* Victoria, BC: Victoria Transport Policy Institute. Retrieved March 26, 2008, from http://www.vtpi.org/london.pdf.

Lopez, R. and G. I. Galinato (2005). Deforestation and forest-induced carbon dioxide emissions in tropical countries: how do governance and trade openness affect the forest-income relationship? *The Journal of Environment Development, 14*(1), 73–100. Retrieved October 19, 2007, from SAGE Publications: http://jed.sagepub.com/cgi/reprint/14/1/73.pdf.

Lovgren, S (2006, December 14). China's rare river dolphin now extinct, experts announce. *National Geographic News.* Retrieved February 27, 2008, from http://news.nationalgeographic.com/news/2006/12/061214-dolphin-extinct.html.

Madrian, B. C. and D. F. Shea (2000). *The power of suggestion: Inertia in 401(K) participation and savings behavior.* Working Paper 7682, National Bureau of Economic Research. Retrieved January 31, 2008, from http://ideas.repec.org/p/nbr/nberwo/7682.html.

Madsen, B., Carroll, N., and Moore-Brands, K (2010). State of biodiversity markets: Offset and compensation programs worldwide. Ecosystem Marketplace Report. Retrieved March 11, 2010, from http://www.ecosystemmarketplace.com/documents/acrobat/sbdmr.pdf.

Mankiw, G (2006, December 9). Pigouvian questions. Message posted to http://gregmankiw.blogspot.com/.

Marshall, J (2008, May 28). Lead exposure linked to violent crime, brain changes. *Discover News.* Retrieved October 24, 2008, from Discovery Channel online: http://dsc.discovery.com/news/2008/05/28/lead-violent crime.html.

Mathews, S (2005). Imperial imperatives: Ecodevelopment and the resistance of Adivasis of Nagarhole National Park, India. *Law, Social Justice, and Global Development Journal (LGD), 1.* Retrieved October 12, 2008, from http://www2.warwick.ac.uk/fac/soc/law/elj/lgd/2005_1/mathews/.

McKibben, B (2007, December 28). Remember this: 350 parts per million. *Washington Post*. Retrieved May 9, 2008, from http://www.washingtonpost. com.

Medema, S. G (2004, July). Mill, Sidgwick, and the evolution of the theory of market failure. *Online working paper*. Retrieved October 12, 2007, from http://www.utilitarian.net/sidgwick/about/2004070102.pdf.

Melosi, M. V (2000). Environmental justice, political agenda setting, and the myths of history. *Journal of Policy History, 12*(1), 43–71. Abstract retrieved October 12, 2008, from Project MUSE: http://muse.jhu.edu/login?uri=/ journals/journal_of_policy_history/v012/12.1melosi.html.

Metcalf, G. E., S. Paltsev, J. Reilly, H. Jacoby, J. F. Holak (2008, May). *Analysis of U.S. greenhouse gas tax proposals. NBER Working paper no. 13980*. Abstract retrieved September 28, 2008, from http://www.nber.org/papers/w13980.

Metrick, A. and M. L. Weitzman (1998, Summer). Conflicts and choices in biodiversity preservation. *The Journal of Economic Perspectives, 12*(3), 21–34. Retrieved March 2, 2008, from Jstor.

Meyers, R. and B. Worm (2003, May 15). Rapid worldwide depletion of predatory fish communities. *Nature, 423*(6937), 280–283. Retrieved October 24, 2008, from Research Library Core database (Document ID: 343927311).

Mill, J. S. (1879). *Utilitarianism*. London: Longmans, Green, and Co. In *The Project Gutenberg* (2004). Retrieved February 20, 2008, from http://www. gutenberg.org/ebooks/11224.

Millennium Development Goals report 2007, The (2007). New York: United Nations. Retrieved November 4, 2007, from http://mdgs.un.org/unsd/mdg/ Resources/Static/Products/Progress2007/UNSD_MDG_Report_2007e.pdf.

Millennium Ecosystem Assessment, 2005. *Ecosystems and human well-being: Synthesis*. Washington, DC: Island Press. Retrieved May 22, 2008, from http://www.millenniumassessment.org/en/synthesis.aspx.

Ministry of Environment Republic of Korea (2005, June 1). Purchase Fewer Disposable Bags, Return More Paper Cups. *Ministry of Environment Republic of Korea* (Press release). Retrieved March 26, 2008, from http://eng.me.go. kr/docs/news/press_view.html?seq=282&page=8&mcode.

Monbiot, G (2006, October 18). Selling indulgences. *The Guardian*. Retrieved May 24, 2008, from Monbiot.com: http://www.monbiot.com/ archives/2006/10/19/selling-indulgences/.

Myers, N (1998). Lifting the veil on perverse subsidies. *Nature, 392*(6674), 327–328. Retrieved October 25, 2008, from Research Library Core database (Document ID: 28288937).

Myers, N. and J. Kent (2001). *Perverse subsidies: How misused tax dollars harm the environment and the economy*. Washington, DC: Island Press. Preview obtained October 25, 2008, from Google Books: http://books.google. com/books?id=mA-t1xAJDDUC&dq=norman+myers+subsidies&printsec= frontcover&source=bl&ots=ATm8ggFz_v&sig=ySiU9q3FaIR5wNqngm9P6 0-Vwzo&hl=en&sa=X&oi=book_result&resnum=1&ct=result#PPP1,M1.

Myers, N., R. A. Mittermeier, C. G. Mittermeier, G. A. B. da Fonseca, and J. Kent (2000, February 24). Biodiversity hotspots for conservation priorities. *Nature, 403*, pp 853–858. Retrieved February 20, 2008, from http://www.ithaca.edu/faculty/rborgella/environment/biodiversity_hotspot.pdf.

National Agricultural Statistics Service (2004). *2002 Census of agriculture: U.S. national level data.* Retrieved March 15, 2008, from http://www.agcensus.usda.gov/Publications/2002/index.asp.

Natta, D. and D. Cave. "Deal to Save Everglades May Help Sugar Firm." *New York Times.* March 8, 2010: A1.

Natural Resources Defense Council (2005). Facts about pollution from livestock farms. *NRDC Issues: Water.* Retrieved March 15, 2008, from http://www.nrdc.org/water/pollution/ffarms.asp.

Nelson, G.C., V. Harris, and S.W. Stone (2001). Deforestation, land use, and property rights: Empirical evidence from Darien, Panama. *Land Economics, 77*(2), 187–205. Retrieved October 19, 2007, from HW Wilson Web: http://vnweb.hwwilsonweb.com/hww/shared/shared_main.jhtml?_requestid=57820.

Newsom, G (2007, July 21). *Permanent phase-out of bottled water purchases by San Francisco city and county government* (Executive directive 07–05). San Francisco: Office of the Mayor. Retrieved March 29, 2008, from http://sfwater.org/Files/Pressreleases/Bottled%20Water%20Executive%20Order.pdf.

Newsweek (2007, July 29). Slaughter in the jungle: Chief threat to world's endangered species no longer habitat destruction. *PR Newswire.* Retrieved March 2, 2008, from ABI/INFORM Dateline database (Document ID: 1311780681).

Nordhaus, W. D (2001, January 4). *After Kyoto: Alternative mechanisms to control global warming.* Joint session of the American Economic Association and the Association of Environmental and Resource Economists, Atlanta, Georgia. Retrieved September 28, 2008, from http://www.angelfire.com/co4/macroeconomics302/c.pdf.

Nordhaus, W. D (2007). Critical assumptions in the Stern review on climate change. *Science, 317*(5835), 201–202. Retrieved January 21, 2008, from http://nordhaus.econ.yale.edu/recent_stuff.html.

Nordhaus, W. D (2007, Winter). To tax or not to tax: Alternative approaches to slowing global warming. *Review of Environmental Economics, 1*(1), 26–44. Retrieved September 30, 2008, from http://nordhaus.econ.yale.edu/nordhaus_carbontax_reep.pdf.

Office of Water Use Efficiency (2008). Agricultural water use program. *California Department of Water Resources.* Retrieved March 12, 2008, from http://www.owue.water.ca.gov/agdev/index.cfm.

Oil spill could threaten S.F. Bay wildlife for years (2007, November 9). *CNN.com.* Retrieved September 6, 2008, from CNN.com: http://www.cnn.com/2007/US/11/09/bay.spill.ap/.

Oil spills and disasters (2007). Retrieved October 12, 2007, from http://www. factmonster.com/ipka/A0001451.html.

Organization for Economic Co-operation and Development (2004a). Producer support estimate by commodity. Compliment database to *Agricultural Policies in OECD Countries: At a Glance.* Retrieved March 11, 2008, from http://www. oecd.org/document/58/0,2340,en_2649_37401_32264698_1_1_1_37401, 00.html.

——— (2004b). Total support estimate. Compliment database to *Agricultural Policies in OECD Countries: At a Glance.* Retrieved March 11, 2008, from http://www.oecd.org/document/58/0,2340,en_2649_37401_32264698_ 1_1_1_37401,00.html.

——— (2007a). *Agricultural policies in non-OECD countries: Monitoring and evaluation 2007-Highlights.* Retrieved March 12, 2008, from http://www. oecd.org/document/5/0,3343,en_2649_37401_38271429_1_1_1_37401, 00.html.

——— (2007b). *Agricultural policies in OECD countries: Monitoring and evaluation 2007.* Retrieved March 12, 2008, from http://www.oecd.org/document/ 0/0,3343,en_2649_37401_39508672_1_1_1_37401,00.html.

——— (2008). *OECD environmental outlook to 2030.* Danvers, MA: Author. Preview obtained September 28, 2008, from Google Books: http://books. google.com/books?id=8YSB8LMpLaYC&pg=PA82&lpg=PA82&dq=global+ gdp+growth+2030&source=web&ots=e2yxcM7ym-&sig=uuSKowx1Z5lMCF zKugzvyTIJUew&hl=en&sa=X&oi=book_result&resnum=10&ct=result#PP A82,M1.

Ortega, E., O. Cavalett, R. Bonifacio, and M. Watanabe (2005). Brazilian soybean production: Energy analysis with an expanded scope. *Bulletin of Science Technology Society, 25*(4), 323–334. Retrieved October 19, 2007, from SAGE Publications: http://bst.sagepub.com/cgi/reprint/25/4/323.pdf.

Parry, M. L., O. F. Canziani, J. P. Palutikof, P. J. van der Linden, and C. E. Hanson, (Eds.) (2007). *Climate change 2007: Impacts, adaptation and vulnerability. Contribution of working group II to the fourth assessment report of the Intergovernmental Panel on Climate Change.* Cambridge: Cambridge University Press. Retrieved January 21, 2008, from IPCC: http://www.ipcc.ch/pdf/ assessment-report/ar4/wg2/ar4-wg2-intro.pdf.

PCB (n.d.a). *Dictionary.com Unabridged (v 1.1).* Retrieved March 18, 2008, from Dictionary.com website: http://dictionary.reference.com/browse/PCB.

PCB (n.d.b.). *The American Heritage® Science Dictionary.* Retrieved March 18, 2008, from Dictionary.com Web site: http://dictionary.reference.com/ browse/PCB.

Pearce, D., G. Atkinson, and S. Mourato (2006). *Benefit-cost analysis and the environment: Recent developments.* Paris: OECD Publishing. Preview obtained September 6, 2008, at Google Books: http://books.google.com/books? id=nTPbxgsvBD0C&pg=PA194&lpg=PA194&dq=health+benefits+dom inate+environmental+benefit-cost&source=web&ots=fyvqo6G4V9&sig=

WJtF3Pbv-VFHDX_IyNEFIzvBs7Y&hl=en&sa=X&oi=book_result&resnum=1
0&ct=result#PPA3,M1.

Pigou, A. C (1932). *The Economics of welfare* (fourth ed.). London: Macmillan and Co. Retrieved November 20, 2007, from http://www.econlib.org/ Library/NPDBooks/Pigou/pgEW.html.

Point Carbon (2008, March). *EU ETS phase II—The potential and scale of windfall profits in the power sector.* Godalming, Surrey, UK: World Wildlife Fund. Retrieved May 25, 2008, from http://www.wwf.org.uk/filelibrary/ pdf/ets_windfall_report_0408.pdf.

Polling Report, Inc (2008a). International trade/Global economy. *Polling Report.com.* Retrieved February 19, 2008, from http://www.pollingreport. com/trade.htm.

Polling Report, Inc (2008b). Problems and priorities. *Polling Report.com.* Retrieved February 18, 2008, from http://www.pollingreport.com/prioriti. htm.

Porter, M. and C. van der Linde (1995). Towards a New Conception of the Environment-Competitiveness Relationship. *The Journal of Economic Perspectives, 9*(4), 97–118.

Regional Greenhouse Gas Initiative (2007, October). *Overview of RGGI CO_2 budget trading program.* New York: Author. Retrieved May 25, 2008, from http://www.rggi.org/docs/program_summary_10_07.pdf.

Regional Greenhouse Gas Initiative (n.d.) *Regional Greenhouse Gas Initiative auction results.* Retrieved October 4, 2008, from http://www.rggi.org/co2-auctions/results.

Resor, J. P (1997). Debt-for-nature swaps: A decade of experience and new directions for the future. *Unasylva, 48*(188). Retrieved March 22, 2008, from http://www.fao.org/docrep/w3247E/w3247e00.htm#Contents.

Reyes, J.W (2007). Environmental Policy as Social Policy? The Impact of Lead Exposure on Crime. *B.E. Journal of Economic Analysis and Policy, 7*(1), 1–41.

Rodgers, G. D (1993). Estimating jury compensation for pain and suffering in product liability cases involving nonfatal personal injury. *Journal of Forensic Economics, 6*(3), 251–262. Retrieved September 14, 2008, from http://www. nafe.net/JFE/j06_3_06.pdf.

Roe, D (2002). Toxic chemical control policy: Three unabsorbed facts. *ELR News & Analysis 32.*

Roe, D., T. Mulliken, S. Milledge, J. Mremi, S. Mosha, and M. Grieg-Gran (2002). Making a killing or making a living? Wildlife trade, trade controls and rural livelihoods. *Biodiversity and Livelihoods Issues No.6.* London: IIED. Retrieved November 6 2008, from http://www.iied.org/pubs/display. php?o=9156IIED.

Rogers, M (2003). Risk analysis under uncertainty, the Precautionary Principle, and the new EU chemicals strategy. *Regulatory Toxicology and Pharmacology, 37*(3), 370–381. Abstract obtained March 18, 2008, from *ScienceDirect* doi: 10.1016/S0273–2300(03)00030–8.

Rowe, J (2008). Our phony economy. *Harper's Magazine*, June, 17–24.

Royden-Bloom (2007, September 18). State greenhouse gas (GHG) actions. *National Association of Clean Air Agencies (NACAA)*. Retrieved October 12, 2007, from http://www.4cleanair.org/Documents/StateGHGActions-chart.pdf.

Sanchez-Azofeifa, G. A., A. Pfaff, J. A. Robalino, and J. P. Boomhower (2007). Costa Rica's payment for environmental services program: Intention, implementation, and impact. *Conservation Biology*, 21(5), 1165–1173. Retrieved March 23, 2008, from EJS E-Journals.

Sandel, M.J (1997, December 15). It's immoral to buy the right to pollute [editorial]. *New York Times*, A19. Reprinted in Hoffman, Andrew J (2000). *Competitive environmental strategy: A guide to the changing business landscape* (pp. 40–42). Washington, DC: Island Press. Preview obtained September 20, 2008, from Google Books: http://books.google.com/books?id=6gxwm h6JTIsC&printsec=frontcover.

Sang, D. L (2003). Waste reduction and recycling law in Korea. *International Environmental Law Committee Newsletter*, 5(1). Retrieved March 26, 2008, from http://www.abanet.org/environ/committees/intenviron/newsletter/feb03/korea/.

Satellite imagery to be used to detect illegal logging, determine sustainability (2006, December 21). *Mongabay.com*. Retrieved September 27, 2008, from http://news.mongabay.com/2006/1221-fsc.html.

Sayre, L (2003). Farming without subsidies in New Zealand. *The New Farm*. Retrieved March 11, 2008, from http://www.newfarm.org/features/0303/newzealand_subsidies.shtml.

Schapiro, M (2007). *Exposed: The toxic chemistry of everyday products and what's at stake for American power*. White River Junction, VT: Chelsea Green Publishing.

Schwabach, A (2002). *National Wetlands Newsletter*, 24(1), 7–14.

Schmalensee, R., P. L. Joskow, A. D. Ellerman, J. P. Montero, and E. M. Bailey (1998, Summer). An interim evaluation of sulfur dioxide emissions trading. *Journal of Economic Perspectives*, 12(3), 53–68.

Sierra, R. and E. Russman (2006, August). On the efficiency of environmental service payments: A forest conservation assessment in the Osa Peninsula, Costa Rica. *Ecological Economics*, 59(1), 131–141. doi:10.1016/j.ecolecon.2005.10.010. Abstract retrieved November 4, 2008, from Science Direct: http://www.sciencedirect.com/science?_ob=ArticleURL&_udi=B6VDY-4HRMV3W-2&_user=10&_rdoc=1&_fmt=&_orig=search&_sort=d&view=c&_version=1&_urlVersion=0&_userid=10&md5=37ca6a40d75d9d6a82f68d76377daf2f.

Silverstein, K (1999). Meat factories—Pollutants from meat factories. *Sierra*. Retrieved March 15, 2008, from http://findarticles.com/p/articles/mi_m1525/is_1_84/ai_53501840.

Simpson, R. D., R. A. Sedjo, and J. W. Reid (1996). Valuing biodiversity for use in pharmaceutical research. *The Journal of Political Economy*, 104(1), 163–185.

Smart meter (2008). *Wikipedia*. Retrieved March 25, 2008, from http://en.wikipedia.org/wiki/Smart_meter.

Smith, K (2007). *The carbon neutral myth: Offset indulgences for your climate sins*. Amsterdam: Transnational Institute. Retrieved May 24, 2008, from Carbon Trade Watch: http://www.carbontradewatch.org/pubs/carbon_neutral_myth.pdf.

Smith, M (2001, November). The unlikely environmentalists. *Phoenix New Times News*. Retrieved March 2, 2008, from http://www.phoenixnewtimes.com/2001-11-22/news/the-unlikely-environmentalists/full.

Smith, S. V (2000, March 22). Jury verdicts and dollar value of human life. *Journal of Forensic Economics*. Retrieved September 14, 2008, from Access my Library: http://www.accessmylibrary.com/coms2/summary_0286-28755781_ITM.

Solow, R. M (1991). Sustainability: An economist's perspective. In R. Dorfman and N. S. Dorfman (Eds.), *Economics of the environment: Selected readings* (third ed.) (pp. 179–187). New York: W. W. Norton.

Soubbotina, T. P (2004). *Beyond economic growth: An introduction to sustainable development* (second ed.). Washington, DC: World Bank. Retrieved November 6, 2008, from DEPweb: http://www.worldbank.org/depweb/english/beyond/global/index.html.

Speed limit and deaths [Letter] (1997, October 19). *New York Times (Late Edition [East Coast])*, p. 14. Retrieved November 2, 2007, from ProQuest.

Spiro, G (1998, May). What's Rosita Arvigo up to now? An update. *The Monthly Aspectarian: The magazine for the New Age* (online edition). Retrieved November 11, 2008, from http://www.lightworks.com/MonthlyAspectarian/1998/May/0598-07.htm.

Standley, V (2005, September 12). New green building materials. *Green Guide*. Retrieved March 29, 2008, from http://www.thegreenguide.com/doc/110/materials.

State of New Jersey, et al. v. Environmental Protection Agency, 2008 U.S. App. LEXIS 2797 (D.C. Cir., February 8, 2008). Retrieved March 22, 2008, from LexisNexis Academic database.

Steed, B. C (2007, Fall). Government payments for ecosystem services—Lessons from Costa Rica. *Journal of Land Use, 23*(1), 177–202. Retrieved November 4, 2008, from http://www.law.fsu.edu/Journals/landuse/vol23_1/Steed.pdf.

Stern, N (2006). Stern review report on the economics of climate change (Pre-publication version). Retrieved November 4, 2007, from HM Treasury: http://www.hm-treasury.gov.uk/independent_reviews/stern_review_economics_climate_change/stern_review_report.cfm.

Sunstein, C (2007). Of Montreal and Kyoto: A tale of two protocols. *Harvard Environmental Law Review 32*. Retrieved February 19, 2008, from http://www.law.harvard.edu/students/orgs/elr/vol31_1/sunstein.pdf.

Szabo, G (2006). *EU ETS—Action 2006*. Retrieved September 21, 2008, from http://www.euets.com/index.php?page=75&l=1.

Szabo, M (2008, July 23). Don't offset your CO_2 emissions, retire them. *Planet Ark*. Retrieved September 21, 2008, from http://www.planetark.org/dailynewsstory.cfm/newsid/494 57/story.htm.

Taxpayers for Common Sense (n.d.). *Tongass logging subsidies—Cost to taxpayers.* Washington, DC: Author. Retrieved March 23, 2008, from http://www.taxpayer.net/forest/tongass/loggingsubsidies.htm.

The support of electricity from renewable sources. Commission of the European Communities. Commission Staff Working Document, 2008. Retrieved March 11, 2010, from http://ec.europa.eu/energy/climate_actions/doc/2008_res_working_document_en.pdf.

The Kyoto Protocol—A brief summary (2007). *European Commission.* Retrieved November 4, 2007, from EUROPA: http://ec.europa.eu/environment/climat/kyoto.htm.

Tietenberg, T. 1998. Disclosure strategies for pollution control. *Environmental and Resource Economics 11*, 587–602, Citation retrieved January 29, 2008, from Sand, Peter H (2002). The right to know: Environmental information disclosure by government and industry. Munich: University of Munich, Institute of International Law: http://www.inece.org/forumspublicaccess_sand.pdf.

Tsuchiya, A. and P. Dolan (2006). Equity of what in health? Distinguishing between outcome egalitarianism and gain egalitarianism. *University of Sheffield Working Paper.* Retrieved December 26, 2007, from http://www.shef.ac.uk/content/1/c6/01/87/47/DP0611.pdf.

U.S. Bureau of Reclamation (2006). Agreement signals start to historic San Joaquin River restoration. *U.S. Department of the Interior: Bureau of Reclamation.* Retrieved March 13, 2008, from http://www.usbr.gov/newsroom/newsrelease/detail.cfm?RecordID=13681.

U.S. Environmental Protection Agency (1999). *33/50 Program: The final record* (Office of Pollution Prevention and Taxes Rep. No. EPA-745-R-99–004). Retrieved November 19, 2007, from http://www.epa.gov/opptintr/3350/3350-fnl.pdf.

――― (2006). SO_2 emissions and the allowance bank, 1995–2005. *Acid rain program: 2005 progress report* (EPA-430-R-06–015). Washington, DC: Author. Retrieved May 20, 2008, from: http://www.epa.gov/airmarkt/progress/docs/2005report.pdf.

――― (2006). *Wetlands: Protecting life and property from flooding* (Office of Water Rep. No. EPA843-F-06–001). Retrieved November 17, 2007, from http://www.epa.gov/owow/wetlands/pdf/Flooding.pdf.

――― (2007). Trends in greenhouse gas emissions. *Inventory of U.S. Greenhouse Gas Emissions and Sinks: 1990–2005.* Public Review Draft. Retrieved November 20, 2007, from http://epa.gov/climatechange/emissions/downloads07/07Trends.pdf.

――― (2007, December 19). *Protection of stratospheric ozone: The 2008 critical use exemption from the phaseout of methyl bromide* (40 CFR Part 82). Washington,

DC: Federal Register (Vol. 27, no. 248). Retrieved March 15, 2008, from http://www.epa.gov/ozone/mbr/2008CUEFinalRule12–19–07.pdf.

———— (2007, January). *OVERVIEW: Office of Pollution Prevention and Toxics Programs*, pg. 7–8, 18–19. Washington, DC: Author. Retrieved March 22, 2008, from http://www.epa.gov/oppt/pubs/oppt101c2.pdf.

———— (2008). *Clean Air Mercury Rule*. Retrieved March 22, 2008, from http://www.epa.gov/camr/basic.htm.

———— (2008). Watershed land acquisition program. *New York City watershed: Watershed protection programs*. Retrieved November 4, 2008, from http://www.epa.gov/region02/water/nycshed/protprs.htm#rules.

U.S. Environmental Protection Agency Office of Water (2002). *Cases in water conservation: How efficiency programs help water utilities save water and avoid costs* (EPA832-B-02–003). Washington, DC: Author. Retrieved March 26, 2008, from http://www.epa.gov/owm/water-efficiency/pubs/index.htm.

U.S. Fish and Wildlife Service (2007). Endangered species. *Rachel Carson: A Conservation Legacy*. Retrieved March 17, 2008, from http://www.fws.gov/rachelcarson/toolkit/Endangered%20Species/index.html.

U.S. State Department (2004). Land management. *Desertification: Earth's Silent Scourge*. Retrieved March 23, 2008, from http://usinfo.state.gov/products/pubs/desertific/land.htm.

Union of Concerned Scientists (2007, June 29). Findings of the IPCC fourth assessment report: Climate change mitigation. *Global Warming*. Retrieved September 29, 2008, from http://www.ucsusa.org/global_warming/science_and_impacts/science/findings-of-the-ipcc-fourth-1.html#3.

United Nations Committee on Economic, Social, and Cultural Rights (2002). *The right to water* (General Comment No. 15 [arts 11 and 12]). New York: Author. Retrieved October 14, 2007, from http://www.unhchr.ch/html/menu2/6/cescr.htm.

United Nations Department of Economic and Social Affairs, Population Division (2003). *World population in 2300*. New York: Author. Retrieved March 23, 2008, from http://www.un.org/esa/population/publications/longrange2/Long_range_report.pdf.

United Nations Division for Ocean Affairs and the Law of the Sea (1998). *The United Nations Convention on the Law of the Sea (A historical perspective)*. New York: Author. Retrieved March 22, 2008, from http://www.un.org/Depts/los/index.htm.

United Nations Environment Program (1999). Economic instruments. *Global Environment Outlook 2000*, p.208. Retrieved March 10, 2008, from http://www.unep.org/geo2000/english/0138.htm.

United Nations Environment Program(2003). *Global Environment Outlook Year Book 2003*. Retrieved March 13, 2008, from http://www.unep.org/geo/yearbook/yb2003/.

United Nations Environment Program/Global Environment Facility (2006, August). Draft regional guidelines for the fifth meeting of the RTF-E in

Sabah, Malaysia. Sabah, Malaysia: Author. Retrieved October 27, 2007, from http://earthmind.net/marine/docs/draft-regional-guidelines-valuation. pdf.

United Nations General Assembly (1948). *Universal declaration of human rights* (Resolution 217 A (III)). New York: Author. Retrieved October 14, 2007, from http://www.un.org/Overview/rights.html.

United Nations Statistics Division (n.d.). United States. *Interest rate, government long-term bond yields, per cent per annum, period average.* Retrieved November 4, 2007, from United Nations Statistics Division: http://unstats.un.org/ unsd/cdb/cdb_series_xrxx.asp?series_code=6310.

United States Climate Action Partnership (2007). *A call for action.* Washington, DC: Author. Retrieved September 29, 2008, from http://us-cap.org/index. asp.

United States of America v. Derrik Hagerman and Wabash Environmental Technologies, LLC, 525 F. Supp. 2d 1058 (2007). Retrieved September 21, 2008, from LexisNexis Academic database.

United States of America v. Sheon DiMaio, 255 Fed. Appx. 537 (2007). Retrieved September 21, 2008, from LexisNexis Academic database.

US-China Joint Economic Research Group (2007, December). *US-China joint economic study: Economic analyses of energy saving and pollution abatement policies for the electric power sectors of China and the United States,* Summary for Policymakers. Retrieved September 6, 2008, from Environmental Protection Agency: http://www.epa.gov/airmarkets/international/china/ JES_Summary.pdf.

Vedantam, S (2007, July 8). Research links lead exposure, criminal activity. *Washington Post Online.* Retrieved October 24, 2008, from http:// www.washingtonpost.com/wp-dyn/content/article/2007/07/07/ AR2007070701073.html.

Vega, C. M (2007, June 22). Mayor to cut off flow of city money for bottled water. *San Francisco Chronicle.* Retrieved March 29, 2008, from http://www. sfgate.com/cgi-bin/article.cgi?f=/c/a/2007/06/22/BAGE8QJVIL1.DTL.

Villar, J. L. and B. Freese (2008). *Who benefits from gm crops?* Amsterdam: Friends of the Earth International. Retrieved March 15, 2008, from http://www. centerforfoodsafety.org/WhoBenefitsPR2_13_08.cfm.

Walker, R (2004). Theorizing land-cover and land-use change: The case of tropical deforestation. *International Regional Science Review, 27*(3), 247–270. Retrieved October 19, 2007, from SAGE Publications: http://irx.sagepub. com/cgi/reprint/27/3/247.pdf.

Walmart goes green on packaging (2005, September 22). *BBC News.* Retrieved March 29, 2008, from http://news.bbc.co.uk/2/hi/business/5372660.stm.

Walmart packaging reduction plan could save $11 billion (2006, September 25). *Environmental Leader.* Retrieved March 29, 2008, from http://www. environmentalleader.com/2006/09/25/wal-mart-packaging-reduction-plan-could-save-11-billion/.

Walsh, D. and T. Barrett (2008, May 22). Problems with Congress override of farm bill. *CNN Politics*. Retrieved June 1, 2008, from CNN.com: http://www.cnn.com/2008/POLITICS/05/22/farm.bill/.

Warren, W (2005, May 5). Comments on OMB draft report and guidelines. [Letter to the Office of Management and Budget]. *United States Congress*. Retrieved September 8, 2008, from http://www.whitehouse.gov/omb/inforeg/2003report/334.pdf.

Washington Toxics Coalition (2004). Many U.S. residents carry toxic pesticides above "safe" levels. *Press Release*. Washington, DC: Author. Retrieved October 14, 2008, from http://www.watoxics.org/pressroom/press-releases/pr-2004–05–11.

Water to flow for salmon, farmers under San Joaquin River settlement (2006). *Environment News Service*. Retrieved March 13, 2008, from http://www.ens-newswire.com/ens/sep2006/2006–09–15–01.asp.

Weiss, R (2003, April 7). Africa's apes are imperiled, researchers warn [FINAL Edition]. *The Washington Post*, p. A.07. Retrieved March 2, 2008, from National Newspapers Core database (Document ID: 321804241).

Weitzman, M. L (2007). A review of the Stern review on the economics of climate change. *Journal of Economic Literature, 45*(3), 703–724.

West, H. R (2008). *Utilitarianism*. As contributed to *Encyclopedia Britannica*. Retrieved February 20, 2008, from http://www.utilitarianism.com/utilitarianism.html.

WildAid (2007). *The end of the line?* (Second ed.). San Francisco: WildAid. Retrieved March 2, 2008, from http://www.oceana.org/sharks/shark-report.

Wiser, R., M. Bolinger, and E. Holt (2000, August). *Customer choice and green power marketing: A critical review and analysis of experience to date.* Prepared for the ACEEE Summer Study on Energy Efficiency in Buildings. Retrieved March 29, 2008, from http://www.eere.energy.gov/greenpower/resources/pub_chrono.shtml.

Woodruff, J (2008, May 15). *Congress passes $290B Farm Bill despite White House opposition.* [Online broadcast]. Arlington, VA: Public Broadcasting Service. Retrieved June 1, 2008, from http://www.pbs.org/newshour/bb/politics/jan-june08/farmbill_05–15.html.

World Agroforestry Centre (2004). *Annual report 2004: Restoring hope restoring the environment*. Nairobi: Author. Retrieved March 23, 2008, from http://worldagroforestry.org/downloads/publications/PDFs/rp13340.pdf.

World Bank fund will pay to leave forests standing (2007, December 11). *Environmental News Service*. Retrieved February 21, 2008, from http://www.ens-newswire.com/ens/dec2007/2007–12–11–01.asp.

World Bank, The (2004). How much is an ecosystem worth? Assessing the economic value of conservation. *World Bank Working paper no. 30893.* Retrieved October 27, 2007, from http://www-wds.worldbank.org.

World Bank, The (2006). *Strengthening forest law enforcement and governance: Addressing a systematic constraint to sustainable development* (Report No. 36638-GLB). Washington, DC: Author. Retrieved November 4, 2008, from http://www.illegal-logging.info/uploads/Forest_Law_FINAL_HI_RES_9_27_06_FINAL_web.pdf.

World Bank, The (2006). *The road to 2050: Sustainable development for the 21st century* (Report no. 36021). Washington, DC: Author. Retrieved May 22, 2008, from World Bank Documents and Reports: http://www.worldbank.org/reference/.

World Health Organization (2007). Data query. *Global Health Atlas.* Retrieved March 17, 2008, from http://www.who.int/globalatlas/DataQuery/default.asp.

World Resources Institute, United Nations Environment Program, United Nations Development Program, and World Bank (1998). *World resources 1998–99: Environmental change and human health.* Washington, DC: Author. Retrieved October 27, 2007, from http://pubs.wri.org/pubs_description.cfm?PubID=2889.

World Trade Organization (2008a, January 22). *DS250: United States—Equalizing Excise Tax Imposed by Florida on Processed Orange and Grapefruit Products.* Retrieved March 10, 2008, from http://www.wto.org/english/tratop_e/dispu_e/cases_e/ds250_e.htm.

———— (2008b, January 22). *DS267: United States—Subsidies on Upland Cotton.* Retrieved March 10, 2008, from http://www.wto.org/english/tratop_e/dispu_e/cases_e/ds267_e.htm.

———— (2008c, January 22). *DS291: European Communities—Measures Affecting the Approval and Marketing of Biotech Products.* Retrieved March 15, 2008, from http://www.wto.org/english/tratop_e/dispu_e/cases_e/ds291_e.htm.

World Wildlife Fund (2006). Role of the Global Ecoregions and how they are selected. *World Wildlife Fund Where we Work.* Retrieved February 20, 2008, from http://www.panda.org/about_wwf/where_we_work/ecoregions/about/role/index.cfm.

———— (2008). Debt-for-nature swaps. *Conservation Finance.* Retrieved February 27, 2008, from http://www.worldwildlife.org/conservationfinance/swaps.cfm.

Worldwatch Institute (2004). *State of the world 2004: Consumption by the numbers.* Retrieved March 23, 2008, from http://www.worldwatch.org/node/1783.

Worm, B., E. B. Barbier, N. Beaumont, J. E. Duffy, C. Folke, B. S. Halpern et al. (2006, November 3). Impacts of biodiversity loss on ocean ecosystem services. *Science, 314*(5800), 787–790.

Worrell, D. (2006, September). Venture capitalists see potential in green businesses. *Entrepreneur Magazine.* Retrieved January 31, 2008, from Entrepreneur.com: http://www.entrepreneur.com/money/financing/venturecapital/article165820.html.

WWF Center for Conservation Finance (2003a). Bilateral debt-for-nature swaps by creditor. *Debt-for-nature swaps*. Retrieved February 27, 2008, from http://www.worldwildlife.org/conservationfinance/pubs/bilateral_ swaps_summary.pdf.

WWF Center for Conservation Finance (2003b). Commercial debt-for-nature swaps summary table. *Debt-for-nature swaps*. Retrieved February 27, 2008, from http://www.worldwildlife.org/conservationfinance/pubs/ commercial_swaps_summary.pdf.

Zweibel, K., J. Mason, and V. Fthenakis (2008, January). A solar grand plan. *Scientific American*. Retrieved September 30, 2008, from http://www.sciam. com/article.cfm?id=a-solar-grand-plan.